JIM THOMPSON
THE UNSOLVED MYSTERY

William Warren

JIM THOMPSON
THE UNSOLVED MYSTERY

Archipelago Press

For Charles Sheffield

Copyright © William Warren 1970, 1998

This edition first published in 1998 by

Archipelago Press, an imprint of
Editions Didier Millet
64, Peck Seah Street
Heritage Court, Singapore 079325

Printed by HBM Print Ltd
Reprinted 1999, 2000

ISBN 981-3018-82-8

Contents

Acknowledgments

A number of people have been helpful to me in the writing of this book, and I should like to express gratitude to all of them. To one, Charles Sheffield, the book has been dedicated, since without his cooperation and assistance it could never have been written. Others who have generously given me their time include Mrs. James H. Douglas, who provided me with information about her brother and about the Thompson family and also read the manuscript; Mrs. Connie Mangskau and Dr. and Mrs. T.G. Ling, who answered many questions concerning the fateful weekend in the Cameron Highlands; and Dr. and Mrs. Einer Ammundsen, Mrs. Lewis Thompson, Mrs. William R. Bond, Miss Elizabeth Lyons, and Mr. Charles Baskerville, who furnished useful memories of the subject. I should also like to thank Mr. Frank Dyckman and Mrs. Joyce Hartman of Houghton Mifflin Company, the former for suggesting the idea of the book and providing constant encouragement during its writing, the latter for her many wise editorial suggestions.

List of Photographs

Introduction

On Easter Sunday afternoon in 1967, an American businessman from Thailand named James H.W. Thompson disappeared, perhaps while on an innocent stroll, perhaps not, in the jungled mountains of central Malaysia. The circumstances surrounding his disappearance were unusual, to say the least, and Thompson was already the subject of a considerable legend; these two factors combined to assure the case of an extraordinary amount of public attention. A number of people involved in the affair, especially those closest to Thompson, thought the interest would die down in time, but for a variety of reasons this has not happened. In 1997, on the thirtieth anniversary, the British Broadcasting Corporation, the International Herald Tribune, and numerous other media outlets featured prominent stories on the mystery, and theories regarding a possible solution still abound, not only in most of the capitals of Southeast Asia, where Thompson was a familiar figure, but also in American and European circles. The disappearance has, in fact, assumed the proportions of a second Thompson legend, which with its tempting array of possibilities, threatens to obscure the very real and remarkable achievements that were the basis of the first.

Jim Thompson, as he was generally known, was sixty-one years old in 1967. His life had not really taken its distinctive shape, however, until he was in his early forties, at an age when radical changes are difficult to make. Paradoxically, this is a restless time for many men, perhaps for the majority; they dream of turning their back on what they have achieved (or failed to achieve) and starting out on an entirely new path, but few ever take even the first step toward translating such vague desires into reality. Thompson was one of those rare few, and that he happened upon the new path accidentally does not diminish the rarity of what happened.

At this midpoint of his life, he abruptly abandoned everything that was familiar to him and moved into a world and a career as exotic as any novelist's creation. What is more remarkable, he found in this new world, again by chance, a fulfillment of certain innate talents that not only brought him personal satisfaction but also profoundly changed the lives of thousands of other people. In the twenty years before his ill-fated holiday in Malaysia, he had accomplished more than most men in a full life. He had built a major industry in a remote and little-known country whose language he never learned to speak; he had become an authority on an art that, previously, he scarcely knew existed and had assembled a collection that attracted scholars from all over the world; he had built a home that was a work of art in itself and one of the landmarks of Bangkok; and, in the process of doing all this, he had become a sort of landmark himself, a personality so widely known in his adopted homeland that a letter addressed simply "Jim Thompson, Bangkok" found its way to him in a city of three and a half million people.

Thompson's career in Thailand became one of the most popular postwar legends of Asia, recounted in dozens of publications and gathering, along the way, all the usual embroideries and distortions common to legend-making—some of them, it is only fair to say, invented by the subject himself. It was quite characteristic that only a week before he went to Malaysia he was interviewed for yet another telling of it by an American television crew. Given such renown, it is not surprising that his disappearance attracted widespread attention. What was less expected was that the disappearance should acquire a legendary life of its own, with even more distortions, one in which the man himself has been all but lost amid the fascinations of the mystery.

The following account has two purposes: to tell the first Thompson story in greater detail than has been possible in other published versions, and to examine the second more closely and comprehensively than has been done. It is based on numerous interviews with people who were close to Thompson, on private letters, on all the material that has been printed concerning his career and disappearance, and on numerous conversations the author had with Thompson over some eight years in Thailand. When it was first written, less than three years after the disappearance, Thompson was still legally alive, and there were various reasons for omitting or playing down certain aspects, particularly concerning his private life. This gave rise to certain misconceptions, some of which seriously affected conclusions drawn from them; in this revised telling of the story, an effort has been made to fill in some of the gaps and produce a portrait more in keeping with the man known to his close friends and associates, as opposed to the numerous impressions, both oral and written, that have come from people who, despite their claims, knew him only slightly at some stage in his life or, in some cases, not at all.

Even a casual reader will soon perceive, however, that Thompson, like most gifted men, was a complex person; and for this reason there are inevitably assorted points of view about different aspects of his life. No account of either the career or the disappearance is likely to meet with complete approval from the many people who admired and the few who disliked him. What follows aims at telling the truth but it does not, it cannot, claim to be infallible.

One could start the Thompson story at several places: with his arrival in Thailand, for instance, which is really the beginning of the first legend, or, more conventionally, with his birth and follow through chronologically. Considering the purpose of this book, it seems more suitable to begin at that dividing point where the first legend came to a sudden, tragic end and the second began its curious growth.

Part One: A Walk in the Highlands

1

The Cameron Highlands is a cool and picturesque hill station, some 6,666 feet above sea level at its highest point, in the central Malaysian state of Pahang. It was named after William Cameron, a British surveyor who in 1885 discovered what he described as "a fine plateau with gentle slopes shut in by lofty mountains" and soon afterwards developed by foreign settlers from the lowlands as a retreat during the hot season, following a practice already well established in other British colonies like India and Ceylon. There is no train or air service; the quickest way to get there is to fly to Ipoh, the capital of neighboring Perak state, and then hire a taxi to make the winding ascent to the resort. Ipoh, however, has little to recommend it to the average traveler, and most tourists who go the Highlands for a holiday prefer to drive from either Kuala Lumpur, the Malaysian capital, or Penang, a pleasant island off the west coast. From the former, the drive takes about five hours, from the latter seven.

Beyond Ipoh the road gradually begins to climb, rice paddies and coconut plantations giving way to jungled foothills; after a small town called Tapah, the climb becomes steep, the road more winding, and the scenery wilder and more forbidding. As one nears the Highlands, the countryside has a definitely untamed look about it, much, one imagines, as it must have appeared to William Cameron. This was particularly true in 1967, before development led to considerable clearing; then the dense jungle rolled away endlessly on all sides, green and silent, roadless and dangerous; tigers were reported to still lurk in it, hidden ravines plunged a hundred feet deep, and there were tribes of elusive aborigines who still hunted with blowguns and poisoned darts and reportedly dug illegal animal traps along the secret trails.

Even today in the midst of all this wilderness the Highlands settlement, centered around the town of Tanah Rata, comes as a pleasant surprise with its neat streets and bungalows and general air of orderly, tranquil civilization. In 1967, there were several modern hotels, of which Foster's Smokehouse—patterned after a Swiss chalet—was the most prominent, a first-class golf course laboriously hewn out of the jungle, a rest home for convalescent soldiers on leave from the sweltering coastal areas, and a school for children of American missionaries which had formerly been located in Dalat, in Vietnam, but moved to the Highlands several years before when the war intensified. Around the golf links and scattered about the surrounding hills were numerous solid, European-style bungalows: Tudor cottages and mock Swiss chalets, with carefully tended lawns and beds of roses that grow with astonishing vigor in the clear, thin air that in the late afternoon becomes chilly and at night often quite cold.

The influence of the former colonial masters is strong. The rose gardens and herbaceous borders are English, and so are the high teas served every afternoon in the grander hotels, the hot water bottles thoughtfully provided on cold nights, the little Anglican church in Tanah Rata, and the overall public neatness of the place. Even the alien jungle that until very recently crowded in on all sides, threatening to take over again, has in a sense been anglicized, for it is hard to believe that any Asian settlers would have gone to all the trouble of cutting and maintaining the numerous paths through the forest to indulge the English passion for a bracing walk. A simplified guide map (p. 14) of the resort shows the major trails that meandered through the jungle in 1967, but innumerable minor ones branched off from these, leading deeper and deeper into the luxuriant greenery. (More detailed maps that showed all the known trails were hard to come by in 1967, possibly, according to one source, for security reasons.) Since walking is second only to golf as one of the major attractions of the Highlands, a regular labor force is assigned the burdensome chore of keeping the main trails clear for hikers, hacking at the grass and vines that reach out like greedy fingers. The local authorities now advise adventurous walkers to carry signal smoke bombs along with them "just in case" and discourage exploration of the side trails, which have a way of petering out or branching confusingly. In the first part of 1967, though, the jungle hackers were rumored to be spending more time maintaining the showpiece golf links than on the trails, and no one was advising smoke bombs and caution for the very good reason that lost walkers were almost unknown—possibly a testament to prudence considering the wildness of the countryside.

Back in the twenties and thirties, during the heyday of British rule, the Cameron Highlands was the largest and most popular of the hot-season resorts scattered around the Malay states, and from February through May it was crowded with the elite of Singapore, Penang, and the vast rubber estates to the south: planters and colonial administrators, missionaries and traders, exhausted by the lowlands heat and hungry for a familiar climate. It was the wealthier of these who built the first cottages and planted the first rose gardens, who achieved a feeling of "back home" in defiance of the inhospitable jungle. The Highlands supplied the English of Singapore with European vegetables and fruits, which were brought down the peninsula at great effort and expense. "Highlands strawberries" were a great delicacy in the colony, and still are in modern independent Singapore.

For obvious reasons, the station suffered a severe decline during the Japanese occupation, and even after liberation, in 1945, its respite from hard times was relatively brief before an even darker period set in. This was the time known in Malaysian history simply as the Emergency, though it was, in fact, a full-fledged war fought by British and Malay troops against a small army of Communist-led terrorists, many of them remnants of mainly Chinese resistance groups who had operated during the occupation period. They would swoop down in sudden murderous ambush on government forces and remote rubber plantations and then vanish into the jungle where there were thousands of hiding places and even secret landing strips. No one knows how many lives were lost during the long and bitter struggle—numerous fighters from both sides simply vanished into the forest and were never seen again—but in the

Cameron Highlands in the 1960s.

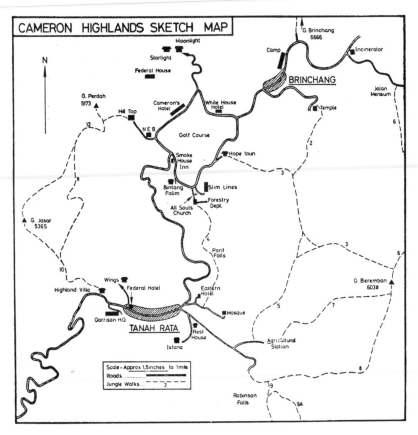

Courtesy Cameron Highlands Tourist Promotion Association, Malaysia

Hints to Walkers

1. Never walk alone.

2. Inform a friend before leaving: —

   a. Route you intend to take.

   b. Your expected time of return.

3. If you are lost, walk either due East or West (i.e. in the opposite direction to that which you left the Main Road), until you meet the Main Road again.

4. If you are uncertain as to the direction of East or West, remain stationary, if possible near a stream, until you are found. It may take over 24 hours to find you. DO NOT PANIC.

5. You should always take the following items on your walk:—

   a. A filled water bottle.

   b. A box of matches (to light a signal fire).

   c. A compass (this may be bought at the tourist board).

   d. A whistle.

   e. A torch.

   f. A little food (e.g. chocolate).

   g. A knife.

6. You should always wear long trousers and long sleeves. This will protect you from being scratched and will keep you warm at night. (Bring warm clothing along.)

7. KEEP TO THE NUMBERED PATHS AS SHOWN ON MAP.

mid-fifties the government got the upper hand, and by 1960, when the Emergency was officially declared over, the remaining insurgents had been forced back to an even wilder area near the Thai border, where there were still reports of their marauding activities as recently as 1967.

Security returned to the Highlands, and with it a renewed prosperity. The creepers that had repossessed most of the rose gardens were hacked away, the bungalows one by one were reopened, and hopeful local promoters dubbed the resort "the holiday playground of Malaysia" and began trying to attract tourists from outside as well as inside the country. The colonial days were over, of course, and most of the old British faces were gone, replaced by rich Chinese from Singapore and Penang, Malaysian government officials, and an increasing number of visitors from neighboring countries like Thailand. By the spring of 1967, when it found itself unexpectedly and unhappily in headlines around the world, the Highlands had fully recovered from its various setbacks and was well established once more as the country's leading resort.

2

Land values at the Highlands understandably fell during the Emergency, and numerous bungalow owners, disillusioned by the long insecurity, sold out for whatever they could get. One such sale was made to a Singapore couple named Dr. and Mrs. T.G. Ling. Dr. Ling was Chinese and his wife, Helen, was American; they met in New York during the twenties, when Dr. Ling was a chemistry student at Cornell University, and later married in China; their son became an officer in the U.S. Air Force. The Lings lived in China until the Communist takeover in 1949, when, leaving most of their possessions behind, they fled first to Hong Kong and finally to Singapore. There Dr. Ling found a good position with a European firm and Mrs. Ling opened a successful antique shop. Both prospered and within a few years were making enough money to live in one of Singapore's more fashionable areas and, looking ahead to eventual retirement, to buy a bungalow in the Highlands.

The property they acquired there consisted of a fair-sized piece of land atop a steep hill overlooking the golf links and a pleasant semi-Tudor bungalow called Moonlight Cottage, one of a pair built before the war by a British company as holiday houses for its personnel. The other of the two, predictably called Starlight, was a short distance down the hill but out of sight of Moonlight, so that both had unusual privacy. In the spring of 1967, Starlight was being used for rest and recreation by British officers on convalescent leave from their units.

Compared with most of the other holiday houses at the Highlands, Moonlight Cottage at the time was uncommonly isolated. The twisting road from the golf course narrowed to a one-car, partially asphalted track, then bordered by thick jungle, and came to a dead end at the Ling property; except for a number of somewhat precarious paths, it was the only way to get down the hill. The isolation of the place was undoubtedly one reason for the low price it sold for, and another, rather more ominous factor may also have been influential. Moonlight, it was rumored, had been used as a headquarters by the terrorists at the peak of their activities, and summary executions had reportedly taken place in the pretty flower garden near the veranda. Later, this grim interlude was recalled by a number of local people, and at least one witch doctor maintained there was a link between the past and the mystery that brought the cottage into the news in 1967; certain spirits in the jungle, he said, were still outraged by the bloodshed that had taken place on their doorstep and were having their revenge at last.

Ghosts notwithstanding, once the terrorists had been cleared out and security returned to the Highlands, it was obvious that the Lings had made a good buy. The house was spacious and comfortable and wonderfully private. There were three bedrooms downstairs, each with its own bath, a large living and dining area with an open fireplace to take the chill off the celebrated Highlands air, and a modern kitchen and storeroom. Upstairs were some more storage rooms. Off the living room was a covered veranda, from which a gravel path led along the lawn to the narrow road down the hill. The ample servants' quarters were separate, to the right of the house and facing the road, though without an absolutely clear view of it. A large garden extended around three sides of the house and the Lings, both plant lovers, set about restoring it with roses and other temperate-zone shrubs they missed in the equatorial heat of Singapore. The jungle, with its mysteries and its dangers, was kept at bay across the road, where it provided a striking contrast to the orderly compound.

Despite regular plane services to Kuala Lumpur and Ipoh, the Cameron Highlands was then not within really convenient weekend distance of Singapore, and the Lings never planned to use Moonlight Cottage for more than occasional holidays until the time came for retirement. Accordingly, they made arrangements with a Dutchman and his wife, who lived in Tanah Rata, to act as rental agents for anyone who might want to take the house for a vacation; a Malay named Mohammed and his family lived in the servants' quarters and acted as caretakers for the place in addition to cooking and cleaning when anyone was in residence. The Lings came up four or five times a year, and one of their visits, almost invariably, was over the long Easter weekend, which fell in the worst part of the coastal hot season and always attracted a large number of visitors.

Twice the Lings had invited two old friends from Bangkok to be their houseguests for this particular holiday, and in 1967 the invitation was extended and accepted once more. The friends were Mrs. Connie Mangskau, the owner of one of Bangkok's leading antique shops, and James H. W. Thompson, or Jim as he was known to friends and strangers alike, who was internationally famous for his highly successful revival of the Thai silk industry and as one of the most colorful Americans living in the Far East. Before the weekend was over, he was also to become the most celebrated guest in the history of the Cameron Highlands, one whose memory still haunts that peaceful resort.

3

On Thursday, March 23, when he left Thailand for Malaysia, Thompson was two days past his sixty-first birthday, a soft-spoken, blue-eyed, slightly overweight man of medium height whose skin was deeply tanned from spending almost every lunch hour beside the swimming pool of the Royal Bangkok Sports Club. He drank sparingly and was trying, not very successfully to cut down on a heavy smoking habit. According to his doctor—a Dane named Einer Ammundsen, who, by coincidence, was also at the Highlands, playing golf, over the Easter weekend—he was in generally good physical condition for a man of his age, though he was not in perfect health. He was unusually susceptible to bronchial disorders—he had been in the hospital with pneumonia twice in the previous three years—and for the past year had been subject to painful gallstone attacks; for the latter he had pills to take in case he felt an attack coming on and had reluctantly agreed with professional advice to have the stones removed in the near future. (He kept his pills in an antique silver box given to him by one of his sisters, which friends in Bangkok had jokingly dubbed his "jungle box," since he had taken to carrying it with him whenever he went on trips up-country.)

Thompson led a highly active life, getting up early in the morning to visit his silk weavers and seldom getting to bed before eleven or twelve at night, and he resented these signs of physical weakness, preferring, whenever possible, to pretend they did not exist. On more than one occasion, friends in Bangkok later recalled, he had needlessly driven himself into a bad cold or a gallstone attack by refusing to slow down his fast pace even when confronted by a variety of warning signals. His "jungle box" was thus something of a concession, though a wise one, for, as he had discovered, the attacks were not as easily dismissed as a cold: when he had his first one, in a London hotel room, he had thought it was a heart attack and had been convinced he was going to die.

Despite such problems, however, his general stamina seemed remarkable to many of the less hardy foreign residents of tropical Bangkok. They marveled at his ability to dash about the city in the hottest part of the day, his refusal to have air-conditioning in his bedroom or, until recently, in his office, and his unwillingness to waste part of a weekend by taking a nap. On Sunday, the one day of the week he took off from his silk business, he frequently made the two-hour drive to the old capital of Ayutthaya or else spent the afternoon browsing about the congested alleyways of the Chinese section where there were a large number of antique shops. He entertained almost nightly in his celebrated Thai-style house and would often get up a dinner party of six or ten people simply to avoid eating alone. One of his special pleasures, which in recent years he had been able to enjoy less and less frequently due to business and social engagements, was walking, preferably in the country and, if at all possible, off the beaten track. In the Thai countryside, he often combined this pleasure with an interest in exploring ancient ruins, and some of his happiest hours had been spent with a few friends who shared these enthusiasms, clambering through thick jungle and scaling precipitous cliffsides to locate a rumored cave, a lost temple, or merely a pretty view—expeditions that he described in great detail in the long letters he wrote to his sister Elinor. He had been with the Office of Strategic Services (OSS) during the Second World War and, towards the end of it, had been with a group scheduled to parachute into Thailand. In preparation for this, he had undergone a jungle-survival course in Ceylon designed to teach a man how to take care of himself for weeks on end in a tropical forest.

Partly because of this training, though it had taken place more than twenty years before, and partly because of his many experiences in the wilds of Thailand, he was justifiably proud of his sense of direction and his knowledge of jungle lore. On at least one occasion in the not too distant past, however, this knowledge had not succeeded in keeping him out of trouble. On his first visit to the Highlands as a guest of the Lings, he had gone for a solitary ramble near Moonlight Cottage and had stumbled on a nest of wild hornets. They had pursued him with a vengeance and only a handy stream had saved him from serious injury. On his second visit, out of curiosity, he had revisited the scene of the near disaster and before leaving Bangkok in 1967 he had remarked to several people that he would like to see it again.

On the day of his departure, Thompson was a tired man and freely admitted it. In addition to his normal heavy load of activities, he had several weeks before moved his silk business into a handsome new building, a copy of an eighteenth-century Thai structure, and had been undergoing the usual strains and confusions of getting settled into new quarters. The Highlands holiday was intended to provide a much-needed rest, though, typically, a brief one, for on the Monday following Easter he was going to Singapore for a round of entertainments and talks with an American businessman who was thinking of starting a fabrics industry there and wanted some expert advice. On Monday evening, Thompson was scheduled to dine with the businessman and the American ambassador, and to make the engagement he and the Lings and Mrs. Mangskau were planning to leave the Highlands early in the morning and drive down the peninsula.

Mrs. Mangskau, his traveling companion, was a fifty-nine year-old widowed grandmother, half-English and half-Thai by birth, who had been married to a Norwegian; despite her age, she could have easily passed as the mother of her grandchildren. She and Thompson had been good friends since 1945, when he first came to Thailand and she had worked as an interpreter for the allied forces. He had been helpful when she opened her first shop, in the old Oriental Hotel; the business had flourished and by 1967, moved to larger quarters in another hotel, she was one of the leading antique dealers in Bangkok. There was no romantic attachment between her and Thompson and never had been, though later a good many people, especially in Malaysia, tried their best to manufacture one. They were simply close friends who enjoyed the same interests, often entertained the same visitors to Bangkok, and sometimes traveled together when their destinations were similar. As noted above, they had been twice to the Cameron Highlands to visit the Lings, as well as to the Middle East and Europe; Mrs. Mangskau had been in London when Thompson had had his first frightening gallstone attack. Thompson, who had been divorced in 1946, was considered a highly eligible bachelor—his personal fortune, mostly family money in America, was estimated at about a million dollars—but Mrs. Mangskau was not among the several women, in Bangkok and elsewhere, who had a serious claim on his affections.

4

The trip to Malaysia began amid a certain amount of confusion. This was not exceptional, for Thompson, despite considerable experience, was singularly absent-minded about the various formalities of international travel and generally left them until the last possible moment. On a few occasions, he had overlooked some of them altogether, and this proved to be the case when he and Mrs. Mangskau arrived at the Bangkok airport to catch their plane to Penang, where they were planning on spending the night. It was discovered there that he had neglected to have his cholera shot, then requisite for travel to any foreign country, and also to get his Thai tax clearance certificate, which all resident foreigners had to produce on leaving Thailand. Either of these oversights could easily have prevented him from going on his holiday, as they had with other travelers, but he was lucky—or perhaps unlucky, as things turned out—on both counts. An agreeable health official at the airport gave him a shot there and backdated it to meet the six-day requirement (Mrs. Mangskau asked the doctor to "make it a light dose" to avoid any reaction), and to solve the tax-clearance problem Mrs. Mangskau signed as guarantor should Thompson fail to return and pay any taxes he might have outstanding. He did remember to bring along some money, though hardly a large amount by the standard of most international travelers. He had about a hundred dollars in U.S. currency—enough to see him through the next week he figured, since the Highlands stay and most of the Singapore visit would involve few expenses.

Neither Thompson or Mrs. Mangskau had ever been to Penang, then a pleasant, faintly seedy island with a colonial atmosphere; established in 1786, it was the first British possession in Malaysia and until the rise of Singapore had been the most important. On their two previous visits to the Highlands, they had gone via Kuala Lumpur. This time, therefore, they planned to stop one night at George Town, the island's principal city, and then hire a taxi the following day for the drive up to the resort, where the Lings would meet them at Moonlight Cottage in the late afternoon.

The following week, when the restful holiday had turned into a nightmare, Mrs. Mangskau would be asked to repeat again and again the details of their brief stay in Penang, for there were many who felt it might hold some clue as to what had happened. If so, the clue was artfully concealed; despite exhaustive investigations, nothing was ever uncovered to suggest that it was anything but the enjoyable little interlude it seemed at the time. They stayed at the Ambassador, one of Penang's newest hotels, which Thompson rather regretted when he saw the Eastern & Oriental, a rambling old place from British days that was more to his architectural taste. Using the same taxi that brought them in from the airport, they made a tour around the island, not stopping off anywhere but returning to the hotel in time for Thompson to get a haircut, something else he had forgotten to do before leaving. That evening they dined at an Indian restaurant and took a stroll. The next morning they made arrangements at the hotel for a taxi to take them to the Highlands, did a little shopping, and went to call on Thompson's local silk agent, only to find the shop closed since it was Good Friday. They were picked up by the taxi a little after eleven and arrived at Moonlight Cottage about five-thirty that afternoon.

In reexamining the events between their departure from Bangkok and their arrival at the bungalow, Mrs. Mangskau could recall only three that were even remotely suggestive. One of these was decidedly minor: Thompson's unexpected decision to have a haircut the evening they got to Penang. At the time Mrs. Mangskau put it down as yet another example of his absent-mindedness—which, in all probability, is exactly what it was—and she was mildly annoyed that they had to cut short their drive around the island so he could go to a barbershop before they met for drinks. The only reason the incident assumed any subsequent interest was that except when they were sleeping, it was the only time Thompson was alone in Penang, a point that could have been significant in several of the theories that were later advanced.

The other two events she remembered seemed, at first anyhow, of potentially more sinister import. Both occurred on the drive from Penang to the Highlands, and both involved changes of drivers. The first took place in George Town on their way to the vehicular ferry to the mainland. Without warning, the driver stopped the car, jumped out, and ran into a nearby building. He was gone about five minutes and when he returned he had another man with him; the new man, he said, would be their driver. Thompson and Mrs. Mangskau did not question this change but they found the second one more annoying. This took place at Tapah, the small town where the highway begins to climb steeply up to the resort, and here they were asked not only to change drivers but also to switch to another taxi, which already had two Chinese passengers waiting in it. The explanation given was that the original taxi had developed engine trouble and was unable to make the climb. They were willing enough to change cars, but Mrs. Mangskau balked at the proposal that they share the new one with two strangers; they had arranged and paid for a private car, she said, and five in a smallish vehicle would hardly make for the comfortable trip they had looked forward to. After a brief discussion the owner agreed, and the other passengers unloaded their bags from the taxi, in which Thompson and Mrs. Mangskau completed their journey.

The possible implications of these two incidents intrigued a number of people during the next week, and the second in particular came in for some imaginative speculation. The *New York Times*, in a long report on the early rumors in the case, suggested it might have been a kidnapping attempt that failed due to Mrs. Mangskau's insistence on evicting the two strangers. It was not for some days that the apparent mystery was cleared up by the Malaysian investigation authorities. It was found that the first change of drivers was due to the fact that the original one lacked a Malaysian driving permit and had therefore turned over his taxi to a friend who did. As for the change of cars, it emerged that drivers from Penang (and from Kuala Lumpur, too) frequently transferred their passengers at Tapah to save fuel and wear and tear on the car. Only the year before, the same thing had happened to Thompson's assistant at the Thai Silk Company, Charles Sheffield, and it would also happen later to some of the investigators going up to the Highlands. By the time these unexciting explanations were revealed, however, the original speculations had already planted some seeds for thought in various fertile minds and these were soon to produce some extraordinary fruit.

5

Dr. Ling had arrived at Moonlight Cottage only about fifteen minutes before Thompson and Mrs. Mangskau, having driven up alone from Singapore. Mrs. Ling, delayed on business, was coming up to Ipoh by plane and then on to the Highlands later that evening. She got there about eight, and after dinner the party retired early.

Thompson was the last to get up the next morning, saying that he'd had the best night's sleep in ages. He looked rested, Mrs. Mangskau remembered later, and was in excellent spirits. Over breakfast, Dr. Ling remarked that he had discovered a new trail leading down the hill to the golf links, and Thompson, of course, was eager to try it. The ladies were less enthusiastic; they said they would drive down later and meet the men at the golf club. The two men left soon afterward and started down the hill.

Around ten the ladies drove to Tanah Rata for some shopping

and arrived at the club at the appointed time. There they met Dr. Ammundsen and several other friends who had come from Bangkok to play golf, but there was no sign of Thompson and Dr. Ling. It was nearly one before they trudged in with a tale of minor adventure. It seemed that not long after they left the bungalow they had gotten lost in the tangled undergrowth that spilled down the hill and, to make matters worse, Dr. Ling had stumbled over a root and sprained a ligament. Given an ideal opportunity to display his jungle knowledge, Thompson had come through; he had spotted a small stream, and by following its course they had eventually arrived in familiar surroundings. The incident had shaken Dr. Ling slightly, but Thompson, characteristically, seemed exhilarated by it.

After a restorative drink at the club, they drove back to the bungalow, had lunch, and all retired to their respective rooms for a rest. The Lings shared a large bedroom on the front corner of the house, with views of the garden and the gravel path that led to the road down the hill; when they rested in the afternoon, they customarily left the windows open to catch the breeze. Mrs. Mangskau had a smaller room next to theirs, and Thompson was in a room at the back of the house.

Did he remain in his room all that first afternoon? The Lings and Mrs. Mangskau were sure he did, though they agreed that if for some reason he had wished to go out unnoticed he could easily have done so; if he did, he never mentioned it, nor did the Lings hear him through their open window. Everyone assembled for tea at four-thirty and inspected the garden, for which Thompson had brought some amaryllis bulbs; after an early dinner they retired.

The next day, the one that ended in horror, began peacefully enough. It was, of course, Easter Sunday, and over the years the Lings had established a sort of Easter tradition at the Highlands, which consisted of services at the little Anglican church in Tanah Rata, a large lunch, and a lazy afternoon. This year the routine was to be varied slightly: after church, they had decided to take their guests on a picnic to a scenic spot inside a military reservation not far from Moonlight

Cottage. It was a pleasant site with fine views of the countryside, and they thought it would appeal to Thompson's love of the outdoors.

While everyone was getting organized for the drive to Tanah Rata, Thompson announced that he was going to walk to the bottom of the hill and would meet the others there. He did so, leaving a little before the rest and prudently keeping to the road this time as he was wearing a dark blue Thai silk suit. This morning walk is significant only in that it disproves one of the several "facts" regularly cited in discussions of the Thompson case—namely, that he was never alone outside Moonlight Cottage all that weekend until Easter Sunday afternoon, a point of some importance since several of the most persistent theories rest on the assumption that he was being closely watched in the hope of catching him alone. Thompson was in fact alone for the ten or fifteen minutes it took him to get down the hill and was for most of it out of sight of the house and its occupants. An alert and well-organized group of men could have abducted him then as well as later.

Presumably, however, no such group was lying in wait that morning or, if they were, they did nothing, for he was waiting for the Lings and Mrs. Mangskau near the golf course when they came down in the car. They drove on to Tanah Rata, attended the church service, and after picking up some newspapers returned to the cottage to get the picnic lunch, which was packed and ready. Here something slightly unusual happened, or at least it seemed unusual later when the others looked back on that fateful day. Thompson, rather surprisingly, seemed to have lost his enthusiasm for the idea of the picnic. He suggested that the garden was just as suitable as the hill they had previously selected, and much more convenient. The others, though, were in favor of following the original plan and, without further protest, he agreed.

The picnic site was on a broad plateau, about three quarters of an hour's drive from Moonlight Cottage. Mrs. Mangskau brought along a camera and took some pictures during the lunch. They are the sort of snapshots one sees of picnics anywhere: the blanket spread out on the grass, the hamper and the Thermos, a lazy, relaxed, summer afternoon mood. What they do not show, but something the others recalled vividly, was Thompson's restlessness. He seemed eager to get the picnic over with; hardly had they finished eating, the Lings remembered, than he began to collect things and put them back in the hamper. He refused to have any beer, as the others did, saying he did not like to drink anything in the middle of the day. The rest assumed he was tired, perhaps from his walk down the hill that morning, and wanted to go back and rest. It was, after all, the last real day of leisure he was to have on his trip, for they were leaving for Singapore early the next morning and a full social and business schedule awaited them there.

(Some theorists were to dwell later on this incident, using it to support a variety of plots, mostly involving Thompson's determination to get away on his own so that he could carry out some pre-arranged plan. Close friends in Bangkok, however, suggested another likely motive. "He was probably bored," one of them said flatly. "He wanted to go off on that walk he'd enjoyed so much before and he was tired of sitting around making small talk, even with good friends. That would have been entirely in character.")

At any event, they packed up and left the plateau shortly after two, reaching Moonlight Cottage about two thirty. Dr. Ling remembered the time because he happened to look at his watch and was surprised they had returned so early.

In the car on the way back, Mrs. Mangskau had announced her intention of taking a nap and everybody, including Thompson, agreed it was a fine idea. When they got to the house, Mrs. Mangskau went straight to her room and the Lings to theirs. The last time they saw Thompson, the last time anyone saw him for certain, he was in the living room, preparing, they assumed, to do the same thing they were.

What happened in the next half hour or so is largely a matter of conjecture, but a few points seem reasonably clear. For one thing, Thompson certainly did not take a nap. His bed had not been turned down, nor, apparently, even lain on. He must have gone out to sit on the lawn in the sun, for a little after three the Lings, resting but not sleeping in their front room with the windows open, heard the sound of an aluminum deck chair being placed on the veranda; a moment later, they heard footsteps going down the gravel path leading to the road. They were not Asian footsteps, Mrs. Ling said firmly later, but those of a European; she was sure she could tell the difference. They heard no voices, either before or after the footsteps; after the steps they heard nothing at all. If anyone had called to Thompson, they would certainly have heard it and would have noted it, for no guests were expected. As it was, they supposed that Thompson was merely going for a stroll, and since this was hardly unusual—he had gone for walks alone on both previous trips—they did not bother to look out the window.

If they had, it might have made a considerable difference in the events that were about to descend upon them and their peaceful retirement cottage. Or perhaps not. Perhaps had they looked out, they might have seen nothing at all unusual: just their old friend from Bangkok, alone, setting out for a walk in the clear Highlands afternoon, as unaware as they that he was about to add a new and sensational chapter to a life already quite remarkable enough.

Part Two: The First Legend

1

In 1959, Somerset Maugham made a sentimental final journey through the Far East, stopping off at many of the places he had used so effectively for his stories and novels in the twenties and thirties. He came to Bangkok (which figured in *The Gentleman in the Parlour*, his only pure travel book), and like most of the distinguished visitors to the city at that time, he went for dinner at Jim Thompson's celebrated Thai house, which was then less than a year old. Other than a brief thank-you note to his host (containing the Maughamesque observation, "You have not only beautiful things, but what is rare you have arranged them with faultless taste") there is no record of the writer's impression of that evening, but one is perhaps justified in saying that the old man may well have recognized in Thompson a familiar character, quite in keeping with the nostalgic nature of the trip.

A recurrent figure in Maugham's work, especially in his short stories, is the seemingly average man who, for some deeply private and often inexplicable reason, suddenly deserts his ordinary, secure world and starts a new life amid totally alien surroundings. He met a number of such characters on his early travels—on remote Pacific islands, in deep jungles and along the docks of raffish seaports—and he never ceased to be fascinated by them; he found them mysterious and romantic (and perhaps enviable), and in story after story he sought explanations for their strange behavior. Undoubtedly his most exhaustive study of the type was in *The Moon and Sixpence*, his novel based on the life of Paul Gauguin, in which the hero, Charles Strickland, abandons his respectable job, his family, and his friends to go and paint on a South Seas island. There is a passage in it that seems to sum up all Maugham's other lone—but rarely lonely—men who find contentment in exotic places. The narrator, trying to comprehend Strickland's remarkable affinity for this distant, unfamiliar place, observes, "I have an idea that some men are born out of their due place. Accident has cast them amid certain surroundings, but they always have a nostalgia for a home they know not. Perhaps it is this sense of strangeness that sends men far and wide in search of something permanent to which they may attach themselves...Sometimes a man hits upon a place to which he mysteriously feels that he belongs. Here is the home he sought, and he will settle amid scenes that he has never seen before, among men he has never known, as though they were familiar to him from his birth."

James Harrison Wilson Thompson's journey to the strange place he was instinctively to recognize as the place he belonged to began, as Charles Strickland's did, in surroundings that could hardly have been more different from the spectacular house in which he entertained Maugham. He was born in Greenville, Delaware, a prosperous community not far from Wilmington, on March 21, 1906, the youngest of five children by fourteen years. The family was comfortably off, prominent in Delaware society, and had roots that went deep into the history of that region and outside as well.

Of a number of distinguished ancestors, perhaps the most interesting, in terms of Thompson's later career, was his maternal grandfather, James Harrison Wilson, after whom he was named. Wilson graduated as an engineer from West Point in 1860, the sixth in a class of forty-one, and soon after his graduation went on an assignment to Oregon, then practically virgin territory, to survey the route from Puget Sound to the Columbia River. The Civil War advanced his military career rapidly; he was a major general at the age of twenty-seven, with the largest cavalry command of any American officer, and an intimate of General Grant. His first encounter with Grant, according to one historian, was not encouraging: "The general's bearing was hopelessly unmilitary; he might have been the proprietor of a country store. One of the other members of the staff sidled up to the newcomer with the information that Grant would be all right if the staff could keep him away from 'bad habits.'" However, Wilson soon perceived Grant's talents as a leader and became a trusted and valuable member of his staff. He fought all the way through the war, winning his greatest victory at the battle of Selma, Alabama, and was one of the party that captured Jefferson Davis; he and Davis spent the evening of the capture exchanging anecdotes of West Point, of which Davis had once serve as superintendent.

With this distinguished military record, together with his friendship with Grant, General Wilson expected a high-ranking position in Washington when the former commander became president; but the two men had some kind of falling out and the job never materialized. Undaunted, Wilson embarked on a career that included extensive traveling about the world, writing, engineering, and, from time to time, more fighting. He made a year-long journey through China for the purpose of building a railroad and produced a popular book called *Travels in the Middle Kingdom.* He also wrote a lengthy autobiography in two volumes, *Under The Old Flag,* in which he described his Civil War experiences and delivered himself of some candid judgments of his fellow generals.

It was through General Wilson, in a somewhat indirect way, that the family got its introduction to Thailand, or, as it was then known to the world, Siam. In 1902, he was appointed by President Theodore Roosevelt as the military representative of the United States at the coronation of King Edward VII, and during this event he met and became friends with the Siamese Crown Prince, Vajiravudh, the son of King Chulalongkorn; later generations of Americans were to become familiar with Chulalongkorn as one of the young princes whom the legendary Anna came to teach in *The King and I.* The crown prince also became friends with the general's daughter, Elinor, and asked her to be his guest at the end of term festivities at Oxford, where he was about to complete his studies.

Later that year, Prince Vajiravudh made his first official tour of the United States and while in the Washington area accepted an invitation to spend a day at the Wilson home in Wilmington. Thompson was not yet born, but his oldest sister, Mrs. Thomas Reath, remembered it well, including photographs taken of the prince amusing himself on a seesaw that belonged to one of the grandchildren. As a child, Thompson used to enjoy looking at the faded pictures and hearing of the garden party for the young man who by that time was King Rama VI of Siam; some forty years later, in the king's own country, he would be having his meals off a pair of ornate gaming tables that were originally made for the palace of King Chulalongkorn.

General Wilson died in 1924, when Thompson was eighteen, and it would probably be romanticizing to suggest that he had much direct influence over his grandson's later career in Asia. Still, the young Thompson was naturally fascinated by the old man's colorful past and later, when he read the book on China, he found it enthralling; certainly some of his love for faraway places must have come from the general and perhaps some of his lifelong enthusiasm for walking and exploring. He also got, as a child, an unusual number of visits to the dentist to have cavities filled, owing to General Wilson's habit of freely distributing candy to his grandchildren. The purpose of this generosity was not to win affection: during his association with Grant, Wilson had discovered that if he kept the commander supplied with sweets he was less inclined to get drunk, and this had led to a conviction that a liberal diet of candy would ward off the evils of alcoholism.

The more emphatic influences on Thompson came from his parents and, during his younger years at least, from his mother, Mary Wilson Thompson, who was by all accounts a beautiful, strong-willed woman. She entertained frequently and lavishly and acted as an arbiter over Wilmington society. She also took a stand on certain political issues, among them the question of suffrage for women, which she adamantly opposed; she made several trips to the state capital at Dover to address the legislature on this burning subject and it was partly due to her efforts that Delaware failed to ratify the suffrage amendment. A more successful endeavor was her proposal to restore the historic town of New Castle, Delaware—long before the Rockefellers envisioned Williamsburg—which led to the founding of the Delaware Society for the Preservation of Antiquities, a forerunner of the National Trust for Historic Preservation. During the early days of the depression, when various suggestions were being put forth about how to best use the Civilian Conservation Corps (CCC) in the area, she again journeyed to Dover and helped persuade the state to use the unemployed workers to drain the marshes and get rid of the mosquitoes, an undertaking that earned her the nickname of "the mosquito woman."

In a memoir, her youngest daughter Elinor recalled: "Mother's fondest quotation was, 'Women's place is in the home'—not that she spent very much time in it, but she thought she did. Another famous remark on hers among her children was, 'I never get my foot outside the front gate.' Between trips to the legislature in Dover, shopping trips to New York when she said, 'I haven't a stitch to put on,' and being driven to Wilmington by our Italian chauffeur for various meetings, there was not much time."

Nor was Thompson's father, Henry B., much in evidence in his youngest son's early years. His offices were in New York, and he only came to Delaware on weekends. He was the president of the United States Finishing Company, with mills in Connecticut and Rhode Island, which printed cottons and, when they were later developed, rayons. As a member of the family later succinctly stated, "It was not a carriage trade business"; the emphasis was on mass production, and it was a very different sort of operation from the one Thompson was to found in Thailand with a very different sort of fabric.

Two other interests of Henry Thompson probably had more effect on his son than his involvement with the textile business. These were architecture and landscape design, neither of which he ever studied but about which, according to one of his daughters, "he knew as much as any layman I have ever known." His knowledge in these areas led to his serving as the chairman of the Grounds and Building Committee of Princeton University, of which he was a life trustee, for twenty-five years; it was during his tenure that many of that university's famous Gothic buildings were added to the campus. His daughter Elinor was inspired by his example to study landscape architecture and Thompson himself decided on architecture as his initial career partly because of his father's interest in the subject.

Home for Thompson as a boy was Brookwood Farm, a large house set in spacious grounds near Greenville. His older sisters, Mary and Katherine, and his brother, Henry, were away at school for most of his boyhood and he was closest to Elinor, the nearest to him in age. As children, they had a number of governesses, from one of whom, a Swiss woman, he learned French; he never lost his love for this language, which was useful to him later in the military and also in Thailand, where many of his early friends were from the former French colonies of Indo-China.

Elinor Thompson Douglas, as she later became, remembered that she and her brother enjoyed roaming the estate and conjuring up imaginary people who lived in a hollow tree and who entertained at lavish parties similar to those their mother gave. "Our imaginary world was full of intrigue," she wrote in a memoir of Brookwood, "and some devious crimes were committed, usually because of a passionate love affair with someone else's wife. Where did we get all these ideas? They were not certainly modeled on our parents' very circumspect life. I was an avid reader and undoubtedly read books in our large library that my mother would have considered much too adult for a ten or twelve-year old."

One of Thompson's childhood enthusiasms that was to remain with him was his interest in bantam chickens. He started raising them when he was about eleven and developed into such an expert that he traveled along the East Coast showing and winning prizes in chicken shows and even wrote a learned pamphlet on the subject for the U.S. Department of Agriculture. In Thailand, many years later, one of his early purchases after moving into his first house was a flock of the jaunty little fowl, which were allowed free and sometimes destructive run of his garden.

He attended public schools in Wilmington and then went on to boarding school at St. Paul's, where he was an enthusiastic oarsman and generally active in school athletics. Princeton, obviously, was the family university, and Thompson entered in 1924, graduating in the class of 1928. He was interested in art and might, his sister Elinor thought, have become a painter of merit had he gone on with it; instead, however, he chose to become an architect and went on to the University of Pennsylvania. He never took his degree from there. The stumbling block was calculus, which he failed twice and finally gave up on.

As a boy, and later in his twenties, Thompson made a number of trips to Europe with his family and with school friends, but he never displayed any particular interest in Asia, despite his grandfather's association with that part of the world and despite the fact that one of his sisters, Katherine, married the son of General Leonard Wood, who was at the time governor-general of the Philippines.

From 1931 to 1940, he was a practising architect in New York City, working for the firm of Holden McLaughlin Associates. Following his failure to win a degree from Pennsylvania, he also failed to pass the New York architectural board exams, a fact that undoubtedly limited his career in that state but that did not prevent him from enjoying a busy life as a designer up and down the coast. His very first architectural project was decidedly untypical: it was a combination public lavatory and bandstand at the summer resort of Rehoboth, Delaware, where his mother had built a large seaside house named "Mon Plaisir" and where the Thompson family regularly passed June and July (in August they went to Maine). This edifice was for many years depicted on one of the postcards sent home by Rehoboth's summer visitors and could thus claim a singularly wide public, if no special aesthetic distinction.

Public lavatories were not, however, to be his specialty. His talent was for country houses of traditional design—colonial and Georgian, mainly—and he built a considerable number of these in Pennsylvania, Delaware, New Jersey, Virginia, and Maryland, often for college and family friends. Besides designing the houses—many of which are still highly admired by their owners—he also often landscaped the gardens and helped with the interior decoration; manifest in the latter was his remarkable flair for color, already suggested in his love of painting and later to find such spectacular release in the silks of Thailand.

Friends of Thompson from his New York period recall him as a good-looking, easy-going young man who liked parties, apparently enjoyed his work, and was a familiar figure at debutant balls in New York and Philadelphia; according to one, he loved foxhunting and had a pack of bassett hounds with which he hunted the countryside outside of Wilmington. Their memories, despite the grim depression around them, are mainly of social occasions, with Thompson cast in the role of the carefree young bachelor, always ready for a dance, a theater party, a hunt, always rumored about to marry this or that young heiress but never quite doing so.

In his later years in Thailand, Thompson, who enjoyed reminiscing, was oddly disinclined to talk about his life in New York. The reason, in the opinion of one friend who knew him in both places, may have been that in retrospect the New York years came to have an air of unreality about them, almost as though they involved another person. The American Thompson and the Thailand Thompson shared many similarities; but there were also certain basic differences between the two and some of them were so great that it is quite possible that to the latter the former came to seem a sort of stranger. Thompson in New York was certainly not a failure in the conventional sense of the word, as suggested by at least one woman whose description of herself as a good friend was possibly inaccurate. He had a good, if not brilliant, career as an architect and thanks to a legacy from a cousin of his father's a more than adequate private income; he was popular among a wide circle of amusing and talented friends; his probable future, to most young men, would have seemed an enviable one. Yet in some inexplicable way, for reasons probably he himself could not put into words, none of it was entirely satisfying.

The only aspect of his New York years that he frequently alluded to later to friends in Thailand was his great interest in ballet. On one of his early trips to Europe with his family he had seen the Diaghilev company in the glory of its prime and had been enormously impressed by the spectacular sets and costumes; he had come across a rare edition of a book of Leon Bakst's costumes in a Paris bookshop and when his mother bought it for him, it became one of his most treasured possessions. This enthusiasm for the scenic effects of ballet, which interested him more than the dancing itself, continued in New York and led, in the late thirties, to his becoming a director of the Monte Carlo Ballet company, an outgrowth of the Ballets Russes and the forerunner of the famous New York City Ballet. Such eminent figures as George Balanchine, Vera Zorina, and Tamara Tamanouva were connected with this company, and the sets and costumes were in the grand Diaghilev tradition. Thompson's association with the group lasted only a few years, but it was in many ways one of the decisive influences in his life. The bold, original colors clung to his imagination, and his friendships with the intensely creative members of the company perhaps increased his vague dissatisfaction with his life and work.

As the thirties came to a close, a combination of things conspired to produce a remarkable change in the thirty-four-year-old architect's view of the world in general and his own life in particular. Partly, it was the storm which was just then breaking over Europe and his conviction that America must sooner or later become involved; partly, it was his growing disenchantment with his social activities and his nagging sense of restlessness. Whatever the causes, the change manifested itself in a series of radical decisions. He changed his politics, from traditional Republican to Democrat. He became critical of people who spent their lives in frivolous pursuits. And he quit his job and enlisted, as a private, in the Delaware National Guard Regiment.

2

Although it cannot have been very easy in view of his age and background, Thompson did well in basic training and by the time Pearl

Harbor was attacked he had become a noncommissioned officer. He went to Officer Candidate School in Florida and after receiving his commission was assigned to duty with a coastal artillery unit based in North Carolina.

About a year after the outbreak of war he met Captain Edwin Black, a West Point graduate and a member of the recently formed Office of Strategic Services (OSS), at Fort Monroe, Virginia. Black urged him to ask for a transfer to the OSS, and since this seemed to offer an opportunity to see a bit more of the war, Thompson eagerly complied.

The OSS, which had been formed by a colorful World War One hero named General William ("Wild Bill") Donovan, specialized in subversive propaganda, intelligence gathering and clandestine warfare behind enemy lines. Though after the war it evolved into the CIA, it was at this stage a very different sort of organization, attracting a wide variety of recruits who ranged from adventurous upper-class types like Thompson to newspaper reporters like Alexander MacDonald, who was also to discover a career in postwar Thailand. Its predominant sentiments were liberal and anti-colonial, which would lead to conflicts with its British equivalent in the Far Eastern theater, and in accounts by former members one is struck by an almost boyish enthusiasm for adventurous undertakings. MacDonald later described his training camp, located in what had once been a country club on the outskirts of Washington:

> "We were taught to lie and steal, kill, maim, spy, deceive, terrify, and destroy. It was the Ten Commandments in reverse. There was, for example, the class in personal combat, led by a former police colonel from Shanghai. He taught a gutter type of karate. He demonstrated how to chop with the hand at an adversary's windpipe, how to grip an arm so that the finger bones could be crushed, how to immobilize a rival by pressing a certain nerve in the neck. 'And don't ever hesitate,' he urged, 'to go after the balls.'"

While some OSS veterans were undoubtedly absorbed into the CIA, most were far too individualistic or ambitious to fit into that tightly-controlled bureaucracy and went on to different, often colorful careers. Many, like both Thompson and MacDonald, were inclined to nostalgia when they talked, and occasionally wrote, about this past period of living dangerously as members of what they regarded as an elite group; on the other hand, as Macdonald wrote in a review of this book when it first appeared, once they had embarked on their new lives in Thailand, "I can say with certainty that neither of us carried on further intelligence work."

Black also influenced Thompson's life in another way. He introduced him to a tall, elegant ex-Powers model named Pat Thraves, who succeeded where the debutantes of Wilmington, Philadelphia, and New York had failed. Besides being blond and beautiful, she had artistic inclinations, and Thompson decided to end his bachelor life. They were married in 1942.

The couple enjoyed only about six months of married life, mostly in Washington, before Thompson was shipped overseas as a member of an OSS group assigned to work with French forces in North Africa. From there, he later went up through Italy and into France following the invasion. His work was of a highly classified nature, so much so, indeed, that even after the war he never discussed it with his family; but from other OSS accounts, one can assume it involved raids behind German lines, liaison with local resistance groups, and probably a good deal of personal risk.

Had the war in Europe lasted another two or three months, Thompson's subsequent career would almost certainly have been very different, for it is unlikely that he would ever have reached Thailand on his own. As a matter of fact, Thailand was not even in his mind when, shortly after V-E day, he volunteered to go to the Pacific; his assignment was to the vast China-Burma-India theater, and he might easily have ended up in one of the dozen or so countries included in that designation rather than in the one he was to make his home. If Fate had a hand in the development of the Thai silk industry, and in the radical transformation of Thompson into a living legend, it operated in the form of some anonymous army officer who as part of his routine duty decided that a captain named Thompson should be assigned to the OSS contingent that was preparing for the invasion of Thailand.

Though few people remember it today, technically Thailand was then an enemy of the Allied powers. In 1941, when the Japanese were preparing for their triumphant sweep down through British Malaya to Singapore, they had enlisted the Thais as rather reluctant allies, offering them the lure of some territory in Indo-China that had been seized by the French and the implied threat of occupation if they failed to cooperate. Thailand, alone among Southeast Asian countries, had retained its independence for centuries, and it was not eager to have the experience of giving up its freedom. Accordingly, in early 1942, the government of the time declared war on both the United States and Great Britian. In Washington, Secretary of State Cordell Hull shrewdly refused to accept the declaration, to the considerable relief of the Thai ambassador, who at once proceeded to organize an anti-Japanese group that became known as the Free Thai. A similar group sprang up in England, where there were also many Thais living, though the British government did acknowledge the war declaration. Initially, the two groups were largely composed of students, diplomats, and a few political exiles, but they were soon joined by a strong underground movement in Thailand itself, headed by a prominent Bangkok leader known to most simply by his code name of "Ruth." By 1945, when Thompson first went to Asia, the Free Thai was a complex organization inside and outside the country, and it was working closely with both the OSS and Force 136, its British equivalent; a number of OSS agents were actually living secretly in the Thai capital, in a former royal palace, and sending messages out to their compatriots.

Soon after the war ended in Europe, Thompson was sent to Catalina Island, off the California coast, for a rigorous training program to prepare him for service in Thailand. Since his assignment would be behind enemy lines, a good deal of emphasis was placed on survival, and one part of the program consisted of leaving him on a deserted island to see how well he could shift for himself. June of 1945 found him in Ceylon, in Trincomalee, a particularly beautiful part of that scenic island, with luxuriant jungle and breathtaking gorges that became widely known to moviegoers some twenty years later when they were used for the background scenes in *The Bridge on the River Kwai*—the story of which, ironically, was set in Thailand.

Both Thompson, then a Major in the Army, and MacDonald, a Naval Lieutenant, were members of a group who had volunteered to be parachuted into Thailand to assist in what they thought of as the liberation rather than the invasion of the country, and jungle training took place in Trincomalee. Later, during speculation about Thompson's disappearance in the Malaysian jungle, much would be made of this supposedly rugged training period. MacDonald, however, who had been fighting in Burma, looked back on it as "vacation time" mainly devoted to survival techniques, demolition tactics, and some rather farcical lessons in parachute jumping from a rickety wooden tower about a hundred feet high.

In any event, after the training was completed the men were divided into groups, assigned to different parts of the country. Thompson was the ranking officer in his team, which was scheduled to be dropped in the northeast near the Cambodian border in the second half of August. At that time only a few people were optimistic enough to think Japan would surrender easily, despite the atomic bomb which had just been dropped on Hiroshima. Its leaders had announced their intention to fight to the last man, abroad as well as on its home islands, and the men who were going to Thailand expected a long and difficult fight ahead of them.

What in fact happened, though dramatic enough in its own way, must have seemed something of an anticlimax. As the C-47 carrying them was crossing the border of Thailand and Burma, one of the pilots appeared in the plane. "His eyes were wide with excitement,"

MacDonald wrote. "He was shouting, his arms waving. 'It's over!' he was yelling. 'The goddam war is over.'" Indeed, by order of the Emperor, Japan had surrendered, and the plane was told to return to recently-liberated Rangoon and await instructions. A few days later, the instructions came. Thompson, MacDonald, and the others (who included several Free Thai members) were to proceed to Bangkok and land there, in full view of the former enemy.

3

A detailed study of Thai politics in the immediate pre- and postwar period is, obviously, beyond the scope of the present book. However, some brief summary of the period and its leading figures is necessary to an understanding of the country Thompson was about to see for the first time, for some of the events, and several of the personalities, were to play important parts in his subsequent life there.

For those whose knowledge of the country is limited to the fanciful tale of Anna and the king, a brief look at the prewar years may be in order. In 1932, the centuries-old absolute monarchy in Thailand (or Siam, as it was then known to the Western world) came to an end when a small group of young men, mostly educated abroad, staged a relatively mild coup d'état and established a constitutional monarchy modeled on that of Britain. Two of the revolutionaries involved were to dominate the Thai political scene for many years to come, though from increasingly divergent points of view. They were Luang Pibul Songgram, a major in the army at the time of the coup, and Pridi Phanomyong, a lawyer and teacher whose name was to figure prominently in later speculations about Thompson's disappearance. The King at the time of the revolution, Rama VII, finally abdicated in 1935, not because he was opposed to constitutional government but because he distrusted the motives of some of the men who came to power in its name. He was in England at the time for medical treatment and continued to live there until his death in 1941. He named no successor and had no male heirs; therefore, under Thai law, the National Assembly on his abdication made the choice from a number of eligible princes. They selected Prince Ananda Mahidol, at the time a boy of ten living in Switzerland with his mother, younger brother, and sister. As the new king was a minor and was completing his studies in Europe, a council of regency was appointed to act for him. In 1938, after steadily rising in power through the military Pibul, then a colonel, became prime minister, thus setting him on a long career as head of the Thai government.

As prime minister, it was Pibul who acceded to Japanese demands for the right of passage through Thailand on their invasion of Malaya in December 1941 and who the following month declared war on America and Great Britain. For this reason, as well as others—he was also an avowed admirer of Hitler and Mussolini and authoritarian government—he was held in low esteem during the war and just after it by most of the Free Thai and their Allied supporters in the OSS and Force 136. Pridi, on the other hand, increased his prestige abroad enormously during the war years, for it was he who organized the underground Free Thai movement within the country and became the celebrated "Ruth" of the wartime codes.

The two men, so radically different in many respects, were alike in others. Both were patriots, doing what they thought was best for their country, though their aims were dissimilar; both had great personal charm and were capable of inspiring fierce loyalties among their partisans; and both were well educated and genuinely talented. To the majority of the Americans who had worked with the Free Thai, the choice between the two was as simple as black and white: Pridi was the good one because he had resisted the Japanese, while Pibul, who had cooperated with the enemy was, in the terminology of the times, a war criminal. That the matter was not quite so simple as it seemed would become clear very shortly after the war ended, but even so, many foreigners never really lost their wartime admiration for the "Ruth" they had heard so much about long before they ever met him. Alexander MacDonald, Thompson's fellow OSS officer, who stayed on to found the English-language *Bangkok Post*, summed up this opinion in his book *Bangkok Editor*, which describes his newspaper days in Thailand. Discussing his disillusionment with certain of Pridi's postwar policies and associates, he nonetheless confessed, "I knew I probably should never be really objective where [Pridi] was concerned." Many Thai leaders, a number of whom were by no means pro-Pibul, took a very different view.

In July of 1944, a year before the hostilities ceased, the Pibul government fell, partly because of various unpopular projects (one of which was a costly scheme to build a new capital in a swampy province far from Bangkok) but mostly, many people felt, because of the efforts of Pridi and his supporters, whose power was increasing as Japan's inevitable defeat became clearer. Pridi apparently felt it would be unwise for him to try to take over the government himself at this time—his anti-Japanese views were not exactly a secret—and so a popular politician named Kuang Aphaiwong became prime minister and Pridi became the absent king's regent, a position from which he could wield considerable influence while waiting for his moment to come.

Thailand was, as we have seen, spared the invasion that many of its citizens expected. Bangkok suffered periodic Allied bombing, and some women and children were evacuated to the safety of provincial villages, but the abrupt end of the war saved it from the horror of becoming a battlefield. Unlike other countries in the region, it emerged with most of its public facilities intact, a government that could go on functioning, and plenty of rice in its fertile fields.

With peace, the Free Thai leaders from Britain and America hurried back home, joining foreigners like Thompson and MacDonald who had arrived there before them. Bangkok was faintly shabby and exhausted from the war, and almost every imported luxury was in short supply, but people who were there then remember it as an exciting time, full of plans for the future and the sense of embarking on a new era. The young King Ananda came back to the acclaim of his subjects, most of whom had never seen him but had, like their ancestors, a deep-rooted reverence for their monarchy that the 1932 revolution had scarcely dimmed at all. Mainly to satisfy the Allies, Pibul was sent to jail for collaborating with the enemy, but was released after a short time; he announced that he planned to retire from politics. Pridi decided the time had come to take advantage of his wartime popularity and became prime minister. He also proclaimed that the declaration of war against the Allied powers had been against the will of the people and was therefore invalid, an explanation that was accepted by the U.S. Secretary of State James F. Byrnes (and also, though a bit more reluctantly, by the newly-elected British Labor government) and that paved the way for Thailand to apply for membership in the United Nations. The application was approved in December 1946, but by that time a major tragedy had shaken Thailand to its foundations, and partly because of it Pridi's days were numbered.

On the morning of June 9, 1946, a gunshot rang out in the ornate Grand Palace in Bangkok, and a few minutes later King Ananda was found dead in his bed, a pistol lying nearby. The circumstances did not suggest an accident, and most people refused to accept the idea of a royal suicide. That, of course, left murder, and as the weeks passed with no clearing of the mystery rumors flew all over Bangkok, many of them implicating Pridi in a plot to kill the young king. Three palace employees were eventually arrested for complicity in the regicide, and after a lengthy trial that lasted until 1955 were found guilty and executed. Today the general opinion seems to be that they, and Pridi, were innocent victims of political intrigue; but at that time Pridi's enemies succeeded in creating such a climate of doubt and suspicion that he found it expedient to step down after only five months as prime minister.

He still retained a large measure of his power and no doubt planned to return as soon as the case could be resolved. This, however, turned out to be a vain hope. Corruption on the part of some of his appointed officials forced food prices to rise, and economic hardship coupled with the dark rumors about the king's death undermined his popular support. On November 7, 1947, Pibul, reappearing from supposed oblivion, staged a successful coup with the aid of the army and the powerful police, and Pridi barely avoided arrest by escaping in a sampan on the river that ran behind his house. He got out of the country with the aid of some of his English and American friends, who acted out of wartime loyalty as well as a firm refusal to believe his guilt. He made one disastrous attempt to return with the support of the navy in 1949, which will be mentioned in more detail later, and thereafter retired into exile. Pibul remained securely in power until he himself was overthrown in a coup by Field Marshal Sarit Thanarat in 1957; he died in Tokyo in 1966.

For all their former admiration of him, Pridi in exile proved something of an embarrassment to both the British and the Americans, partly because of his alleged involvement in the king's death and also because both countries recognized the Pibul government. A place of refuge was thus a fairly delicate matter and might have become even more delicate had Pridi not resolved the problem by going to China on the eve of the Communist victory. He remained there, living in Canton until 1970, when he was granted asylum in France where he died in 1983. While in China he was often accused by the military-dominated Thai government of playing an active role in the insurgency that plagued the country; as late as July 1968, a senior Thai official on a visit to Malaysia publicly named him as the architect of the Communist underground movement, making specific reference to the insurgents operating along the Thai-Malaysian border.

4

Thompson and the other OSS men arrived in Bangkok only a few days after the surrender. The airport, MacDonald remembered, was still full of Japanese soldiers with weapons, but they had accepted the emperor's orders and were not hostile. The city was in a state of some confusion, but the newcomers had a place to stay, a former royal palace known as Suan Kularb, which for the past year had secretly housed Howard Palmer, an OSS operative who had been broadcasting intelligence reports to Ceylon. Palmer's father had been a missionary in Thailand, and he had grown up in the country, speaking the language and knowing many people. Suan Kularb was a rambling Victorian structure and a pleasant alternative to a parachute drop in the northeastern jungle. There were dozens of rooms, comfortable beds, and an enormous staff of servants who treated the visiting Americans as if they were royalty.

There was little time, though, to enjoy these amenities. Palmer departed for the States a few weeks later and Thompson assumed the duties of OSS station chief. Together with MacDonald, he also set up a temporary American consulate to handle various pressing affairs until a more permanent office could be established with bona fide diplomats. There were almost nightly festivities, at which he enjoyed the hospitality of his Thai friends and got a first-hand look at the traditions and culture he had heard to much about. Pridi, the legendary "Ruth," came to call during the first week, and like most of the other foreigners Thompson was greatly impressed by his intelligence and charm. Moreover, he was enchanted by Bangkok itself, with its numerous canals (which had inevitably led earlier visitors to call it "the Venice of the East") and its incredible, glittering temples, of which Somerset Maugham had written, "It makes you laugh with delight to think that anything so fantastic could exist on this sombre earth."

It was also in those last months of 1945 that Thompson met Connie Mangskau, a vivacious young widow in her thirties. She and one of her sisters worked for a time as interpreters for the Allied forces in their dealings with the Thai government, and they were also included in many of the social activities. Later Mrs. Mangskau remembered his obvious enthusiasm for Thailand and its exotic wonders. He enjoyed rummaging through the shops and markets in his spare time, buying beautiful things that caught his eye: old Thai paintings, then scarcely known outside the country, porcelains, antique jewelry, pieces of lacquerware, and, occasionally, lengths of the shimmering silk that was then being made by only a few weaving family, Most of the things he bought, Mrs. Mangskau recalled, were intended as presents for his wife, who, he frequently said, was an artist and would admire them as much as he did.

It is impossible to say exactly when Thompson began to seriously consider coming back to Thailand and go into business after he received his discharge from the service, but it was probably in early 1946, when it became clear that his orders to return to the States would be coming through soon. Several factors undoubtedly played a part in these thoughts. One may have been the quite normal sense of anticlimax that afflicts most war veterans when the danger and excitement abruptly end and the bland vistas of normal life replace them—a sense that is possibly stronger in intelligence agents, with their feeling of behind-the-scenes participation, than in ordinary soldiers. This may have been intensified by the fact that unlike other cities in Asia, haunted by ruins and hunger and nightmare memories, Bangkok still retained much of its glamour and splendor. Another factor may have been Alexander MacDonald's decision, at about the same time, to get his discharge in the Philippines, return to Thailand, and found an English-language newspaper—a project in which he was encouraged by a number of Thai government officials. Finally, and probably most importantly, he had fallen in love with Thailand and its people and, more practically, he foresaw great things for the country in the future and yearned to be a part of them. As one of the few countries in the region relatively untouched by the war, it would certainly enjoy some measure of prosperity simply by exporting foodstuffs to less fortunate neighbors. As the only non-colonial power in Southeast Asia, it would also very likely assume an important strategic position in the end-of-empire struggles that were already giving off warning rumbles in Malaya, Indonesia, and Indochina. Thompson was developing a particular interest in the latter through friends he had made in the Laotian, Cambodian, and Vietnamese nationalist groups who were seeking temporary refuge in Bangkok.

Another development he saw as likely, and one that started him thinking about a particular project, was that with the inevitable improvements and expansion of air travel, peace would surely bring more and more tourists to the Far East. These travelers, he reasoned, were going to need somewhere to stay, and in Bangkok that presented a problem. In 1945, there were few hotels that even approached acceptable international standards and of those only one was in a really convenient location for tourists. This was the venerable Oriental, built in the 1880s, which overlooked the great river flowing through the capital and which, in prewar days, had been to Bangkok what Raffles was to Singapore and the Peninsula to Hong Kong: a meeting place for almost everyone who traveled in the area and a social center for the local foreign community. Charlie Chaplin had stayed there, and so had Noel Coward and assorted members of European royalty; Somerset Maugham had almost died there, of a fever contracted upcountry, and while recuperating on the riverside terrace had written a charming and surprisingly little-known children's tale laid in the royal court of a mythical Siam. The Oriental had history and tradition, and a good location just off New Road, the center of what shopping and travel agencies there were in those days.

When Thompson first saw it, though, these were about the only assets it had. Its vast, old-fashioned rooms had swinging doors and mosquito nets and were ranged along endless open verandas that the guests referred to as "the bowling alleys." Although it had once boasted a French chef, the kitchens were now primitive and the staff small and poorly trained. The plumbing was antique and rarely worked; instead of bathtubs, there were huge water jars with dippers and on a least one famous (though probably apocryphal) occasion, a hapless lady tourist had climbed into one under the mistaken impression that it was a bathtub and had to be extricated by force. Much of its china and silverware had been looted or broken during the war by the Japanese, who requisitioned it as an officer's club and forbade entry to local people. In brief, it was going to take a lot of work as well as a lot of capital to take its place among the great hotels of postwar Asia.

At that particular moment, it was not even functioning as a hotel, as it had been appropriated as a billet for Allied personnel, most of whom were scheduled to be sent home soon. Inquiries, however, revealed that the hotel might become available to outside bids. Thompson, of course, had never had anything to do with the hotel business and knew next to nothing about it, but the idea of renovating the Oriental and putting it back on its feet appealed to him for a number of reasons. For one thing, while there were certainly risks involved, it was a generally sound economic project providing things developed in the way he and most other people expected them to; there was a good chance that one of the international airlines like Pan American (which had just been given the rights to fly into Bangkok) might be willing to invest in it. For another, it would give him a chance to use his proven talents as an architect and designer since additional construction would obviously be necessary. And, of course, it provided an excellent excuse for staying on in Thailand for a while instead of returning to New York and a life that no longer appealed to him

The idea was also attractive to a Frenchwoman named Germaine Krull, a former correspondent for a French news agency who had arrived in Bangkok shortly after Thompson; her job had ended with the war, and she was looking about for something to do. She and Thompson already had several things in common—she had spent some time in Indochina and was interested in political conditions there—and their interest in the Oriental drew them closer together. After several months of discussions and some consultations with influential friends in the Thai government, they ultimately formed a partnership of six rather assorted people, which included, besides Thompson and Miss Krull, a Thai prince, a prominent local lawyer, an American who had worked in the Free Thai underground during the war, and a Thai general; each of the group put up $250 to get the venture off the ground.

Of the six, Thompson and Miss Krull were by far the most enthusiastic, and they spent many hours drawing up plans for improving the hotel and concocting schemes for raising the necessary capital, since it was quite clear that $1,500 was not going to go far in solving the Oriental's numerous problems. Miss Krull, it was agreed, would take up the management and reopen the hotel with whatever was available. Thompson, still in the army, could not yet devote himself fully to the project, but he could still give some assistance and soon he would be free to do much more.

Late in 1946, he left for America to get his discharge, find some investors for the Oriental, and, he expected, persuade his wife to come back to Thailand with him. With the last he found bitter disappointment awaiting him. Pat Thompson greeted him with a request for a divorce. It was an unexpected blow—all the more so when he discovered that part of the reason was someone he had regarded as a friend—and a harsh one; and it very likely removed whatever lingering doubts Thompson had about returning to the Far East. (It did not, however, as some writers on the subject seem to believe, end his interest in women; there would be other relationships in his life, some of them intense, and if none ended in marriage at least one persisted for more than a decade.) After the divorce he did not see his former wife for nearly twenty years. A year before his disappearance, he passed through San Francisco where she was living after a second divorce, and they had a friendly reunion. By this time Thompson had become famous, and she expressed a desire to see the country where he had made his home. Before she could make the trip, however, she suffered a severe brain hemorrhage and lapsed into a coma from which she never emerged.

To take his mind off his divorce, Thompson spent his time in America talking to prospective investors and thinking more about the development of the Oriental. It was an intensely unhappy period for him, and it must have been with a great sense of relief that he boarded a place in 1947 that was to carry him back to his improbable future.

5

The Bangkok that so captured Thompson's imagination was a very different place from the booming, modern, highly Westernized metropolis that a tourist finds today. It was smaller for one thing, at least to a foreigner, for the community of *farangs*—a Thai word coined in the 16th century that covers all Europeans—was sufficiently limited in those days that everyone knew everyone else, and parties were generally comprised of familiar faces. Almost every important street was bordered by a canal, called a klong, and these waterways—black and stinking in the hot season, miraculously clean and flowing when the rains came— played a major role in the city's life and commerce. All the major ones connected sooner or later (more often later) with the Chao Phraya River, and they were usually crowded with a colorful assortment of boats plying back and forth between the city's markets and the orchards and paddy fields of the countryside; most of the older houses in the city faced, or had faced, either the broad river or a klong.

There were few cars, mostly belonging to higher government officials, a fleet of elderly buses, and a tram line that ran along New Road. The most popular form of transportation was the jaunty little pedicab, or samloh (literally "three wheels"), the memory of which still inspires acute nostalgia among old-timers. The pedicabs were equipped with jingling bicycle bells, which the drivers sounded at the slightest provocation, and at night the shadowy dim-lit streets resounded with the musical sound, like a chorus of strange insects calling to one another. (Progress, inevitably, caught up with the samlohs and in 1959 they were banished to the provinces, followed by a surprising number of their highly individualistic drivers who turned down a government offer to help them switch to more modern motorized vehicles.)

Bangkok had but two or three proper hotels, none of them very comfortable, and few tourists. There was no shortage of living space and therefore no apartment houses; the more prosperous residents lived in vast rambling houses with spacious verandas that overlooked tropical gardens and numerous servants who remained over generations. The area now known as Bangkapi, which would become the most fashionable residential section of the city, was largely rice fields, and the splendid British Embassy, now in the center of things, was looked upon as being rather inconveniently located. For less than fifty dollars a month one could get a sizeable house, plus a staff.

Then as now, Bangkok was a perplexing place for a Westerner accustomed to the capitals of Europe, since it had no clearly defined center, no great square or intersection of major avenues where the heart of the city could be reliably located either in fact or sentiment. Instead it had several centers, and the question of which was the center depended on who one was and what one's business was.

For most Thais the spiritual and cultural center was probably the large oval field known the Pramane Ground, or Sanam Luang, located a few hundred yards from the riverbank at the city's original site and overlooked by a number of major government buildings and by the soaring rooftops and gilded spires of the old Grand Palace and the Temple of the Emerald Buddha, the most sacred of the capital's innumerable Buddhist temples. Spectacular fairs were held here in the cool season, as well as important ceremonies like royal cremations and the Ploughing Ceremony, which insured a bountiful rice crop each year; on Saturdays and Sundays there was a marvelously varied weekend market that attracted thousands of people from all over the city and the surrounding countryside.

Not far away were two other centers. One was the area along Yawaraj Road, where the bulk of the city's Chinese population lived, a district of narrow, twisting alleyways and curious smells and signs lettered in Chinese rather than Thai. The other center was for the army, already powerful and steadily growing more so. Here tall, medieval-looking walls protected barracks and headquarters, and along peaceful, tree-lined streets were the homes of most of the leading generals, without whose support no civilian government could at that time hope to survive for long. During coups or times of national unrest, this section bristled with armed soldiers and resounded to the heavy crunch of tanks.

For the *farangs*, both visiting and resident, the center of Bangkok was further down the river, along New Road. This was the first proper road built in the city, constructed in the mid-nineteenth century especially to accommodate the carriages of early Western diplomats, whose embassies overlooked the river and who complained to King Rama IV about not having any place to walk or drive in the cool of the evening. New Road has probably never been a really handsome thoroughfare—one visitor called it "the meanest Main Street in Asia"—but in 1946 there was considerably more to it than the shabby, dingy souvenir shops one sees today. Most of the stores that catered to foreigners were then located on or near it, including the Silom Grocery Store, which was not only one of the few purveyors of Western foodstuffs but also had a claim on the affections of older residents because it had reportedly smuggled food to interned foreigners during the war. Several important embassies were on the narrow lanes that led off New Road to the river, and so was the Oriental Hotel, which, by the time Thompson returned, had been re-opened to paying guests by Miss Krull and had become a popular meeting place as well as a semi-permanent home for a number of Western residents, including Thompson.

For those *farangs* who decided to seek their fortunes in Thailand, relations with the natives were for the most part pleasant and unrestrained. The country had managed to steer clear of the colony-hungry European powers of the last century, and thus no deep resentment of Westerners had taken root; the atmosphere in Bangkok was distinctly different from that which the returning Dutch, British, and French were finding in their restless former possessions.

There were, however, many inconveniences for anyone used to Western comforts. Air-conditioning, which has made life in the tropics bearable for many today, was virtually unknown. The electricity was highly erratic, and everyone kept a supply of candles within easy reach for the almost nightly power failures. There were no gas stoves, and in palaces as well as ordinary homes the cooking was done on primitive charcoal braziers. All drinking water had to be boiled, for cholera was still an annual hot-season threat. Sanitation for most depended largely on the nearest klong, which, fortunately, was usually not very far away. Many residential streets were permanently in a deplorable condition, and in the rainy season it was hard to distinguish between them and the canals; it was a commonplace for ladies in evening dress to come wading up flooded drive, shoes in hand, for a formal dinner party. Imported foods were rare and expensive, and one either developed a taste for the highly-seasoned local cuisine or dined meagerly.

Yet for all these discomforts, there was clearly a tremendous charm about the city in those days that old-timers find sadly lacking today, when power failures are rare enough to rate a newspaper mention and American-style supermarkets carry frozen foods and French cheeses. Survivors of the forties look back wistfully on such bygone pleasures as the American ambassador's annual Fourth of July party, to which the entire American community was invited—hardly possible today when they number in the thousands—and the gala charity balls where every face was familiar, from the highest government officials on down. To newcomers, they trace the courses of the old klongs now mostly transformed into six-lane avenues, and lament the vanished rain and mahogany trees that once made leafy tunnels along streets now harshly exposed to the sun. They recall the wonderful sense of adventure that accompanied an excursion of more than a few miles outside the city. Even undeniable inconveniences have acquired charm with the passing years, and they will recount tales of souffles achieved in charcoal ovens, of the unexpected ingenuity of amateur electricians, and of the enterprising hostess who used to hire fleets of samlohs during the rainy season to transport her dinner guests from a main road down her flooded lane to her relatively dry doorstep.

No old resident viewed the past with more nostalgia than Thompson in the latter part of his life in Bangkok, and he stubbornly clung to many of the old ways long after they had become avoidable. Indeed, as the Westernization of the city increased, he seemed to take an almost perverse pleasure in shunning those conveniences others were beginning to take for granted. He refused to sleep in an air-conditioned room or, for many years, to work in an air-conditioned office; when he built a new shop, shortly before his disappearance, he reluctantly consented to allow the entire building, including his office, to be cooled but he resisted the improvement by spend most of his time away from it at a hot factory where his silks were printed. He also refused to modernize his kitchen to the extent of investing in a gas stove even when most of his friends had gladly abandoned their charcoal contraptions. In his palatial Thai-style house which became a landmark of the city and in which he entertained an endless procession of eminent guests, his Chinese cook continued to turn out elaborate dinners for ten or twenty on a three-hole charcoal stove and did so, Thompson proclaimed, at a fraction of the cost other foreigners were paying with their luxurious ways. Similarly, guests averse to mosquito bites learned to spray themselves liberally before arrival since he would have no screens defacing his splendidly proportioned living room.

As Bangkok became more and more like an American city, he sought relief by going out to the provinces, where life was more to his taste—more, that is, as it was when he first took up residence in the country. He enjoyed the clamorous provincial Chinese hotels, the flyspecked little restaurants that served superior noodles, and the problems of coping with unexpected emergencies. He came back from such trips with renewed energy and advised the same therapy to newcomers who expressed disappointment with the capital's modern aspects. Still another link with the past was his preference for "Siam"— the European name for the country before the war and, for a brief period, after it—to the more generally used "Thailand". He did allow his future business to employ the adjective "Thai" in its title, but in conversation he habitually used "Siamese."

6

If Thompson's plans had worked out to his satisfaction when he came back he would, in all probability, be known today as a hotel entrepreneur, and Thai silk might still be known only to a select few in Bangkok. As it happened, of course, they did not work out.

There are at least two versions of what went wrong with the Oriental Hotel venture: his own and that of Miss Krull, who went on to develop the hotel and later wrote a book about it. The two are markedly dissimilar, and at this stage it would probably be impossible to untangle all the charges and countercharges and arrive at a really accurate picture of what happened. Fortunately, this troublesome chore is not worth attempting, since for all its seeming importance at the time and for all the lasting bitterness it engendered on Thompson's part, the hotel affair, in retrospect, figures as a decidedly minor event in his Thailand career; it is significant merely because it did not work and therefore left him free to discover the silk. The trouble, basically, may have stemmed from the simple fact that both he and Miss Krull were strong personalities, with very definite ideas about what should be done with the hotel and how, and that they were probably bound to clash in time. The clash came fairly soon, was accompanied by a good many harsh words, and ended with Thompson pulling out of the project entirely. Miss Krull, in her book, claimed that the final break was due to a dispute about the plans for the proposed annex to the old building about which Thompson, as an architect, had strong feelings. Despite the quarrel, he continued to live at the Oriental for more than a year, carefully avoiding Miss Krull whenever possible. Some twenty years later, after Miss Krull was no longer associated with the hotel, Thompson was asked to decorate two of the suites named after famous authors in the old wing, a chore he performed free of charge and from which he derived a good deal of personal satisfaction.

At the time the Oriental business was moving to its unhappy conclusion, Thompson was also serving as a sort of unofficial political advisor to the American embassy, then headed by Ambassador Edwin Stanton, who was also a good personal friend. Thompson had learned a good deal about the political complexities of Southeast Asia in his OSS work toward the end of the war. His particular area of interest, outside Thailand itself, was the nationalist movements in Laos and Vietnam, for both of which Bangkok became a convenient headquarters in the second half of the forties, partly because of its location and partly because the Thai government was exceptionally lenient about giving them refuge. As a result the city sheltered a great many Laotians, Vietnamese, and Cambodians plotting for their countries' independence from the French—among them were several destined for high positions in the future—and since they were frequently being plotted against as well by French intelligence agents, the situation was more than a little murky. In time, a number of dissident groups came under Communist influence (this was especially true of the Vietnamese) and this contributed to the increasing suspicion with which they were to be regarded by the Thai authorities after the Pridi government was overthrown by the army forces in 1947.

Of all the refugee nationalists with whom he had contacts, Thompson liked the Laotians best, perhaps because they were most like the Thais. Laos borders a substantial part of northeastern Thailand, and the Thais from that part of the country are very often pure Laotian ethnically, if not nationally; movement back and forth across the border, at least in the late forties, was a relatively simple matter and a common one, too, since almost everyone in the northeast had relations in Laos. (Field Marshal Sarit Thanarat, who deposed Pibul in a 1957 coup, came from the northeast; one of his cousins was the Laotian premier.)

With his Laotian friends, Thompson made a number of trips through the border region and saw a good deal of its life and customs, about which he wrote enthusiastic letters to friends and members of his family back in the States. This may be regarded as somewhat unusual, for Issan, as the northeast is commonly called by other Thais, was in those days almost roadless and enjoyed little of the natural bounty characteristic of other regions. The soil was poor, droughts were frequent, and the crops that grew so freely almost everywhere else were produced only by long and hard labor; it was no coincidence that during the 1960s and 1970s, Issan became the most serious center of Communist insurgency within Thailand. One plant that did do well in the arid soil, however, was the mulberry tree, and because of this the production of raw silk was a traditional, if not very profitable, source of income for many northeastern families. In the old days, the raw silk had been sent to Bangkok to supply weavers there, but with the rise of cheap, machine-made textiles from abroad and changing fashions—both dating from the early decades of the present century—by the time of Thompson's visits the demand was almost gone. Some silk was still being woven, much of it of high quality and beauty, but principally for family use; according to local custom a young girl was expected to weave at least two superior pieces, one for her wedding costume and another for her bridegroom.

On his visits, Thompson developed a great fondness for the northeasterners, in whom were combined, rather unexpectedly, a passive acceptance of their hard lot and a strong sense of regional pride that often took the form of political radicalism. He also undoubtedly got his first look at the source of some of the lovely silks he had noticed soon after he first came to Bangkok, for some of his Laotian friends had relatives engaged in silkworm cultivation, and the industry he later founded may well have been born on one of these expeditions.

By the middle of 1947 he was certainly in a receptive mood for a new project with which to occupy himself. The collapse of his hopes for the Oriental, following so soon on the heels of his divorce, had been a severe blow to his pride as well as to his hopes of staying on in Thailand. He was not really interested in making a career of his political advisory work, even in the unlikely event that he could have done so, nor did he want to go back to America and a life he no longer wanted. He turned—almost inevitably, one would like to say, were one not aware of a great element of chance in such moves—to the brilliant fabric that would make his reputation.

7

Contrary to the belief held by a large number of foreign tourists, and even perhaps by a few Thais, Jim Thompson did not invent Thai silk. Weaving and the production of raw silk had for many years been one of the few industries of the northeast, and in the past there had been an active group of silk weavers in Bangkok, working on simple, hand-operated bamboo looms and passing the silk down from one generation to another. In fact, silk weaving has been a traditional handicraft in most Southeast Asian countries at one time or another, one of the numerous cultural legacies received from China, and it was certainly being practised in the earlier Thai capitals of Sukhothai and Ayutthaya.

There is, on the other hand, some justification for the widespread misconception with regard to Thompson's role in Thailand, for prior to his discovery and promotion of it, it was an ailing art with very small prospects of recovery. The twentieth-century advent of cheaper textiles from the mills of Europe and Japan had dealt the Bangkok weavers a body blow, increased by the growing preference for Western-style clothes by upper-class Thais; and by 1947, the few weaving families left were learning other, more profitable trades. The majority were scattered and unorganized, and none of them could be said to be earning a living from silk. Their fellow countrymen, for the most part, regarded the shimmering material as being too old-fashioned to be smart or as exorbitantly expensive and therefore suitable only for special, ceremonial occasions. Neither view was conducive to large sales.

One of the largest collections of weaving families who were reasonably close was clustered in a run-down district of Bangkok called Bangkrua that had once been a village on the outskirts of the city. They were held together not so much by their devotion to silk weaving as by the fact that they were Moslems (of Cambodian descent) in a country that is 95 percent Buddhist. Because of their distinctly minority religion, with its strict ritual and dietary demands, they had remained unusually close-knit over the years, intermarrying and retaining their old skills much longer than they would probably have done otherwise. They were not, however, much more optimistic about the silk trade than their non-Moslem competitors in other parts of the city, and the grim economic realities had prompted most of the Bangkrua weavers to either abandon their looms or start seriously thinking about it. The idea of a foreign market for Thai silk, if it ever entered their minds, was quickly dismissed. The organizational skills needed for such an operation, not to mention the money, were formidable, and there was more than a little doubt that a Western market even existed in view of the fact that the celebrated Japanese silk industry would probably soon recover from its wartime devastation.

This was the situation when Thompson came on the scene, and the prospects for success were approximately as dim as those in the Oriental Hotel project had been bright. It would appear that the idea of starting a silk industry had very little to recommend it to a man past his fortieth birthday, who had never worked in the textile business and knew nothing whatever of its production end, who did not speak the language of the country, and whose knowledge of marketing a product like silk seemed only marginally greater than that of the discouraged weavers. What happened surprised most of his friends and possibly even Thompson himself.

Ever since his arrival in Bangkok, he had been picking up lengths of silk here and there, partly because by nature he was an almost compulsive collector of anything that struck his fancy and partly because he had a genuine admiration for its lustrous, lumpy texture—what he called its "humps and bumps"—and its often startling color combinations: a plaid of acid green and magenta, for example, or deep blue and shocking pink. The pieces he bought were mainly in lengths of about a yard and a half and were intended for use as sarongs for women (called "pasins") or for men (called "pakomas"). Those for men were relatively simple affairs, though often in brilliant plaids; women's pasins were frequently brocaded in rich gold and silver threads and were worn only for important ceremonies such as weddings and royal receptions; both were later to become best-selling items, used with Western fashions as stoles. It was rare, in 1947, to find longer pieces of the material, for the weaving process on traditional looms was slow and laborious and there was, of course, little demand for non-sarong lengths. The colors came mostly from vegetable dyes and faded, sometimes disappeared completely, with repeated washing. This was not really a serious problem as far as the Thais were concerned, however, since the most expensive pieces were rarely if ever washed, but were kept folded in scented chests, sometimes for generations.

Thompson later told various stories about how he decided to start a silk business, but in most he mentioned a commercial attache at the U.S. embassy named James Scott. Scott had previously served in Syria, where he had seen an active export trade developed from silk brocade which, like Thai silk, had previously been a little-appreciated traditional art. He had seen and admired Thompson's small collection of local silks and mentioned over dinner one evening that he thought they held similar possibilities. As commercial attaché he was able, of course, to offer some useful information on the business side of such an enterprise.

Whatever the source of inspiration, once the seed was planted Thompson began to look at the silk more closely. He consulted his Thai friends on the subject; he studied a collection of rare old pieces in the National Museum; he tracked down some of the weavers through the shops in which they sold their material. He discovered the weaving enclave at Bangkrua—little suspecting that one day he would be living across from it—and talked with some of the families who lived in its crowded houses. The weavers were no doubt highly skeptical of this curious *farang* who seemed to think people in Europe and America might be interested in their handiwork, but like most Thais they were polite and tolerant of his eccentric ideas. Some forty years later one of them still remembered the novelty of being offered a check for several lengths she had woven and refusing to accept such a dubious substitute for real money. Another, who was working part-time as a plumber (and who later became a prosperous shareholder in the company Thompson founded) was sufficiently intrigued to weave a few long pieces in various typical colors so Thompson could test their potential. He thus became, in effect, the first employee of the future Thai Silk Company, and the silk he wove—about a hundred yards in all—can be regarded as the real beginning of what became a major industry.

With several suitcases full of silk, Thompson, who was then forty-one, boarded a plane for America to see what enthusiasm he could stir up for it in New York, the world's principal marketplace for such luxury items in those immediate postwar years.

The most important encouragement came from the redoubtable Edna Woolman Chase, then editor of *Vogue* and general arbiter of what was and was not acceptable in the small but potent world of high fashion. Thompson got his introduction to her through Frank Crowninshield, the former editor of *Vanity Fair*, who had been an acquaintance during his party-going New York years and who was the only person Thompson knew who might have some connections in the fashion industry. Crowninshield generously made a phone call, and soon Thompson was sitting in Mrs. Chase's *Vogue* office, his load of Bangkrua silks spread out across her desk.

Like many of the people involved with fashion, Mrs. Chase had a keen sense of the theater and she employed that now for Thompson's benefit. According to his account, she took one look at the pile of glowing material, stepped back, and announced to her secretary that none of the staff was to leave the offices that day without seeing this magnificent new discovery. Thai silk had arrived, at least as far as *Vogue* was concerned.

Nor did Mrs. Chase limit her enthusiasm to theatrical scenes. She asked Thompson to leave the silks with her for a few weeks so she could show them around, and during that time she persuaded Valentina, the dress designer, to buy a length in pale mauve for a dress. The designer was later photographed for *Vogue* in her Thai silk dress, Thompson was given a credit in the caption, and his unlikely plan took a major step toward success.

8

The possibility of a foreign market for Thai silk was thus confirmed in one rather spectacular act. This was not exactly the same thing, however, as starting a Thai silk industry. Some months later, when Thompson had returned to Bangkok, the distance between the primitive looms of Bangkrua and Mrs. Chase's elegant office must have seemed incredibly vast, and no amount of enthusiasm on the part of fashion editors and dress designers could conceal the size of the difficulties that now confronted him if he was to be serious about developing the silk into something more than a small-scale business.

He proceeded cautiously at first and it was, in fact, nearly a year before he went so far as to form a proper company to produce and sell the silk. In the meantime, he operated out of his room at the Oriental, trying to drum up interest among his local friends and additional contacts in New York. These initial probes were educational—he soon began to fill in some of the many gaps in his knowledge of silk-making—and also encouraging: nearly everyone who saw the material was enthusiastic about it, and he was able to keep a fairly steady flow of orders going to his handful of weavers. Stimulated by his confidence, the weavers, too, began to revise their pessimistic view of the future and gradually increased their output.

Before long, it became apparent that the whole operation ought to be put on a more businesslike basis, and Thompson began to give thought to the idea of setting up a company with adequate capitalization to expand. About the time he started considering this, a friend from California named George Barrie came through Bangkok on a trip. Barrie was a well-to-do and adventurous businessman, and he liked the challenge of investing in unusual but likely enterprises. When he saw what the weavers were producing and heard about the reactions to the silk, he decided the project had real possibilities. He urged Thompson to form a company and sell shares, saying that he would be willing to buy a block of them.

Thompson decided to take the plunge and in late 1948, about a year after he had first become interested in the possibilities of the fabric, the Thai Silk Company, Ltd., came into being. There was nothing secret about the company's organization, either at the beginning or later, yet in the future there were a remarkable number of mistaken impressions concerning it. Even more people came to believe that it was wholly Thompson's property than those who thought he was the inventor of Thai silk, and this error led to a widely held conviction that the millions made by the silk company went principally to him. As a matter of fact, it was not until his disappearance in 1967 that many otherwise knowledgeable people in Bangkok became aware of the facts of the finances and organizational structure of the Thai Silk Company.

The misconception was perhaps understandable in view of the enormous amount of personal publicity given to the founder over the years, during which such terms as "silk king" were freely employed and people who were going silk shopping were inclined to say, "I'm going to Jim Thompson's"; but it did not reflect the opinion of Thompson himself, who never pretended to be the sole owner. In almost every interview he gave about the business—and he gave hundreds, from Stockholm to New York—he made a point of emphasizing that controlling interest in the company was held by Thai nationals rather than by *farangs*. Another misconception, this one included in most of the stories written about him, was that the company was founded on a shoestring of a few hundred dollars. This appealing little Horatio Alger touch may have had its origins in a desire to make a good story better, or it may have resulted from an honest confusion over the two or three hundred of his own money that Thompson invested in the silk he took to New York; or, just possibly, he may have been guilty of encouraging it himself, since as time went on he developed a distinct flair for publicizing his product as well as for romanticizing his adopted homeland. (A year or so before his disappearance, on a visit to New York, he allowed a *New York Times* reporter to get the impression that he went to his office every morning by klong; he did in fact have to cross one to visit his weavers in Bangkrua, and he may have rationalized that a slight extension of his water travel was justifiable since it certainly made for more fascinating copy.)

Actually, the Thai Silk Company's original capitalization when it was formally incorporated in 1948 was $25,000, raised by selling 500 shares at fifty dollars each. It is true, however, that the company had only half this amount to work with, since the shareholders paid up only twenty-five dollars on each of their shares at first; the balance was paid six years later out of company profits.

The company paid dividends from the very first year of its operation and the value of the shares steadily increased, so that a shareholder who invested twenty-five dollars in 1948 had an equity in the company of $860 twenty years later; one of the original investors received a million dollars each for shares sold in the late 1980s. Of the 500 shares sold, 51 percent were owned by Thai citizens, and the remaining 49 percent by foreigners, of whom the two largest holders were Thompson and George Barrie, each of whom took ninety shares. Over the years that followed, Thompson gave away six of his shares for various reasons; two, for example, were given to a silk weaver who supervised the construction of his Thai-style house in the late fifties. In 1967, therefore, he held only eighty-four of the total 500 shares.

If his ownership of the company he founded was less absolute than many people thought, so, too, was the money he earned from it. He took the title of managing director, and his starting salary was $3000 a year. It increased, of course, as the business grew to be a phenomenal success, and when he went to the Cameron Highlands he was getting approximately $33,000 plus bonuses based on sales, a comfortable enough income to be sure but scarcely in the millionaire class that the newspapers, and perhaps a majority of people in Bangkok, supposed him to belong to. The directors of the company remained to the end slightly mystified by Thompson's attitude toward money, for in view of his singular role in the success of the business (people generally referred to it as "Thompson's Silk Company") and its increasing sales (about one and a half million dollars in 1967), he was clearly worth more than he was getting. They repeatedly offered him raises in salary, which he repeatedly refused, saying he made enough. (It is only fair to note that Thompson was indeed a millionaire at the time of his disappearance and that the newspapers were thus technically correct. It was not, however, due to Thai silk. Several years after he started the business a wealthy cousin died and left him a considerable estate, which he invested and rarely touched except when unusual expenses arose, like the construction of his Thai house.)

In comparison with the majority of foreigners—and natives, too, for that matter—going into business in Asia, Thompson held some rather unconventional notions of how things should be done. For example, at the back of his mind in the beginning he had a fairly radical scheme that he confided to a number of close friends. This was an idea that once the business was on its feet and capable of being run without his help, he would pull out of it entirely, turn it over to the silk weavers, and try his talents on one of several other Thai handicrafts he considered likely prospects for development. He was not a Utopian dreamer, but neither was he a practical, hardheaded businessman; he once described his job as "being like a missionary but with better visual results." His real object, he frequently maintained—and there is no evidence to suggest that he was not sincere—was not to make a fortune out of Thailand's underdeveloped state but to make some positive contribution to its improvement, and to accomplish this he had an old-fashioned, nineteenth-century faith in the free enterprise system as taught by clear, easily emulated example. Through his Laotian friends, he had seen the results of the French colonial system, and some of its obvious evils had made a deep impression on him; whatever he did in Thailand must be of practical benefit to its people, arising out of their own skills and returning most, if not all, of the profits to them. He was unimpressed by the vast aid programs that were just then getting underway in Thailand, particularly those that dispensed great sums of money and attempted to create unfamiliar industries overnight, and he was strongly opposed to those foreign companies whose principal purpose it was to drain as much money as possible out of the country. As far as he was concerned, the real measure of the Thai silk industry's success was not so much in the profits of his own company as in the rival companies that soon began to spring up all over Bangkok, the majority of them freely copying his designs.

Thompson never went through with his plan for abandoning silk and taking up another industry, but he never entirely forgot it. It was one of his reasons for limiting his holdings in the company to such a small number of shares and for underrating his own importance, and it also lay behind his unorthodox system of payment to the weavers. The latter amounted, in the beginning, to a cooperative arrangement, whereby the silk was placed on consignment by the weavers, who were paid for it after it was sold; later this was changed so that most of the silk was bought for cash before retail sale. The weavers worked independently, for the most part in their own homes, and the extent of their profits depended entirely on how much silk they were willing to produce. If they were inactive, their monthly income showed it; if they installed more looms and produced more silk, their prosperity increased. Thompson visited the Bangkrua weavers regularly and others near the northeastern city of Khorat whenever he could, inspecting the quality of the material, trying out new color combinations, and generally establishing a close rapport with the families; in a number of cases he made sizeable personal loans to ambitious weavers who wanted to enlarge their production or to company employees who wanted to set up their own looms and join the competition.

In the early days this sort of informal arrangement was a necessity because of the uncertainties of the new business, but it was also very much a part of Thompson's philosophy about how things should be done and it remained substantially the same when silk had become a major industry. He still made his daily visits, he still knew all the people who wove for him, and he still retained the competitive system. More than once, efficiency-minded friends urged him to abandon the cottage industry scheme and install all his weavers in a modern factory where they would receive a standard wage and could be better controlled. Efficient production was not the only reason such a proposal could be made to sound attractive, at least on paper. For one thing, a common weaving factory would help eliminate the occasional feuding that broke out between various families, leading to accusations that the silk of one was being given preference over that of another. In addition, it would prevent certain of the families from growing so prosperous that they could afford to strike out on their own in direct competition with the Thai Silk Company, as quite a few of them did when the industry proved so successful. Thompson, however, detested the very idea of factory-style production, no matter how many theoretical advantages it offered, and he never even seriously considered it. His refusal may, as some people suspected, have been due in small part to the romantic side of his nature that enjoyed the morning visits to Bangkrua: crossing the klong in a tiny boat and then going about the narrow boardwalks from house to house with cheerful greetings called out along the way, the village-like atmosphere that remained oddly untouched by the rapidly changing city around it and that served, especially in later years, as a constant reminder of the Bangkok he had first come to love. But there was also a practical side to his distrust of silk factories. He felt that the competition between the weavers, for all its problems, was basically a healthy thing, spurring them on to greater efforts and thereby benefiting the economy in general, and that, furthermore, the impersonal routine of a factory was contrary to the native Thai character and would ultimately lead to inferior silk. A number of years later, when a rival silk company put the factory idea into practice, he did not conceal his satisfaction when they quickly ran into difficulties with the quality of their silk, which never equalled that of his own.

(Ironically, but perhaps not surprisingly, it was the company Thompson founded that later demonstrated that under the right circumstances a factory could produce high-quality silk. In the 1980s, faced not only by demands for far greater quantities than independent weavers could meet but also by new techniques that required expert supervision, it established the largest hand-weaving facility in the world and, at the same time, maintained its high standards. Whatever his misgivings, Thompson would surely have approved of its location in a small, peaceful village not far from Khorat and of the fact that it provides much-needed employment in a traditionally poor region.)

Certainly Thompson's silk weavers never had any cause to complain of his policies. Very soon after he started his operations, all of them were prospering beyond any dreams they could have had before, and some of them had become wealthy. Among the Moslems of Southeast Asia, one of the more prominent signs of affluence is the wearing of a fez, for it is a visible indication that the owner has enough capital to have made the long and expensive pilgrimage to Mecca. Before Thompson, fezzes were as rare as refrigerators in Bangkrua, and the hopes of making the journey were exceedingly dim even for the most devout; within ten years both fezzes and refrigerators were common in the village, and many weavers went to Mecca not once but several times. Weaving children who might, at best, have looked forward to a sixth-grade education suddenly found themselves on planes headed for Britain, France, and the United States, and families that had been principally concerned with making ends meet on a monthly budget of around twenty-five dollars found themselves wondering where they could park a new automobile and which kind of television set they should buy. For them, at any rate, Thompson's methods were not wasted.

9

Most of this, of course, lay in the very uncertain future in early 1948 when Thompson set himself up as a silk distributor. At the time, he operated through an independent retail outlet with the engaging name of La One, which sold various souvenirs in addition to silk. (The former owner of La One would become a shareholder in the Thai Silk Company and serve on its board of directors.) With the help of an interpreter, Thompson made the arrangements with the weavers, tried to drum up business by mail to potential customers abroad, and kept a supply of silk in his room at the Oriental in case any of the tourists who were beginning to pass through expressed an interest in the fabric and couldn't make it over to La One.

A good many visitors did express an interest. This was not surprising in view of Thompson's favored sales technique, which was to stand about the hotel lobby whenever he was free with a mass of silk conspicuously draped over one arm; sooner or later a curious stranger was bound to ask him what it was or where it could be bought and a few fast-talking minutes later the silk weavers had another customer.

Though he insisted on keeping the weaving as a cottage industry and retained many of the old methods of manufacture, Thompson did in time introduce several innovations that resulted in a marked improvement in the quality and quantity of the silk. The most important of these was his insistence on the use of high-quality, color-fast chemical dyes from Switzerland instead of the traditional vegetable dyes. Unpredictable colors might have been an insignificant matter to the old Thai wearers of pasins and pakomas, but the question was vital in a successful conquest of American and European markets.

It took some time to teach the weavers how to use the new dyes—indeed, it took a little while for Thompson to learn how to use them himself—but they caught on remarkably fast considering the radical novelty of the idea. Today, the old dyes are almost never used except in remote upcountry weaving villages that are unconcerned with the export trade, and the foreign dyes have become so familiar that many Thais are unaware they are not local. In putting them to use, Thompson's exceptional color sense—which had been noticeable years before in America—at last found a worthy outlet, and he put it to work with breathtaking effects. The great majority of the brilliant and often audacious combinations for which Thai silk became famous were entirely his creations, though they were so widely copied by numerous rival companies that they have come to be regarded as traditional. He got many of his original inspirations from old designs, and some of his combinations from the Bakst ballet costumes he had admired so much in the thirties, but he changed them in sometimes subtle ways, working with the spindles of colored thread much as a painter uses a pallet, trying first one combination, then another, until some instinct told him it would work. In making literally thousands of combinations for plaids and, later, prints, his instinct rarely failed him.

Thompson also gradually persuaded the weavers to switch to a faster, foot-operated shuttle on their looms, which sped up their production considerably and made it possible for them to turn out more than the few yards a day that had been the average in the old days. One tradition he did not change was the practice of washing the silk thread in the inky waters of a neighboring klong that in the hot season tended to get distinctly odoriferous. This was probably due to practical considerations as much as to nostalgia, for the water supply was a problem in Bangkrua, but later Thompson blandly informed an interviewer that the klong water was responsible for some mysterious chemical process that gave the silk its special luster.

In working with his weavers and learning the ways of his new trade, Thompson found his Laotian friends in Bangkok extremely useful and, in the beginning anyway, even indispensable. A number of them were familiar with silk weaving from their past in their own country and in northeastern Thailand and they were able to give invaluable advice and assistance on such matters as weaving techniques and supplies of raw silk. Some even set up looms of their own and earned a living by working for Thompson while going on with their various political activities. "When they are not busy revolutionizing," Robert Trumbull reported in the *New York Times* early in 1949, "many devote themselves to weaving silk for an American exporter, James H.W. Thompson of Greenville, Delaware. Mr. Thompson...buys up fine Siamese, Cambodian, and Laos silks and ships them to the great couturiers of New York. These beautiful cloths—spectacular plaids and designs shot with gold and silver threads—cost two or three dollars a yard here. In New York, after shipping costs and import duties, they usually show up advertised in the smartest fashion magazines over some of the most famous names in the ladies' wear world."

One of the Laotians, a man named Tao Oum, who had plans of becoming a part of an independent Laotian government once the French could be persuaded to leave, became Thompson's personal assistant and also one of his closest friends. They made many trips to the northeast together to talk with silk farmers and buy up thread and Thompson got, in addition to an increased knowledge of the silk trade, a thorough grounding in the complexities of the Laotian power struggle. It is possible, even likely, that he passed on some of this information to his friends at the American embassy, but spying was certainly a minor activity during this busy period.

Thompson threw himself into the silk business with an energy and an eagerness to learn that surprised numerous people in Bangkok, some of whom had tended to regard him as a well-to-do playboy who would soon become bored with the exotic East and go back to the familiar pleasures of New York. Despite his father's connection with a textile-printing company, it was really a completely new world for him and there was so much to learn, not just about the silk itself but about the customs and working habits of the country, that many far younger men would have gotten discouraged early in the game. He discovered, for example, that the quality of the silk produced had to be constantly checked to weed out inferior lengths that found their way into the work of even the best and most reliable of the weavers. A family squabble could delay an important order for days, and during Ramadan, the Moslem fasting period, practically nothing was produced by the Bangkrua families since the weavers claimed the lack of food made them too weak to work in the daytime; and at night, when they could eat, they over-feasted. Once an order was finished, there were the various problems of international shipping to consider. He could not depend on much official assistance. The government was pleased that someone was starting up an industry that might result in a new export trade and bring in needed dollars, but it had far too many grave political and economic problems to contend with to provide much practical aid to the novice. Furthermore—and this remained in the background, more sensed than actually felt—Thompson was rather too closely associated in many official minds with the by now disgraced and overthrown Pridi administration.

Thompson had, as a matter of cold fact, only two major assets when he began his company, but they were to prove all-important in its success. One was the color sense already described, which amounted to something a good deal more than a mere talent. The other—and perhaps more important in the early days—was a genuine enthusiasm for the silk, and this went beyond a simple desire to dispose of the weavers' products. It has been said that all successful businessmen are successful salesmen, and Thompson's case was no exception; the development of the silk industry was due in great measure to his astonishingly persuasive salesmanship, which he exercised at every possible opportunity. This manifested itself early on, when he haunted the Oriental lobby in search of stray customers, and it did not diminish with success, when he had a sales staff of eight or ten people. Even then, he still spent every free hour in the shop, working harder than anyone else, and it exhilarated rather than tired him; on more than one occasion, he went down and opened the shop on Sunday to satisfy a customer whose desire for silk he had stirred up over dinner the night before. Women customers were his specialty. He would drape them in swaths of the shimmering fabric, stand back critically for a moment, and then give them a look of such rapt approval that they invariably succumbed. It could be, one woman in Bangkok remembers, a rather unnerving experience. "It was like being hypnotized in a way. Many times he would show me a piece of silk I really didn't want at all and couldn't afford. Then he'd do that draping bit and start telling me what it did for my eyes and my hair and the next thing I knew I'd be out on the street with three and a half yards of the damned stuff. I've still got masses of silk I bought that way."

Hypnosis or not, many Bangkok women refused to buy silk from anyone else in the shop, convinced that only Thompson knew the proper colors for them. Others, in foreign countries, requested in their orders that he personally select the material to be sent to them.

His periodic trips to Europe and America were rarely much of a rest since he usually carried along an ample supply of new designs, and orders picked up along the way would flow back to Bangkok. On one of these trips, his enthusiasm for the silk led him to give some of it away under singular circumstances. This took place at a dinner party in Paris, where one of the guests was the actress Paulette Goddard. Miss Goddard expressed great admiration for the Thai silk suit he was wearing and said she wished she could get one like it for a gentleman friend. Without a moment's thought, Thompson gallantly made her a gift of the suit and went back to his hotel wearing a raincoat provided by his host.

Though Thompson's development of Thai silk came, in later years, to be ranked as one of the great success stories of postwar Asia, it was not achieved as easily as many people believed. In the early stages, there were regular crises, some of them sufficiently serious to threaten the whole structure of the young industry, and the letters that Thompson wrote home to his family frequently reflected a discouragement that he took pains to conceal from friends and associates in Bangkok. There were problems over supplies, difficulties with overseas agents, and all sorts of minor frustrations that were probably inevitable, but nonetheless maddening, in a business where there were practically no local precedents to follow. On several occasions in the early fifties, Thompson discovered

abstract ideologies and movements and, moreover, in terms of people he knew rather than distant leaders. He was incapable of real detachment, and thus he was frequently shocked by the cynical approach of governments, to whom the personalities of the men involved were secondary to national interests and who were able to switch allegiances quite blandly when it seemed expedient to do so. The British, for example, for all their former admiration of Pridi (whose escape in 1947 was assisted by the naval attaché of the British Embassy) and their branding of Pibul as a war criminal, lost no time in recognizing the Pibul government after the 1947 coup, much to the disgust of people like Thompson and Alexander MacDonald. The Americans (who were also instrumental in the prime minister's escape) held out a little while longer, but in time they, too, extended recognition and aid. To a man like Thompson such reasoning, however realistic, was difficult to accept, since his own loyalties were firmly grounded in personal friendships. Almost his entire view of the power struggles in postwar Southeast Asia derived from men he knew and admired—many of them men he had met in his OSS work—and he was seldom greatly interested in movements that did not involve friends.

In the immediate postwar years, he and the other OSS people who stayed in Thailand remained on close terms with the old Free Thai leaders with whom they had worked so closely. The 1947 coup had, of course, been a severe blow to most of these leaders, who had counted on coming to power with Pridi; but still the majority of them suffered no real misfortune and many even continued to be openly loyal to the exiled premier and to advocate his return. On the first day of the long-delayed trial of the king's death case, for example, a high naval officer took the opportunity while giving testimony to state that he was convinced the former prime minister had nothing to do with the case and that he considered Pridi to be an honorable man and a good friend. Such outbursts were naturally resented by the Pibul government, who were saying that Pridi had not only been involved in the regicide but had actually engineered it; however, they remained more tolerant than might have been expected, possibly because they were as yet unsure of the extent of pro-Pridi sentiment in the country and, more important, in the armed forces. They were given an opportunity to find out toward the end of February in 1949.

All through the first two months of that year there had been rumors of an impending coup, but no one seemed to know exactly who was plotting it. When it finally came, it took most people by surprise, including Thompson. He went that night to a gala benefit dance for the American University Alumni Association—the sort of charity affair that made up most of Bangkok's social life in those days—and took part in a theatrical performance that preceded the ball in an airy pavilion in Amphorn Gardens, not far from the National Assembly building. He played a silk merchant who was pursued by intelligence agents in a nightclub called the Golden Banana. Bangkok society was present in force at the ball, including most of the high-ranking ministers and the chief of the Thai intelligence service; the only really prominent figure missing was Prime Minister Pibul. Around one o'clock in the morning, when the festivities were reaching their climax, the dancers heard gunfire from the vicinity of the river, only a mile or so from the pavilion. Soon afterward, someone ran in and said that a new government had been announced over a captured radio station in the city. The government officials left the ball hastily; the other guests, with little idea of what was going on, sat around in groups speculating.

An hour or so later, with still no definite news, Thompson and his Laotian friend and assistant Tao Oum left with some ladies who were concerned about their children back home. The group had a hair-raising trip through the city, stopped periodically by nervous policemen who seemed as uninformed as they were about the progress of the coup, but they finally accomplished their mission and the two men went back to the Oriental Hotel, where Thompson was still living. By this time, Thompson had begun thinking about the safety of certain of his political-minded northeastern and Laotian friends whose activities were being looked on with increasing disfavor by the government, and he persuaded Tao Oum to stay on at the Oriental; if the government really felt threatened, it might use the coup as an opportunity to settle old scores.

Through the rest of the night and for most of the next day, the situation in Bangkok remained unclear, though it soon became apparent that the coup had been organized by pro-Pridi elements in the navy and that the exile was in fact attempting a personal comeback. According to rumors, he was actually in the city leading the fight, though exactly where was a mystery. The army was solidly backing Pibul and Thompson later described the efforts of the hotel residents to find out what was going on as being like listening to the Army-Navy football game on radio. It was clear, however, that what was going on was far more deadly than any game. For the active Pridi supporters it was, in fact, a desperate last chance: a failed coup on top of the grave charges in the matter of the king's death would irreparably damage his prestige as far as the mass of Thai citizens was concerned, and for the supporters themselves it would certainly mean an end to government tolerance of their open dissent. For some it would mean death.

What Thompson and most people did not know during those first hectic days that followed the ball was that the coup had been doomed to failure almost from the beginning. It was poorly organized, certain key figures chose, at the last minute, not to join it, and the two most powerful organizations in the country, the army and the police, were strongly united in support of the present government. Pridi did, as the rumors claimed, succeed in returning and was reported to be among a party of men who took over the Grand Palace, but his stay was brief. He soon realized he lacked the necessary support and managed to leave Bangkok, this time forever. As a number of observers as foreseen, his failure did indeed complete the destruction of his former image, at least for many years to come. The majority of his followers later retired from public life in disillusionment or disgust or ended up in jail during the mass arrests that followed once the coup had been suppressed.

It was the aftermath rather than the coup itself that proved so shattering to Thompson. Among those picked up in a widespread series of arrests that followed were three of his close friends, all from the anti-Pibul northeast and all former members of the Pridi government. One had been minister of industry, another assistant minister of commerce, and the third a member of Parliament. They were taken on suspicion of having been involved in the attempted coup.

A week after the fighting stopped, Thompson went with Tao Oum to the ministry of foreign affairs to discuss an exhibition of Thai silk that was being planned for a forthcoming international trade conference. He had dealt with this ministry a number of times before in connection with similar exhibits, and the protocol chief was a friend. As they were talking, an aide came in and handed a slip of paper to the official, who read it with apparent shock. The news, he told Thompson, was bad: the three former government men, together with a fourth, a former assistant minister of finance who had been arrested on similar charges, had been killed.

Horrified by the news and its implications, Thompson went immediately to U.S. Ambassador Stanton's residence, where a luncheon party was in progress. There the report was confirmed with a few telephone calls, and the probable truth of the tragedy, as it gradually emerged over the next few days, was even worse than Thompson had feared.

The story given out by the police was that the prisoners had been ambushed and shot while being taken to a jail outside Bangkok. There were certain inconsistencies, however, which did not exactly inspire belief in this official version, and in his Bangkok Post, Alexander MacDonald brought them out in brief report that, under the circumstances then prevailing, was remarkably courageous. The story was headlined POLICE DESCRIBE 4 MEN'S DEATHS and recounted, in a perfectly straight-forward manner, what the police said had happened, along with a description of the men's bodies.

The police said that the prisoners, accompanied by twenty guards, had been en route to the jail when they were attacked by two cars; in the shooting that followed, the four politicians were riddled with bullets, and the mysterious assassins had escaped. MacDonald closed his article with the following paragraphs:

"Weren't any policemen shot?" a reporter asked Luang Pichit. "No," he said.

He said there were more than 80 bullet holes in the station wagon [in which the men were being transported].

Another reporter asked why Dr. Thongplaew [one of the dead men] had bruised and swollen eyes and ears. The officer said it might have happened in the firing.

He said a further official report would be turned in by the Bangkhen police.

The bodies of the four men were at Makutkasat Monastery where they were taken at 4 P.M. yesterday.

Dr. Thongplaew's face was battered and his legs riddled with bullets. Nat Thawin's left leg was broken and his right leg shot. Nai Thong-in's right leg and Nai Chamlong's left leg were broken. Nai Chamlong's ribs were broken. All were riddled with bullets.

MacDonald ran the story inside a black mourning border, and for the benefit of those who may not have been able to read between the lines of the report he also wrote an editorial condemning the shooting and reminding the government that the rest of the world was watching closely. Very soon afterwards, he found the *Post* under censorship and his own position in Thailand highly delicate.

The 1947 coup which restored Pibul to power had been a bloodless one; by contrast, there were numerous casualties in the 1949 attempt, and the murder of the four officials was only one of a number of similar tragedies that darkened Thailand in the months that followed. Some placed the blame on the overzealous police, which (with the help of arms supplied by the U.S.) had become almost an army in itself and which took charge of most of the investigations—sometimes, it was said, without the knowledge or consent of Pibul. Whoever was responsible, the days of tolerance were clearly over and, as Thompson had feared, old scores were being settled in a lethal manner and potential troublemakers were being eliminated.

A former Free Thai major was shot while being interrogated by the police. A colonel, also a Free Thai alumnus, was shot by the police while shaving, apprehended, they reported, while in the act of escaping. The pretty pavilion where the gala AUA ball had been held the night it all began was turned into a police court to deal with the hundreds of suspects who were being brought in.

For some, their fate did not come immediately but was delayed for several months. One of these was a close friend of Thompson's who often went with him on his trips to the northeast. When this man was arrested, he and Thompson were on such a trip; the police picked him up at their hotel and only much later did Thompson learn that he had been shot.

His friend Tao Oum had been close to several of the murdered government officials and had reason to suspect his days might be numbered as well. He decided not to take the risk but, instead, to return to his native Laos. He had been asked by the French to come back and help draw up a new agreement that would supposedly lead to the liberation of his country, and though he had some misgivings about their sincerity he was revolted by the conditions in Bangkok and accepted.

One by one, most of Thompson's original friends were disappearing.

11

The effect of these grim events on Thompson was profound in at least three ways. First—and, at the time, obviously the least important— it meant a fairly drastic change in the conduct of his silk business, which was just beginning to get on its feet. Tao Oum he considered his most valuable assistant as well as his closest friend, and a number of the men who were dead, in prison, or threatened were friends who had helped him set up the contacts with the silk growers of the northeast and had been available to give him useful advice. Their abrupt departure from the scene would mean a good deal of reorganization.

This was a minor concern, of course, compared with the horror of seeing those he described in a letter as his best Asian friends killed or imprisoned or driven into exile on charges that he believed to be untrue. These were some of the men who first taught him to love Asia, who had offered him encouragement and help when he badly needed it, who had given him his first real glimpses of life behind the Eastern facade; and now many, if not all, of them were gone. With MacDonald, Thompson went to the Buddhist temple where the rites for the four officials were held, and the memory of it remained with him to the end of his days in Thailand: the formal photographs of the dead men beside their funeral urns, the terrified wives and children clustered about the crematorium, the ubiquitous policemen and plainclothesmen watching every arrival carefully in search of more suspects.

The final level on which he was very probably affected was political. He had learned most of what he knew of Southeast Asian politics from some of these men, and to him their removal appeared a tragedy of major proportions. The intensity of his feelings is plain in the despairing letters he wrote to various friends at the time, smuggling them out with travelers to avoid censorship; they were the letters of a man shaken to his depths and abruptly aware of the frailty of idealism. Whether he was right or not in his deep conviction that the old Free Thai leaders represented the best hope for Thailand's future is, in the context of this book, immaterial; that is a question best answered some day by a Thai historian with a better knowledge of the events and men involved. What is relevant here is that Thompson's disillusionment was acute, and almost certainly there must have been moments when he seriously considered leaving his young business and cutting himself off from this part of the world he had come to love so much. That he did not is perhaps indication that, in the end, the love was greater than the disillusion. In the years that followed that nightmare period, however, he seemed to draw farther and farther away from the politics of the region so that when, in the late fifties, the Pibul government was overthrown (without bloodshed this time), there were no close friends to be put in jail or shot and no emotional letters to be written. In fact, beyond a natural sense of relief that his old enemies were at last out of power, that, in a sense, a certain sort of vengeance had been exacted, his view of the matter was largely objective: he was principally concerned, this time, with how the change of government would affect his business, not with its effect on his personal life.

The reactions discussed above are pertinent to the later story of Thompson's disappearance in that they tend to disprove a popular theory that he was an active spy for the CIA throughout his Thai career, passing on valuable knowledge of high-level activities. All the evidence is quite the contrary. He appeared to lose interest in Thai politics and even in that of neighboring Indo-China, had few contacts in official circles, and rarely even commented privately on the shifts of power in coming years. One of his friends commented, "If Jim Thompson was a spy, one has to wonder what sort of information he could possibly have passed on, he was so isolated from the people in power and therefore from any alleged secrets."

A former CIA agent, who prefers to remain nameless, is more specific. "I've seen the file on Jim Thompson," he said recently, "and while it confirms that there was contact during his early years in Thailand, it also reveals that the agency regarded him as being far too liberal for its tastes, particularly on such subjects as Indo-China. Contacts declined and soon stopped completely, long before he disappeared."

Throughout the remainder of 1949, having made up his mind to stay in Thailand, he devoted himself to the development and promotion of Thai silk with increasing determination, for to his natural enthusiasm was now added the need to keep busy and erase the memories of the spring. A welcome visitor that year was a friend of his brother's named Charles Baskerville, a fashionable painter from New York whose clients included numerous international celebrities. He came to Bangkok from a stay in India, where he had been doing portraits of Prime Minister Nehru and of the King of Nepal. Baskerville was a man of great charm and sophistication (for a time in the mid-twenties he covered night-clubs for the *New Yorker* magazine), and his company must have been a great relief to Thompson after the trying times just past.

"We both stayed at the Oriental Hotel," Baskerville remembered, "which was rather simple at that time with swinging doors like barrooms in the old days on the bedrooms, and great jars of water with a tin pan on top to use in douching yourself instead of bathtubs or showers. I made watercolors, went sightseeing, and went to the silk weavers with Jim. He gave a birthday party for me on the edge of the river where the swimming pool is now. Mr. and Mrs. Peng [a Laotian couple who had become associates of Thompson's in the silk business] gave a dinner in their garden on my last evening and we all danced the ram wong [a Thai folk dance] with music on those tall reed pipes played by the husband-samloh-driver of one of the weavers. It is a gay memory of an unspoiled world."

Baskerville had a wide circle of prominent friends in New York, including the fashion editor Diana Vreeland, and when he left Thailand he took with him a large quantity of silk to circulate among them and stir up interest. Thompson, too, made semi-annual visits to New York to hold showings of the silk and arranged for a distributing agency called Thaibok to handle the fabric in America, the first in what was to become a worldwide network of silk agents in various countries.

Thanks to all these efforts, more and more people were being introduced to Thai silk and one of them, the costume designer Irene Sharaff, was to provide a powerful stimulus to sales. She decided to use the material for Rodgers and Hammerstein's musical comedy, *The King and I.*

Actually this was not the first use of Thai silk on a Broadway stage. Some time before, shortly after Thompson first started production, it had been introduced to the theatrical world in Mike Todd's *Peepshow*. When he was putting together this refined burlesque (one of the numbers featured girls in a huge bubble bath), Todd happened to read in *Time* magazine that the young King of Thailand was an accomplished jazz musician who had written a number of popular songs. Todd decided it would be a fine idea to use one of the king's songs in the show, no doubt reasoning that it would give some class (as well as some publicity) to an evening that was, otherwise, on a more basic level of entertainment. As usual, he got what he wanted and the king's number, entitled "Blue Moon," was given a decorous production in which the girls wore blue-and-green plaid Thai silk pakomas. (That in Thailand they would have been worn by a man passed unnoticed on Broadway.) It was Miss Sharaff, costumes designer for that show too, who had discovered the silk at Thaibok, and when she later got the assignment for *The King and I* she knew at once what material she wanted to lend authenticity to the piece.

The musical was based loosely on a work entitled *Anna and the King of Siam*, by Margaret Landon, which had been made into an earlier, non-musical movie with Rex Harrison and Irene Dunne. Mrs. Landon was the wife of an American State Department official who had spent a number of years in Thailand; her book had been based, even more loosely, on a memoir written in the late nineteenth century by Anna Leonowens called *The English Governess at the Court of Siam*, recounting her experiences as a teacher in the Grand Palace. The ruler at the time of her stay was King Mongkut (Rama IV), father of King Chulalongkorn, and he was not only a remarkable monarch but one who is still revered by the people of his country. The crude caricature of him in Anna Leonowens' book so offended Thai sensibilities that it is, even today, still unwise to bring up the subject of her work in certain Bangkok circles. The musical was even more offensive to them, one result being that the original movie version was banned in Thailand and not available to the general public until the advent of video tapes. (Neither the Landon nor the Leonowens books was ever banned, however, perhaps on the assumption that few Thais were likely to read them.)

Thompson worked closely with Miss Sharaff on the costumes for the show, suggesting designs from old books on Thai life of the period, and weaving special weights and colors to her specifications. Other materials were also used—from China, India, and Japan, for example— but it was by far the most challenging assignment the Thai Silk Company had yet faced, and Thompson was well aware of its immense publicity value.

The star of the musical was Gertrude Lawrence, who had first drawn the attention of Rodgers and Hammerstein to the material. As she prepared for the part (which was to be her last; she died during the New York run), she developed an interest in the character she was to portray as well as in Thailand itself; she met Thompson on one of his trips to New York and they quickly became friends, with the result that she gave introductions to him to people like the director Joshua Logan and the critic Ward Morehouse when they came to Bangkok. In the end, her glowing and elegant Anna bore little resemblance to the real one, whose books reveal her to have been ill-tempered, prejudiced, and more than a little ridiculous, even by Victorian standards. Nor did Yul Brynner's sexy king remotely resemble the austere Rama IV, who had served as a monk for 27 years before becoming king, was in late middle age when he met Anna, and would no more have contemplated a romance with her than he would have danced the polka through the halls of the Grand Palace, as he was portrayed as doing.

Whatever its historical failings, the musical was a tremendous success, both on stage and film, and the costumes were magnificent. A flood of new orders poured not only into Thompson's company but also to other independents who by that were getting organized, as can be seen in the fact the exports of Thai silk jumped from around half a million baht in 1950 (the year before *The King and I*) to nearly two million in 1952.

12

By the early fifties, it was apparent that the silk business was a going concern. Thompson had opened a small shop of his own on Suriwong Road, a few steps off New Road, and the weavers, seeing in unmistakable material terms the results of their efforts, were expanding and producing more silk in a month than ever before in Thai history. Seeing that his stay in the country was likely to be at least semipermanent, Thompson began seriously thinking of a place to live which he would allow him more room than the Oriental.

He first took a small house at the top end of Sathorn Road, about halfway between his shop and the Bangkrua weavers. When this proved not big enough for his growing social needs, however, he decided to build a house of his own on a small plot of land not far away, which was owned by a Thai friend. In those days, before the price of land in Bangkok ascended to heights rivaling that of a major American city, such empty plots were common in the sprawling capital, and it was a fairly common practice for the owners to allow friends to build on them and live rent-free for an agreed period, after which the property and its improvements would revert to the owner. Thompson and his friend agreed on a ten-year lease on a pleasant site bordered by a klong (now gone) that ran along Rama IV Road across from Lumpini Park, after which he put up an inexpensive wooden frame house whose main charm was its airy, pavilionlike openness. In designing it, his first exercise in tropical architecture, Thompson tried to duplicate on a smaller scale the spacious feel of the older Bangkok houses. The living room and the dining room were entirely open on one side, facing the klong, and were unscreened to allow a free flow of air. (There was also a free flow of mosquitoes, but this never bothered Thompson, or so he claimed; for less hardy visitors there were burning mosquito coils at strategic places and bottles of a locally made repellent with a potent odor.) Upstairs there were two bedrooms, which were screened, and a Thai-style bath containing an enormous jar from which one sluiced down with cool water. The compound contained several large flame-of-the-forest trees (*Delonix regia*), covered with a mass of red-orange flowers in the hot season, and Thompson set about planning and planting a small garden with an enthusiasm inherited from his plant-loving mother. It was in this house that he began to assemble the famous antique collection that was to become almost as famous as his silk business and also to assume his role as Bangkok's leading farang host.

In the fifties and sixties, Bangkok was as close to being a paradise for antique collectors as almost anywhere in Asia, and the steep present-day prices are due in large part to the numerous visitors who have seen or heard of the Thompson collection. ("Jim Thompson has one just like it" became a familiar sales pitch in many shops.) When Thompson began his serious buying, the beautiful antiquities of Southeast Asia were little known to the West beyond a small world of experts and a few major museums, and in Thailand itself, only a few rich Chinese and members of the nobility took any great interest in them. Outside the National Museum and a few Buddhist temples, there were probably not more than ten really first-rate collections of local art, and several of these were not so much real collections as masses of dusty relics that had been handed down through generations and kept out of ancestral devotion rather than real admiration. As a result of this general lack of interest (and in the early fifties, comparatively few tourists), the shops of Bangkok, particularly those in a congested part of the Chinese section called Nakorn Kasem, were rich in undiscovered and mostly unwanted treasures: Buddha images and fragments (shunned by most Thais for their religious associations), scenes from Buddhist legends painted on cotton banners, Chinese and Thai porcelains, and intricately carved furniture and pieces of wood that had once graced older houses and temples. As more and more of the old palaces gave way to Western buildings, their contents found their way into the shops, as did much older pieces regularly unearthed in the ancient capitals of Ayutthaya and Sukhothai; there was, theoretically, a law preventing unauthorized excavation of the older sites, but in view of the vastness of the ruins and the incredible number of them all over the country, it was impossible for the cash-strapped Fine Arts Department to exercise any real control. It was not until later, when prices began to rise and organized looting posed a threat, that really effective action was initiated to protect the country's treasures.

Thompson took to spending almost every Sunday afternoon— the only day he took off from work—rummaging about the alleyways of Nakorn Kasem picking up things that interested him, and he also often went up to Ayutthaya, where there were other shops that sold, quite openly, the results of the annual plowings. His buying, from the very beginning of his collection up until his disappearance, when he had achieved international fame, was, like his politics, an intensely personal affair. No one could ever have accused him of being a pedant. Though he read every available book on the art of the region and became, with time and sheer experience, something of an authority, he was never an expert like his Princeton classmate Alexander Griswold, another ex-OSS man, who went on to write several definitive works on Thai art and later established a private museum in the U.S. that continues after his death. Thompson occasionally seemed to feel that this was a deficiency on his part and sometimes got defensive about it, but there can be little doubt that if even he had had the temperament for the role of a scholar—which he did not—he would not have enjoyed it very much. He learned, as all collectors do, to admire certain objects and periods that might not have impressed him at the beginning of his collecting days, thus upgrading his collection gradually, but he continued to buy mainly because of emotional response.

The collection he amassed over the years was thus a varied one, including both extremely rare objects and others that were valueless except for the pleasure they gave to their owner. He kept some known fakes and several other pieces of dubious ancestry simply because he enjoyed them. His house was not, as it was sometimes called, a museum, but rather a home; and the things displayed in it were not collected so much for their rarity or potential market value as because he wanted to live with them.

Most of the items he bought at first were Thai, but as his interests widened he began to collect things from other Southeast Asian countries; not for many years did he become seriously interested in Chinese art, especially porcelain, and he never found Japanese antiquities to his taste. (As a matter of fact, rather remarkably, he never went to Japan until the year before his disappearance, when he stopped off for a few days in Tokyo and Kyoto. He also managed to stay in Asia nearly twenty years before he made his first visit to Hong Kong, which is only a few hours by air from Bangkok.)

Soon after arriving in Thailand, he had been struck by the highly decorative and relatively unknown traditional Thai paintings, and these were among the first things he began to collect. As an art form they were in danger of dying out, and because of his admiration Thompson felt that someone should collect as many as possible of the old ones before they were lost entirely to the ravages of the tropical climate. Most of these paintings were on cotton, ranging from fairly small to tapestry size, and the subject matter generally dealt with either the life of the Buddha or the popular Jataka tales about the Buddha's previous incarnations. Their primary purpose was religious instruction, as well as decoration of the temples on festive occasions, and they were the creations, mostly, of anonymous priests or artists commissioned by devout Buddhists who wished to earn merit by presenting a gift to their temple. They varied widely in quality; the majority were as crude, though often as charming, as the creations of imaginative children; but the best of them were genuine works of art, with a wealth of architectural and decorative detail and bold, original composition and coloring. Many of the designs Thompson used later when he began making printed silks came from these superior works. Over the years, he managed to build up what is probably the finest collection of such paintings to be found anywhere. He was also instrumental in giving most Westerners their first look at the little-known art, for he sent a group of his best paintings on a tour of American museums, sponsored by the State Department, and also donated a number of them to museums that had Southeast Asian collections. A happy side effect of his interest was that a number of younger Thai painters went back to the traditional style in order to supply a new demand from visitors who had seen Thompson's collection.

He was not at first interested in collecting Buddha images, but in time he developed a great admiration for them, especially for delicately wrought bronzes. Nowadays, thanks to the tourists who crowd the antique stops of Bangkok (and despite an official ban on the export of Buddha images) the manufacture of fake antiques, in bronze, stone, or whatever is most in demand, is not only a profitable industry but also an exceedingly skillful one, at times even fooling experts with artfully contrived reproductions of rare styles which occasionally end up on display in respected museums abroad. When Thompson began going to the shops of the Nakorn Kasem, however, fakes were a minor buying hazard, and very fine pieces were available for low prices for anyone who had an eye for them. He became more and more fascinated by the degrees of subtlety on the seemingly stylized faces, which ranged from the almost peasant simplicity of the earliest periods to the haughty elegance of Sukhothai and Ayutthaya, and an increasing number of images joined the paintings in his house.

Thompson came to conceive of the collection as something more than a personal affair, however much it might represent his own taste. He began to look upon it as one way of preserving a few of the country's treasures from possible loss or destruction. In almost every part of Thailand there were—and, indeed, still are—literally thousands of ruined and virtually unexplored temples and city sites, some of them going back to prehistoric times and most of them rich in artifacts. The governmental Department of Fine Arts, which is theoretically in charge of excavating the sites and collecting the antiquities for the nation, is chronically short of funds and trained personnel to deal with this mass of raw material, and the National Museum was, at that time, far too small to store or display even a fraction of it. The same lack of funds, complicated in many cases by ignorance and indifference, prevailed in many of the country's provincial temples, where beautiful murals and unique old buildings were allowed to slowly fade and rot away through successive rainy seasons. The problem was not helped by the conviction of devout Buddhists that more merit was to be gained in rebuilding than in restoring, so that money that might have been used to save a fine old structure was employed instead to build a bright, modern replacement that rarely, if ever, contained workmanship of comparable quality; whatever was left from the older buildings was often simply stacked in some corner of the temple compound and forgotten. Even the less perishable objects, those of stone or bronze for example, were not much safer, for it was not too difficult for a wily dealer from Bangkok to persuade a simple country abbot to exchange a fourteenth-century image for a newly-minted copy or perhaps enough money to put a new roof on the meeting hall. The image then appeared in the Nakorn Kasem and, shortly thereafter, was bought by a passing tourist who carried it off to Cleveland or Mexico City.

To Thompson, all this seemed a terrible waste of the nation's artistic heritage, and he reasoned that it was far better for private local collectors to have the pieces. Whether on public view or not (later he did open his own house to the public and today it is a registered museum), they would at least be preserved from destruction and they would remain in the country. This was, of course, an entirely admirable idea from a purely objective standpoint, but it failed to take into account certain deeply-rooted attitudes that would, some years later, result in a bitter clash with the Fine Arts Department and that also brought him criticism from certain other Thais. Part of the problem was that to most Thais, Buddhist art is not viewed simply as art. It isn't even primarily art. It is religious and in many cases it is believed to possess supernatural powers. Practically no Thai, even the most sophisticated and Westernized, regards a Buddha image as merely an object of beauty, and certainly not as a decorative object. In Thai homes such an image is given a place of honor, often in a little shrine or separate room dedicated to it, and regular offerings are made; its symbolic value far outweighs its material or artistic worth.

Some more scholarly Buddhists have complained that attaching so much importance to images is, in fact, contrary to the teachings of the Lord Buddha, but such arguments have had little effect on most people, for whom the reaction is in any case emotional rather than intellectual. When the invading Burmese captured the great city of Ayutthaya in 1767, they not only sacked and burned it but also, in search of treasure, decapitated and otherwise mutilated most of the numerous images in the old capital (which is one reason so many Buddha heads were available in shops later). To present-day Thais, looking back on the greatest catastrophe in their history, this vandalism seems even more dreadful than the destruction of the city, and it accounts for much of the anti-Burmese feeling that still lingers, particularly among country people. But not only among the provincials: a well-educated, much-traveled Thai businessman suggested to a Western friend not long ago that Burma's current economic and political problems may well be delayed vengeance for their desecration of the Ayutthaya images.

Even in museums, the display of Buddha images in Thailand is a very delicate matter—if the building has a second floor, for example, the images will be placed there rather than on the first, where visitors will be walking above them—and in a private home, especially in the private home of a non-Buddhist foreigner, it becomes delicate in the extreme. For all his genuine admiration of the artistic creations of the country, Thompson never quite overcame the vague resentment that these complex feelings engendered, although he took considerable care not to offend in the way such objects were displayed in his house. Eventually, after his trouble with the Fine Arts Department, he disposed of almost all his Thai Buddha images and tried to limit himself to objects from neighboring countries like Burma and Cambodia, which for some reason disturbed people less.

Some of his most decorative treasures were Burmese, which he picked up in that country when he made several visits in the fifties at the joint invitation of the Burmese government and the United Nations to give advice on starting a silk industry there. He was most impressed by the quality of Burmese silk, which he thought compared favorably with the Thai product, and assisted in the setting up of a number of looms. Subsequent political problems, however, killed the industry before it could really get started.

On one of his trips upcountry in Burma, he found a collection of extraordinarily beautiful wooden nats, or spirits, in a temple near Amarapura, which were gradually rotting away in the open air. Thompson donated sufficient funds to build a shelter for them, and, in gratitude, the authorities gave him several of the figures for his Bangkok house. He also developed an enthusiasm for ornate Burmese tapestries, known as kalagas, which have elaborate designs sewn on velvet and studded with glass and seed pearls. In an effort to revive this almost dead art he rounded up a group of aged artisans and commissioned them to make a collection of kalagas, which he then sent on a tour of the States to stimulate potential buyers. Although the display found numerous admirers and several prospective buyers of future production, conditions in Burma were unfavorable to starting even such a relatively small cottage industry. Not until recent years has kalaga-making started up again, though the new versions tend to be crude compared with those in Thompson's collection.

13

With his growing silk business and his art collection, Thompson was also acquiring, perhaps inevitably, an expanding personal reputation that was attracting more and more attention outside Thailand. The invitations to Burma as a cottage-industry advisor were indications that his remarkable success with the silk had gained him recognition as one of those rare businessmen who had solved the difficult problem of turning traditional handicrafts into profitable industries. In the years that followed, similar invitations came from groups and individuals in other countries, among them Syria, West Pakistan, and Malaysia, and it was, in fact, on yet another such advisory mission that he was supposed to go to Singapore after his holiday in the Cameron Highlands in 1967. The reputation was further bolstered by its obvious and irresistible elements of romance; for had not Thompson, with little but imagination and courage, done what many a middle-aged man dreamed of doing?

The *Readers Digest* was one of the first publications to recognize the appeal of the story and introduced its large readership to the legend of the soft-spoken American who had performed a minor miracle in a distant country of which the average Westerner was only dimly aware. This produced not only a flood of orders for silk but also a surge of journalistic interest; *Time, Life, Newsweek*, and the *New York Times* followed with stories of their own, and articles about Thai silk also turned up in such fashion magazines as *Vogue* and *Harper's Bazaar.* Traveling authors like Philip Wylie and Santha Rama Rau met Thompson while they were in Bangkok and wrote about him and his business in the accounts they later published of their journeys. In time, Thompson, Thai silk, and, later, his Thai-style house were written about in magazines, newspapers, and books all over the world, and after each one appeared the company's mail volume increased appreciably, mostly with silk orders but sometimes with highly personal letters to Thompson himself; a number of ladies from Europe and America generously offered themselves as business assistants or as comforters in his declining years, and several included photographs to back up their written claims.

Affluent tourists were beginning to come to Bangkok in increasing numbers in the early fifties—most at first on cruise ships that anchored at the mouth of the river, later on one of the airlines that stopped at Don Muang Airport—and many of them headed straight to the Thai Silk Company shortly after they checked into their hotels. The modest little shop that he had opened on Suriwong Road—an air-conditioned sales room on the ground floor, hot, cramped offices and store-rooms on the upper floors—was nearly always crowded with people, many of whom used it as a convenient meeting place since it was close to most of the hotels. An astonishingly high percentage of them brought letters of introduction to Thompson, often from people he barely knew, and many who didn't simply introduced themselves, partly out of curiosity and partly out of relief at finding a familiar Western face in a country where foreigners were still comparatively scarce. In short order, Thompson found himself cast in the role of a colorful character and, soon, as the best-known foreigner in Bangkok and perhaps in all of Southeast Asia.

A more retiring type might have been taken aback by all this growing celebrity, and Thompson did, sometimes, complain that he was left with practically no time of his own. Basically, however, and in the circumstances fortunately, he was a naturally gregarious man who enjoyed meeting different kinds of people and who, moreover, strongly disliked spending an evening alone. Nearly everyone who came with an introduction got invited for dinner, as well as many who came with nothing much more than an engaging personality and an interest in Thailand. Accordingly, the airy little frame house he had built, with its increasingly rich furnishings, became the setting of almost nightly dinner parties, to which came a remarkable number of visitors. Barbara Hutton, whom he had known in New York, came and so did Senator William Fulbright. Truman Capote, Cecil Beaton, Joseph Alsop, and a colorful assortment of other visiting statesmen, theatrical people, social leaders, publishers, newspaper reporters, art authorities, diplomats, and others who were distinguished mainly by the fact that Thompson found them interesting. A Bangkok resident who was present at many of these gatherings still marvels at Thompson's sheer physical fortitude, which rarely seemed to flag even after an exhausting day of work, and at his unfailing hospitality.

"Night after night," the friend recalls, "he would be asked the same questions, about himself, about Thailand, about this and that. And night after night he would give the same answers as politely and as enthusiastically as if he had never given them before. It sounds easy enough, but actually it isn't. Something curious happens to people when they become tourists, no matter who they are back home. Even those who are most intelligent and sophisticated become almost incredibly naive when they get in a completely strange culture. I never knew anyone who could be as endlessly patient with this phenomenon as Jim could. No one will ever know how many people first developed an affection, sometimes a passion, for Thailand simply because of having spent an evening with him."

The same friend found some of the later theories about Thompson's disappearance amusing: "People who never knew him have written that he was an active, well-known spy during this period and later. I presume a spy has to have a bit of time to himself to collect information and accomplish other things. Jim had practically no time alone, day or night. If he was engaged in espionage, it would have been an achievement even more remarkable than his work with Thai silk."

It was also at this period that he assembled the staff of servants who were to remain with him throughout his stay in Thailand. The mainstays of the establishment were the Chinese cook, Tun, and the houseboy, Yee, both of whom adjusted without apparent difficulty to Thompson's unpredictable social life, in which the only really constant factor was the probability that somebody was coming to dinner—just how many was often not known until the last minute. Neither the cook nor the boy could speak much English and since Thompson spoke no Thai it might be thought that domestic chaos would prevail; somehow, though, they worked out a system of sign language, which they perfected over the years, and the house ran smoothly.

Considerably before the lease on the property had run its ten-year course, it became apparent that the smallish house was hardly adequate for Thompson's social life, not to mention his collection of antiques, which was expanding at an alarming rate. Within a few years after he moved in, practically every square inch of wall space was covered with paintings and woodcarvings and the effect, while undeniably charming, was getting a bit congested. Furthermore, he went on buying, and it was clear that before long he would either have to enlarge the house or move to more spacious quarters. After some thought, he decided on the latter course and, moreover, decided to build a house that would provide a properly splendid setting for both his collection and his entertaining.

None of his friends in Bangkok can recall exactly when the idea of putting up a traditional Thai-style house came to him, but very likely the thought had been with him for some years, as a remote possibility if not as a definite plan. Thai architecture is one of the great joys of the country, and all the earliest European visitors filled their journals with admiring descriptions of it: the swooping, multilayered roofs of the fabulous temples, all gilded and flashing in the tropical sunlight; and along the rivers and klongs their domestic equivalents, simpler and more practical but with the same distinctive elegance that made them something more than mere shelters. In the past, the religious and domestic architecture of Thailand had many similarities, the principal difference being that the latter, having less of a symbolic weight to carry, was much better adapted to the needs and climate of the country. Wood, of course, was the principal building material for the houses, and, in the best ones it was the hard, long-lasting teak from the vast forests of the north. Like the temples, the houses had steep roofs that seemed to be straining upward to the sky, with curving decorations at the tips of the bargeboards, and in both—as least in the central region— the walls inclined slightly toward the center which added to the illusion of height and gave them a particular grace they might otherwise have lacked. Both, too, had a fanciful quality that went beyond either practical or symbolic requirements and that may be described as an architectural sense of humor; they were startlingly beautiful, but they were also amusing.

The traditional Thai house was well adapted to the habits of the country as well as to the climate. One of its most practical features was the ease with which it could be put up and taken down, for the Thais had devised prefabrication long before it was thought of in the West. The houses were built in sections, each forming a wall, which with very little trouble could be fitted together and hung on a frame of wooden pillars without the use of nails. If the owners decided to move, as they frequently did in the distant past, the walls could be taken down, neatly stacked on a raft, and floated down the nearest waterway to a new location.

Nearly always, the houses were elevated from the ground, a practice that made them cooler, protected them from floods and unfriendly animals, and provided a handy space to keep livestock or do such part-time work as weaving silk. In the living quarters openness and simplicity were the principal characteristics: the walls were generally left unpainted, though sometimes oiled and paneled with scraps of leftover wood, and there were plenty of doors and windows to allow a free circulation of air. Privacy was not highly valued, and often whole families would sleep in a single room, though in some cases this was partitioned off into cubicles to accommodate the various generations. There were few decorative touches, in striking contrast to the dazzling temples and palaces; these were largely confined to carved panels under the windows and sometimes over the doors, and the curving roof-ends that were probably adaptations of the more elaborate ones on religious structures. The thresholds of the doors were raised, possibly for superstitious reasons—i.e., to keep evil spirits from creeping in at night and disturbing the sleep of the inhabitants—but more likely as a structural aid in holding the wall sections firmly in place on their frame; it was regarded as bad luck to step on the thresholds when entering or leaving a room.

Before the war there had been thousands of these traditional houses all over Bangkok, and even when Thompson arrived there were quite a few in older sections of the city. There were a number, for example, in the weaving village of Bangkrua, and some of his silk weavers lived in them. Upcountry, especially around Ayutthaya, there were many more. With the relentless march of progress, though, they were fast vanishing, victims, like the silk itself, of the increasing demand for more "modern" amenities—which, as translated, usually meant Western ones. The great majority of post-war Thais looked upon such houses as old-fashioned and out of tune with the great changes that were going on in the country, and when they built a new residence it was nearly always a copy of a Western model; American ranch-style houses have been particularly popular, often copied from books or magazines down to the picture windows which, without air-conditioning, turn the structure into a stifling hothouse. A few upper-class Thais owned traditional houses in Bangkok but almost never lived in them, using them for ceremonial or entertainment purposes but preferring to take their leisure in a nearby European-style residence. In the mid-fifties, Bangkok landlords busily putting up houses to rent to the foreigners pouring into the city would have considered it the height of madness to build anything remotely resembling a classic Thai structure. What the newcomers wanted, they were certain, was a replica of what they had left behind them at home.

One measure of Thompson's considerable influence can be seen in how this attitude changed after he erected his Thai house, which quickly became one of the sights to see in the capital, as celebrated in its way as the temples and the floating market. Directly or indirectly due to his experiment in using the traditional for modern purposes, it soon became quite fashionable to have a Thai-style residence, preferably assembled from really old ones, and remote provincial villages grew accustomed to eager buyers from Bangkok offering them huge sums for ancestral homes. When the supply ran out, companies opened to make new ones, crafted by skilled carpenters. Quite a few traditional homes, and many more that might charitably be described as semitraditional, have been built for rent to foreigners, not all of whom, it turned out, wanted Levittown on a klong. Several prominent Thais, too, have given up their modern, Western homes and gone back to their native architecture. Most of them would balk at the suggestion that they have done so because of an American who led the way, but there can be little doubt that the house he built exercised some sort of influence on the trend, if only by proving that old houses could be adapted to suit contemporary needs without destroying their essential character. Thompson may not have "saved" Thai domestic architecture, as he certainly saved Thai silk, but he played a powerful role in restoring it to a prominence it had not enjoyed for many years outside temple compounds. In the building of his house, he embarked on a project that gave him more satisfaction than anything he did outside the silk business. At the same time, he added yet another chapter to his growing legend.

14

Once Thompson decided to build he faced a variety of unfamiliar problems, the first of which was where. Under Thai law at the time, foreigners were allowed to buy up to one rai (about half an acre) of land for residential purposes, providing Thai citizens had the same privilege in the buyer's home country or state. Delaware met the requirement, which meant that Thompson was free to buy his rai if he could find one that suited him. A plot he had had his eye on for some time was just across the klong from the weaving village he visited almost every morning. Not too many years before, this part of Bangkok had been considered country, and the land Thompson had been looking at had once been part of a large estate where a princely family kept a summer palace, to which they retreated when the weather in the old city became uncomfortable. The rural aspect had been largely lost, the estate chopped up and sold off for houses and rowshops, but the location still had several features that appealed to Thompson's nostalgia for the unprogressive Bangkok of the past. There was the klong, one of the few large ones left in the city, and along it the sort of scenery that used to be so familiar: great rain trees arching over the water, a daily clutter of boats selling a vast variety of wares, wooden houses, some of them traditional, hugging the water's edge and, with their open rooms, providing theatre-like glimpses of ordinary Thai life. Though it was now squarely in the middle of the modern city, only a block away from the National Stadium, it still retained a flavor of its country past, the city noises muted by trees and the pace perceptibly slower.

It was, in brief, very much Thompson's sort of place, and after some negotiations, he bought it. He then turned his attention to the problem of the house itself. He had already decided not to build a completely new house; many of the fine old houses he had seen were as strong after a hundred years as they were when they were built, and it would be prohibitively expensive—if, indeed, it were possible—to match them in materials and workmanship on the scale he envisioned. He had thus decided to buy a group of old houses and reassemble them, making necessary architectural changes, to form one large residence for himself and several smaller ones in the garden for his servants.

The house he eventually built was composed of all or parts of six separate buildings from a variety of places and owners. The most important section, which became his drawing room, was an early nineteenth-century house from Bangkrua. It had served several generations of one of the weaving families, and, when he bought it, had fallen into the possession of five heirs, all of whom were eager to sell the old structure and put the money into smart Western models. Thompson had been admiring the house for several years on his regular visits to the area, and his architect's eye saw in it possibilities that may have been less evident to others. For one thing, although it had been partitioned off into a number of small rooms for the convenience of the sizeable family living in it, he noted that it had truly magnificent proportions and that it was, moreover, in excellent condition. The paneled teak walls were solid, there was delicate carved work under the windows, and the broad floorboards had been given a beautiful satiny patina by the thousands of bare feet that had padded back and forth across them. When he reassembled the house across the klong, Thompson reversed the walls so that the carvings faced inside; thanks to the practicality of the traditional architecture, this made no difference structurally since the walls were otherwise the same, inside and out. The future kitchen also came from the weaving village. It dated from around the middle of the nineteenth century and had been part of an old palace which had been sold and moved to Bangkrua fifty years before.

To get the remaining parts he needed, Thompson had to go further afield. He found that the province of Ayutthaya, upriver from Bangkok, was particularly rich in old houses, and he spent many pleasant Sundays going about in boats inspecting them—at the same time, of course, buying more antiques, which he now reasoned he would need to furnish his spacious new establishment. He found most of what he needed in a village called Pak Hai, northwest of the old capital. After the sales were made, the houses were taken down, stacked neatly on barges and brought by river and klong to the building site. In Ayutthaya he also found some large, soft-colored seventeenth-century brick, which he later used to pave his terrace overlooking the klong, and some handsome green Chinese tiles, brought as ballast on junks returning from trade in China, which he set in the parapet of the terrace.

The job of putting all these materials together to form the kind of house he wanted was extremely complicated, partly because nothing quite like it had ever been done before. Traditionally, each room of a Thai house was a separate unit, and while there might be several arranged around an open veranda it was always necessary to go out of one to reach another. Thompson wanted to connect them with doors and hallways to create a single structure, an especially tricky task when it came to the steep roofs, and to help him on some of the technical details he hired a young Thai architect friend. What resulted in the end, though, was really his own creation, since it turned out that the Thai associate, having been trained in Western methods of construction, was just as unfamiliar with many of the fine points of traditional architecture as Thompson was. The same was true of the Bangkok workmen who were brought in to repair some damaged parts of the old houses and provide new segments necessary to join them all together; they had long since forgotten the old methods, if they ever knew them, and ultimately a group of carpenters had to be brought down from Ayutthaya, where the ancient skills were still practised.

Thompson wanted his house to be as authentically Thai as possible, but there were certain Western comforts he decided not to do without and this required several structural departures. There was, for example, the stairway from the ground to the main floor, which in a true Thai house would be outside and exposed; Thompson put his inside a stairwell, which became one of the most impressive rooms in the place. Similarly, he installed proper bathrooms with Western toilets in lieu of the customary outhouse with a hole in the floor.

On one point, however, he decided to be completely Thai, and this was in the observance of various semi-religious ceremonies which attend the construction of most buildings in the country. These ceremonies are not strictly Buddhist, which does not acknowledge the existence of good and evil spirits, but in Thailand, as in other Southeast Asian countries—and, of course, in most Western countries, too—the older beliefs have stubbornly refused to fade away and have been accommodatingly absorbed into the faith. Thus one finds fortune-tellers and spirit houses in most temple compounds, and priests take part in ceremonies designed to placate the invisible world.

Three separate ceremonies were deemed necessary to the successful construction of Thompson's house. The first was held at precisely 9 A.M. on September 15, 1958—the most auspicious time and date according to astrological reckoning—when the initial teak column of the house was installed. At this event, which was attended by a sizeable number of Thompson's friends and silk weavers from across the klong, a Brahmin priest and nine Buddhist monks from Ayutthaya chanted prayers at the site as the column was raised, and bowls of food were later placed at strategic points about the compound to encourage the earth spirits to keep the house, its builders, and its future inhabitants safe.

The second ceremony came near the end of the construction and concerned the placing of the spirit house. These little abodes are charming replicas of Thai-style houses or temples and are believed to provide a residence for the guardian spirit of the compound, whose powers are considerable. When the human residents encounter a rash of difficulties—servant problems, say, or frequent burglaries, or a run of bad business luck—the cause can very often be traced to spiritual dissatisfaction, perhaps with the location of his house (which should never be touched by the shadow of the main building), perhaps with the quality or quantity of the daily offerings of food and flowers made to him. It may not even involve laziness on the part of the owner, as indicated by the experience of one businessman who, though diligent in his duties to the spirit, continued to have misfortunes, not only in his home but also at his office. In the circumstances, the only thing to do was to call in an expert spirit doctor, who went into the problem at some length and came up with the rather startling diagnosis that the particular guardian of that compound, for some unexplained reason, was Moslem instead of the ordinary kind; his discontent stemmed from the fact that pork was being included in the daily food offerings.

This dietary affront was quickly corrected, and from that time on the businessman's luck changed for the better. Another example of the supposed power of guardian spirits, though with a less happy ending, came after Thompson's disappearance. One of his leading silk weavers came to the conclusion that possibly one cause of the tragedy might lie with the antique spirit house Thompson had bought for a new silk shop he had just opened. She asked permission to replace it, at her own expense, with a newer model. This was done, though without apparent result.

To site his spirit house, which, like the main dwelling, was a graceful Thai-style structure, Thompson employed the services of a Brahmin priest who specialized in such matters. It took the better part of a morning to find the most suitable location, which by happy chance was exactly where Thompson hoped it would be, in the far corner of his compound overlooking the klong. The priest also consulted a complicated set of astrological charts and came up with a genealogy of the compound spirits that traced their ancestry back 2,000 years.

The third, and final, of the house-building ceremonies was by far the most elaborate and important, the one marking the official completion of the house. In Thailand, there are lucky and unlucky days and months for moving into a house—as there are for starting the construction of one, for getting married, for having an operation, and for taking a trip, among other things—and the selection of a propitious date is a job involving complex calculations. It may not coincide with the wishes of the owner, or even with the real completion of the building, though some effort is made to be accommodating. In Thompson's case, the house was several weeks away from being really habitable on the date chosen, but he went ahead with the ceremony anyway and spent one night on the floor of the unfinished bedroom to satisfy the residence requirements.

The completion ceremony was held on April 3, 1959, a little less than seven months after the first column had been raised. Nine priests performed the requisite chanting, sitting in their saffron-colored robes in a row facing the klong from the open drawing room, and a senior priest, the abbot of a temple, gave his blessings on the house. A symbolic cord was stretched around the perimeter of the property and connected to each of the buildings; this had to be left until it rotted away or its magic protection would be lost. Applications of gold leaf and sandalwood powder were placed above all the principal doors and also on Thompson's forehead, and lustral water was sprinkled generously about the premises. The place having been thus blessed, purified, and protected, the priests were then served a large luncheon, and what was soon to be described in tourist guidebooks as, simply, "Jim Thompson's Thai House" was officially ready.

15

Long before this final ceremony, the house had become the talk of Bangkok, and almost daily visitors came to watch its progress and exclaim over it. The movie actress Anne Baxter stopped off in Thailand on a Far Eastern tour—bringing an introduction to Thompson, as did so many others—and was taken for an inspection of the partially finished structure; she was so enchanted she insisted on coming back at night so she could view it by moonlight from a boat in the klong. A documentary film company came and made a movie about the building. The weavers across the water, of course, were regular spectators and greatly enjoyed the continuing show. Later, when Thompson moved in and began his almost nightly round of entertainments in the stagelike drawing room, the show was even more amusing; and there were usually half a dozen waterside viewers for the exotic goings on. (They must have been startled one evening when Ethel Merman serenaded Thompson's pet white cockatoo to the tune of "Hello, Dolly", rustling the leaves outside with her famous voice.)

The antique dealers, scenting new sales, stepped up their visits as the house neared completion, bringing splendidly carved tables and doors that would obviously suit the new house perfectly, and Thompson spent even more hours than usual in the Nakorn Kasem searching for other furnishings. He was, a friend recalls, overjoyed to be able to buy at last without wondering where he was going to put the things.

In late April, a week or so after he really moved into the house, he gave a housewarming party. There have been few other housewarmings like it in Bangkok, and those who attended still remember their vivid introduction to what was soon to be one of the city's most celebrated social centers.

From a graveled courtyard, they entered what was, architecturally, the rear of the house, but Thompson had accepted the unhappy fact that few guests would be likely to arrive properly by klong and had built a handsome entrance hall off the court. It was floored with black-and-white Italian marble from one of Bangkok's nineteenth-century palaces, and the darkly gleaming teak walls provided an ideal background for a group of tapestry-sized Thai paintings, matted in silk, that rose with the stairwell to the second level. Even those who had admired the vast drawing room while it was being erected were unprepared for its completed splendor: the walls lightly waxed to bring out their mellow grain, an immense crystal chandelier (also scavenged from an old palace) glittering from the lofty ceiling, the Burmese figures from Amarapura looking down from niches that had been made from four of the original windows, brilliant silk cushions on the chairs and couches, a great ornately carved Thai bed in the center of the room, and, scattered everywhere, the treasures of all those afternoons in the Nakorn Kasem. Separating the master-bedroom wing from the rest of the house was a beautifully carved wall that had once been the entrance to a Chinese pawnshop, its grilled doors lined with orange silk, and in the bedroom there was another Thai bed, a tiger skin on the floor, and a painted Chinese screen of the Ming period. On the terrace overlooking the klong, a classical Thai orchestra, dressed in traditional costumes, played in the warm, humid night.

Dinner was served in the breezy open area under the house, and afterwards there was a performance of Thai classical dance given by performers from a theater owned by one of Thompson's old Thai friends. They danced on the seventeenth-century brick of the terrace in their dazzling jeweled costumes and headdresses and lurid masks, with angular yet oddly graceful movements, to the tinkling music of xylophones and cymbals. Nearly all the guests had seen the dances many times before, but rarely in such a perfect setting, with the slow-moving water flickering in the moonlight behind and above, the soaring roof of the house silhouetted against the sky, its dark-red color caught by the light of coconut-oil torches.

This was the kind of setting the dances had been created for, rather than the bare stage and harsh electric lights of a theater; one felt, a guest recalls, as if time, in cinema fashion, had slowly dissolved into the tropical night and as if Thompson and his lovely house had been drawn gently back into the age to which, that one night at least, they seemed to belong.

There were few, if any, criticisms of the house that magical first evening. Those came later, most the product of jealousy or ignorance and thus not worth consideration, but some—even from good friends— that were the result of a fundamental misunderstanding of Thompson and the house he had created.

The burden of this group's misgivings was that it was not a liveable house. It was not the sort of house they would have been at ease in, the sort in which one could curl up on a sofa on a rainy night and read; as a matter of fact, there wasn't really a satisfactory place to read in the entire place. What such comments overlooked was the fact that Thompson's house was never intended to be that sort of residence, for the quite simple reason that Thompson was not that sort of person. When he undertook the creation of his house, he was not thinking so much in terms of comfort and convenience, the two qualities uppermost with most home builders, as in terms of effect. He approached it as a painter might approach his canvas, or, to probably come closer to the truth, as a stage designer approaches a setting. In the thirties, when he had been associated with the ballet in New York, he had been more interested in the sets than in the dancing itself, and his favorite ballets were those with spectacular sets and costumes. His house was put together in much the same spirit, not as a home, really, but as a sort of museum theater. This is not the approach most people would take, even if they had Thompson's flair for design, which may be why so few of the Thai-style houses that have been built since in Bangkok can equal it in dramatic effect and also why it continues to have such a powerful effect on visitors.

Like a theater, too, Thompson's house by day was not really at its best: then one saw the wiring stretched rather crudely across the ceiling, the inevitable dust on the great chandelier, the flaking paint on the antique cupboards. One noticed in the merciless sunlight of a Bangkok mid-afternoon that the weaving village across the klong looked uncomfortably like the dismal slum it would certainly be called in any American city, and that unspeakable objects were drifting past in the murky water. Thompson, however, was almost never home in the daytime, and with evening, enchantment set in, as it does when the lights dim in a theater at curtain time. The deliberately soft lights may not have been good for reading, but they made the bold colors of the drawing room glow and picked up the dull gilt of the pawnshop doors leading to the bedroom. The overgrown jungle garden became a place of luxuriant tropical mystery with its dangling creepers and its carefully illuminated statuary. The weaving village became exotic, with its spicy scents and its waterfront houses that glowed like little stages presenting scenes from an alien culture: here a pretty girl in a pasin sitting at a loom in a bare room, there a baby swinging rhythmically in a tiny hammock, a family lounging on the floor around a low table having supper. Even the klong itself, bathed in moonlight or peppered with a monsoon shower, looked like a black river that led to strange and marvelous places. It was at this time that a visitor saw—or should have seen, if he were perceptive—the true purpose of Thompson's house, and the true measure of his achievement.

16

In his new house, Thompson entered the most active and the most successful period of his life in Thailand. Thai silk, thanks to him, was now world famous, and it could be found in all sorts of places. The producers of the movie *Ben Hur* used it for the principal costumes, commissioning Thompson to create special weaves. Paintings handsomely mounted in the silk were prominent in one scene in the movie *Kind Sir*, starring Ingrid Bergman. In London, the Savoy Hotel used the material when it did over its suites, and Windsor Castle placed an order to refurbish the Canaletto Room. Barbara Hutton used it through her houses in Morocco and Mexico. The Reynolds Metal Company, in America, decorated its executive suites using a silk interwoven with aluminum thread, and a men's clothing manufacturer used it for a line of neckties. The Hong Kong Hilton ordered hundreds of yards for its ballroom and its hundred-dollar-a-day suites. Perhaps the most celebrated and influential customer was the beautiful Queen Sirikit of Thailand, whose Pierre Balmain wardrobe for the visit she and the King made to America in the early sixties included many special Thompson silks. Her Majesty remained a steady customer of

Thompson's company, and he produced a number of costly silks brocaded in gold for her exclusive use; Balmain, too, continued to use Thai silk extensively in his Paris creations.

The Thai Silk Company no longer had the field to itself in Bangkok—there were nearly a hundred companies, small and large, by the mid-sixties, most of them freely copying Thompson's designs—but it did the largest export by far, with representatives in thirty-five countries, from Australia to Sweden. Every year saw an increase in profits. The company's staff had grown steadily and now included a number of other farangs, including a Texan named Charles Sheffield, who was later, after Thompson's disappearance, to be named managing director. In charge of the sales staff was a volatile French woman named Andrée Burrow, whose love of silk was nearly as intense as Thompson's. The small shop on lower Suriwong Road was clearly becoming inadequate for the company's demands, and there were discussions of a new building in the near future.

Socially, too, the pace increased. The fairly large stream of guests that had enjoyed Thompson's hospitality in his former house became a flood in his palatial new residence, which was photographed for numerous American and European magazines. Thompson never lost his zest for entertaining, and just about anyone who came with an introduction got invited to the house for at least a drink. This did not satisfy the popular demand to view the place, however, and on more than one occasion he awoke on Sunday morning to find perfect strangers wandering through the garden on the assumption that the house was a public attraction. Thompson was generally polite with such intruders, but he came to the conclusion that something would have to be done if he was ever to have any privacy, He decided, therefore, to open the house two days a week for the benefit of the Blind School, a local charity whose founder, a blind American named Genevieve Caulfield, he admired greatly. A group of local ladies volunteered to serve as guides, a donation of twenty baht (at the time, one dollar) was requested for admission, and so successful was the undertaking that the school soon found itself able to buy all kinds of much-needed equipment as well as to erect several new buildings.

Something should be said here about Thompson's private life, if only to correct what became a rather prevalent later assumption. Within a decade or so of his disappearance there were suggestions, sometimes in print, that he was homosexual; still later, this came to be accepted by many as fact, to such an extent that one British journalist, in a long article, wrote that he was "well-known among friends for his like of rough trade."

None of his close friends, in fact, ever said such a thing, for the simple reason that it was untrue. He enjoyed liaisons with a number of women over his years in Thailand, some of them socially prominent, and from the late fifties until he disappeared he had a more or less open relationship with a married foreign woman whose husband appeared to accept the situation; she frequently served as Thompson's hostess at dinner parties and, when her husband was transferred to a post in a neighboring country, would come for long stays in the Thai house. All of Thompson's circle knew about the affair, just as they would have known if his tastes had run in another direction. The woman in question would probably have divorced and married him if he had asked, but he never did; nor did he ask another who he regularly saw on trips to America and who possibly entertained similar hopes.

Connie Mangskau, the friend who accompanied him to the Cameron Highlands, later suggested that one reason for the allegations could have been that he had a number of homosexual friends and associates, but she firmly denied her own belief in such stories, as did his doctor and close friend, Einer Ammundsen, and others who knew him well. One of them says, "It's all due to the silly but remarkably common belief that anyone who has creative talent and isn't married must therefore be gay. Jim didn't want to be married, but not because of that. I don't know what his reason was, probably the very unhappy experience marriage turned out to be when he tried it, but it had nothing to do with his sexual tastes."

Only one event cast a shadow on those last years before the Cameron Highlands, but it deserves mention here since it was a dark shadow—the darkest, in fact, since that terrible spring of 1949, though in a very different way. This was what might be called "The Episode of the Five White Heads." It had a profound effect on Thompson and, amid considerable bitterness and possible misunderstanding, it led him to take a step that was to have repercussions long after his disappearance. In retrospect, one can see several ways in which the difficulty could have been mitigated, if not avoided altogether, but at the time these were not so apparent; and when the danger was realized the damage had already been done and too much face, Asian and Western alike, had been lost to go back and start over again.

The episode took place in the fall of 1962, but its origins lay some eight years before, when Thompson and several friends had gone on an expedition to see the ruins of an ancient city called Sri Thep, in Petchaboon province. It was the sort of trip Thompson enjoyed most, and that he made whenever he had the time and willing traveling companions: a ruined and almost forgotten city, surrounded by legends and lying sufficiently off the beaten track to be unappealing to all but the most dedicated ruins lover. This particular site was very much out of the way, and it took the party hours to reach it down terrible roads. At the old city, they fell into conversation with some villagers who lived nearby and who had an interesting story to tell. They said that in a mountain called Khao Sam Rot, not far away but guarded by a dense stretch of jungle, there were wonderful caves of great antiquity, filled with very beautiful sculpture. Here again was an adventure made to order for Thompson's tastes. Were the villagers telling the truth or merely repeating folklore? Were there really treasures in that thickly-forested mountain they could see in the distance? The only way to be sure, of course, was to go to the mountain, and he was eager to do so immediately. Nature, however, was against the idea: the rainy season was well advanced and the single track that led through the jungle was impassable even for their jeep. Regretfully, the party abandoned the search and made plans to come back again when the rains were over.

One thing and another conspired to prevent Thompson from returning until early in 1962. He had not forgotten the rumored caves, though, and two things that had happened since he went to Sri Thep had served to increase his interest in them. One was the reading of book entitled *Towards Angkor* by Quaritch Wales, one of the foremost authorities on Asian art. There were several chapters on the Sri Thep area in this study, and in one of them there was a legend that caught Thompson's attention. In the distant past, it seemed, two powerful hermits had lived on a mountain near Sri Thep and had taught the king's son. One of the hermits had become angered with the king and had brought about the destruction of the city. For reasons having more, perhaps, to do with his romantic imagination than with historical fact, Thompson became convinced that the mountain on which the hermits lived and the one pointed out by the villagers were one and the same, and that the "wonderful" caves had been their sanctuary; if so, then the caves and their statuary must be very old indeed.

The other event was considerably more suggestive. In 1960, one of Thompson's antique-dealer friends, a man from Ayutthaya who maintained contacts with a number of upcountry people who brought him pieces, offered for sale three exceptionally beautiful white limestone heads. They were said to be of the Srivijaya period, which, if true, would make them about a thousand years old. One was the head of a Buddha, one was of a Bodhisattva (or Buddha-to-be), and the third was an unidentified deity. Thompson was impressed by their fine workmanship and bought them for a good deal more than he usually paid for pieces. He justified it on the grounds that he had few Srivijaya pieces in his collection and certainly nothing as beautiful of the period. The next year two other heads were brought to him by the same dealer. One of these, the finest of all the five, was from a Buddha image, and the other was of a Bodhisattva; both were also of white limestone, and it was obvious from their style and material that they had come from the same area, and probably from the same place, as the other three heads.

All five heads were in almost full relief, but a rough area at the back suggested that they had originally been attached to a wall.

By now Thompson's curiosity was thoroughly aroused. The Ayutthaya dealer was inclined to be somewhat evasive as to exactly where the heads had come from and how he had got possession of them, but after a good deal of questioning he said they came from a cave in a mountain near Sri Thep. The villagers, apparently, had been telling the truth after all: there were caves in the mountain and, if the five heads were representative, they did indeed contain treasures.

If at this point Thompson had notified the government's Fine Arts Department of his probable discovery, much, if not all, of the subsequent unpleasantness might have been avoided. He did not do so, however, probably for several reasons. First, the heads had in all likelihood been stolen from the caves, and, if so, the villagers—who would have been almost certainly aware of, if not involved in, the theft—would take fright at the first appearance of anyone connected with the Fine Arts Department and simply deny the existence of the caves. Second, he considered the Ayutthaya dealer a friend as well as a supplier of antiques, and to have notified the government at this point would have exposed him to possible danger from the police. Third, Thompson, characteristically enough, no doubt wanted the privilege of discovering the caves himself after so much preliminary speculation. In justification of such reasoning, it should be pointed out that the Department in Bangkok, while staffed by some very able people and unquestionably sincere in its efforts, operated on an absurdly small budget considering the vast quantity of potential archaeological sites in the country. Even if they had been informed of the caves they may well have lacked the funds to do much about exploring them, much less giving protection to whatever treasures might be left in the mountain.

Another reason, possibly the most important, was that rather surprisingly, Thompson had never established any really close relationships with people in the Department. Most of the experts he invited to see his collection and help him with his identification problems were either visiting authorities or nonofficial local friends. Among the latter were several members of a local research organization called the Siam Society. Thompson was a member of the council of this society and had, in the spring of 1961, taken the important step of drawing up a new will leaving his house and collection to it, along with his interest in the silk company. His desire to keep the collection intact after his death had by that time become firm, and he had decided that the Siam Society, as a nonprofit group dedicated to the study of the country's culture and natural history, would be the most suitable administrators of it.

In any event, for whatever reasons, he did not tell the Department about the caves yet, though the heads themselves had been photographed and published in a booklet he had printed about his house when he decided to open it to the public, so their existence, at least, was no secret. In February of 1962, during the dry season, he and two friends set out to reach Khao Sam Rat and its alleged wonders, armed with an old military map of the region and considerable determination. At length they reached the foot of the mountain—which, in fact, was more like a sizeable hill—where they found a lumber camp and a group of children, one of whom said he could lead them up to the cave. This proved to be more of a boast than the truth: after an hour and a half of hard climbing through steep undergrowth, he finally admitted he was lost. The search might have ended there but for the lucky appearance of two hunters, who also said they knew the way to the cave.

They were as good as their word. There was indeed a cave, a very large one, with an immense stalagmite rising to the roof in the center and in front of it a number of Buddha and Bodhisattva images without their heads carved in relief on a wall. At first glance, it seemed almost certain that this was the cave the heads had come from, but a second look was less encouraging; the first three heads Thompson had acquired were in almost full relief, whereas the bodies in the cave were in rather flat relief. A closer inspection showed that the last two heads could possibly have come from the cave, but that the first three very probably did not.

Was there another cave? They asked the boy, who had come along, and to their delight he said that yes, there was another. The prospect of going to it, however, did not appeal to him: a gigantic snake lived in it, he said, and guarded its treasures. The hunters, who had stood by silently during this exchange, now spoke up and volunteered to lead the foreigners to the cave. Something obviously changed their minds, though, for before Thompson and his friends realized what was happening they were halfway down the hill and clearly going back to the lumber camp rather than to a second cave. The hunters made a vague excuse about having misunderstood and wandered off. Without guides, there was nothing the party could do but return to Bangkok and plan yet another trip to complete their mission.

This trip was set for three weeks later, but on the eve of it Thompson came down with a severe cold and his two friends, together with a Dutchman named Jan Boeles, of the Siam Society, made the journey without him. They made photographs and measured drawings of the first cave but, as before, failed to find anyone willing to show them the other one. To this day, the second cave has still not been found, or at any rate it has not been measured and photographed. Thompson lost interest in the project and never resumed the search, nor, it seems, did anyone else.

This, then, was the situation at the end of September, 1962, by which time the Fine Arts Department had been informed officially of the caves by Boeles, at Thompson's request, in the hope that steps might be taken to preserve the remaining figures and whatever treasures there might be in the unfound second cave. The Department, however, elected to take a rather different course of action. It sent two men to call on Thompson at his office, and they said—or possibly only implied—that the Department was concerned about the five heads in his collection as rumors were circulating that they had been stolen from the cave; there was also a suggestion that the heads ought to be turned over to the Department, and Thompson got the impression that if this was not done, police action might be forthcoming.

He was both shocked and alarmed by the implications of this visit. The idea that anyone would suspect him of being a party to such a theft shocked him profoundly, and he was alarmed by the thought of the ugly publicity that would certainly result from any official action whether the charge was sustained or not. He thereupon wrote a long letter to the then director general, setting down in detail how he happened to get the heads in the first place (though omitting the name of the dealer who had sold them), his growing interest in the caves, and his discovery of the first cave. His letter concluded with the following statement:

"I have elected to make Thailand my permanent home, and as I live here and am very interested in the artistic heritage of the country, I have tried to build up as fine a collection as I can to leave to this country. I know that the museum does not have funds to buy many of the fine pieces that turn up, and rather than see them leave the country, I have tried to buy the really exceptional ones to keep them here. I have paid very high prices for many of them, but I know that if I did not, they might have gone for good. I hope that you will believe that I am deeply interested in the archaeology and the preservation of the beautiful things of this country, and am not making a collection for financial advantages or selfish purposes. As much, or perhaps even more, than well-known Thai collections, this house and its contents will belong to the Siamese people since I have already willed it to them by way of the Siam Society."

In the next few days, there followed a series of complex maneuvers, many of which are still not entirely clear and probably never will be. One or two things, however, are clear enough: the director general did not reply to Thompson's letter, some policemen did come to his house to identify the heads, an official order was issued demanding their return, and Thompson did, one day, put the heads in the back of his automobile and take them down to the National Museum, where they were later placed on display. No attempt was ever made to reimburse him for any of the money he had paid for them.

This was by no means the end of the affair. Thompson's shock had changed to anger by the time he delivered the heads to the museum, and, characteristically, he shared it freely with anyone he encountered. One of the people he met was a reporter from the *Chicago Daily News* service, who wrote it up as a story that ran in a number of American papers under the headline GOOD AMERICAN GETS UGLY DEAL IN THAILAND and quoted Thompson as saying, "First they decorate me and then they raid me"—a reference to the fact that earlier that year he had received the Order of the White Elephant, in recognition of his development of the silk industry. The article generally reflected Thompson's feeling that he had been unjustly singled out for official action despite the fact that his was one of the very few local collections that was clearly destined to remain in the country because of his will.

In an effort to ease, and hopefully to remedy, the situation, some friends arranged a luncheon with the director general, but it was not a very successful meeting, for both parties were by that time in a stubborn mood. The only gleam of hope that emerged was a suggestion that if Thompson registered his house officially as a museum, the heads might be returned to him. He did so soon afterward, but the heads were not returned, which only increased his bitterness. A number of people in Bangkok were of the opinion, not too openly expressed, that the incident might conceivably have political, or at least business, connotations, a sentiment that the *Chicago Daily News* reporter reflected in his rather delicately worded final paragraph: "Thompson single-handedly built Thai silk into a thriving export industry. When he started he had the field to himself. Today he has 86 competitors, including the prime minister's wife." The wife in question was that of Prime Minister Sarit Thanarat, the military strongman who had overthrown Pibul. She was a lady of singular determination who had entered the silk business in a big way, with a weaving factory and a large new shop, and it was rumored that she did not much like Thompson's preeminence in the field. There was, and is, no evidence that she had anything to do, directly or indirectly, with the confiscation of the heads, but she was sufficiently unpopular in some circles for the rumors to be taken seriously.

In the weeks that followed the seizure, Thompson's sense of outrage increased rather than abated, and it led him into taking two drastic steps that must both have been extremely painful to him. The first was to revoke his will leaving both his house and collection to the Siam Society and to resign from the Society's council. He did this out of anger at the apparent indifference of the Department of Fine Arts to his bequest and also because he felt that the Society itself, having, as it were, a vested interest in the property, might have done more than it did on his behalf in the dispute. Whether the council members—some of whom were very prominent figures—really could have done anything is a debatable point, and whether they should have may be debatable, too, in view of the extremely complex rules that govern Thai etiquette in such matters; but Thompson was not in the mood for debating at that point and he destroyed his will, informing the council of his action. In 1965, shortly before leaving on a trip to America, he made out a second will, which was witnessed by three people at the silk company, leaving his Thai property to his brother Henry's son. This second document was to become the center of a considerable controversy after his disappearance.

The other step he took was a sudden and probably emotional decision to dispose of his entire collection of Thai Buddhist art—"the artistic heritage of the country," as he described it in his letter to the director general—and keep only the paintings and objects from other parts of Southeast Asia, principally those from Burma and Cambodia. The emotional aspect of this decision is suggested by the fact that when it came to actually putting it into practice, his great attachment to the pieces he had collected over the years proved, in a number of cases, to be stronger than his anger. He ended up keeping quite a few of the larger and rarer pieces. Nonetheless, he did dispose of many, mostly smaller bronzes and stone heads, some of them of great value. For the most part, he sold them back to the dealers he had bought them from originally, for prices barely covering his original investment but that undoubtedly delighted the dealers since the objects had greatly increased in value due to the growing interest in Asian art in Europe and America.

It would be difficult to exaggerate the distress these actions caused Thompson. It was evident even to casual acquaintances, and his closer friends were frankly alarmed at the depth of his reaction; to one or two he talked of leaving Thailand and going to one of the several other countries that had asked for his assistance in cottage-industry development. The sentiments he expressed in his letter to the director general were deeply felt, and his sense of betrayal was just as deep. It seemed, for a brief period at least, to negate much of what he had done for Thailand, not only in preserving its art but in its silk industry as well, and intermingled with his anger was a fleeting sense of futility. The house, which he had conceived as a sort of personal monument, was not, after all, going to the Siamese people as he had planned; and to a collector as intensely devoted to his objects as he was, the empty spaces on shelves and cabinets must have been continual and harsh reminders of his loss.

Certain of his friends were not just alarmed but also a little surprised at the extent of his bitterness. He was obviously justified in feeling that he had been dealt with less than openly, and not in a manner befitting his prominent position in the foreign community of Bangkok or the public nature of his collection; but, for all that, the other side did have a legal point. The heads had very likely been stolen from the caves by someone—by whom was another matter—and the Department, as official custodian of national treasures, did have a legal right to them. That they had not made similar raids on other private collections or been very successful in stopping the large-scale and quite open trade in antiquities through the many dealers did not really make the point invalid. Furthermore, Thompson had acquired a reputation for being remarkably tolerant in seemingly comparable situations over the twenty years he had lived in Thailand. Less temperate friends had grown accustomed to being philosophically reminded by him that different cultures did things differently—a commonplace enough observation but not always easy to accept when one is on the receiving end. He had been able to accept the discovery that at least two of his most trusted employees were systematically robbing the silk company but could not, for reasons of face, be prosecuted, and had seen his silk designs calmly appropriated by almost every other company in Bangkok without going into a rage or even filing a test court case. Several of his silk weavers had used their profits to set up rival companies—employing, of course, Thompson's weaves and colors—and he had not felt deeply betrayed by these defections. Why, then, did this present example drive him to such extremes? Was it so very different from the others?

According to people close to him, it was. He was able to view his silk business with surprising objectivity, in large part because he had never really considered it in purely personal terms; the idea of turning the industry over to the weavers had never entirely left him. His house and antique collection were different matters. He could not be objective about them, any more than he had been able to be objective about the fate of his friends in the nightmare period following the 1949 coup. The confiscation of the five heads—with its implication of misdeeds on his part—affected him personally rather than professionally, and, moreover, it affected him in an area in which he was particularly sensitive. He was well aware that some people in Bangkok resented a foreigner displaying Buddha images in his home; some of them were also saying that he was trafficking in antiques, and that this was the real source of his supposed wealth. It had been at least partly to put an end to such slanders that he had decided to will his house to the Siam Society, thereby publicly declaring his desire to keep the collection permanently in Thailand. The episode of the five heads suggested that hostile feelings about the collection was possibly not, as he had thought, confined to his known enemies—for like most successful men, he had acquired some—but were shared by some of the people he had thought would be on his side on such an issue. It was a combination of these feeling, perhaps complicated by a series of bronchial complaints, that plunged him into a depression lasting several months.

17

It might have gone on longer and been even more serious had it not been for the same two factors that kept him on after 1949. The first was his genuine, and deep, love for the country he had decided to make his home. Nor was this a one-sided affair: for every Thai who begrudged Thompson his success in their country, there were hundreds, perhaps thousands, who saw him as the ideal "good American," concerned with them not as some nameless official dispensing aid without understanding or sympathy, but as a participant—and this despite a number of seeming paradoxes. Thompson lived in a Thai house, preferred Thai food, and was passionately interested in everything concerning the country, yet he had never "gone native" as the old colonials used to put it; he had never even learned the language, beyond a few polite phrases. (He did make a couple of stabs at it over the years, but finally gave up, claiming, not without some justice, that it was more dependable to work through good interpreters.) However, these attainments are actually not as welcome in Asia as some might suppose: the average Thai reaction to a farang who wholeheartedly adopts their culture is one of mystification rather than admiration, and he is generally looked upon as the misfit he usually is. An anthropologist would say that Thompson had kept his cultural identity—he had, in other words, remained himself—but even so he had become as intimately involved in the country as probably any other foreigner living in Thailand, and far more than the "language experts" and "cultural affairs" people who had supposedly been trained for the job. By gradual steps, and in spite of occasional harsh disillusionments, a bond had been forged between him and Thailand, one that proved too strong to be broken even by an event that hurt as much as the clash with the Fine Arts Department over the heads. It did alter his life in certain significant ways; he never again had any further dealings with the Department of any kind, he never revoked his second will leaving his house to his nephew, and he never regained his former interest in building up a representative collection of Thai art. But it did not really affect his fundamental affection for the country, and he found other collecting interests to at least partially compensate for the loss of his original passions.

He discovered, for instance, a new interest in porcelains, a field he had been rather wary of before since it so clearly belonged to experts and, unlike Thai art, was crammed with authoritative opinion that went back centuries. He decided to concentrate on lesser-known Chinese export ware, mainly blue and white, of which numerous pieces had come to Thailand in the sixteenth and seventeenth centuries, and also on a brilliant pentachromatic porcelain called Bencharong (which means "five colors") that had been made in China exclusively for export to Thailand—following Thai designs—several hundred years ago. He applied himself to learning as much as he could about both kinds with the same determination he had once devoted to Buddhist art and also, of course, buying them. A friend from America named Dean Frasche, a vice-president of the Union Carbide Company, started coming to Thailand regularly on business around this time, and being a porcelain collector himself, he encouraged Thompson in his new interest and helped him evaluate pieces. By the time Thompson went to Malaysia in 1967, he had built up admirable collections of blue and white and Bencharong—an entire room of his house was devoted to the latter— and most of the spaces that had been emptied of Buddhist art were filled with porcelains.

His fascination with his famous house also continued to provide him with new projects, and over the next five years he made a number of additions to it. One was a new guest-bedroom wing, which he decided was needed for houseguests who found it inconvenient to tidy up and vacate twice a week when tour groups invaded the place; the new wing was off limits to the tourists. Another addition was a charming little picture gallery, a single old house, which he put up on the klong. This was built to house an unusual collection of paintings that he had come across in, of all places, Connecticut, where they had rested for the better part of a hundred years. They had been commissioned in the mid-nineteenth century by an American missionary in Thailand named Dr. J.H. Chandler, who, like a surprising number of the missionaries who came to that country, was active in quite a few nontheological enterprises. Chandler clearly loved the country, and among the mementos he took home with him was the collection of paintings he had asked an unknown artist to render around 1860, showing various scenes of everyday Thai life. The pictures had remained in his family after his death and Thompson, hearing about them, felt that they were unique and belonged in the country of their origin. He bought them from the missionary's heirs and built the little gallery to give them a proper setting.

The silk business was prospering, with sales, both local and export, steadily climbing each year despite all the new competition; the year of Thompson's disappearance, they amounted to around one and half million dollars. Charles Sheffield had been able to take most of the business side of the operation off Thompson's hands, leaving him free to concentrate on the creative aspects. His talents in this area found a new and considerably broader outlet when, in the early sixties, he began to make printed silks, using some old designs—taken from paintings, porcelains, and old pieces of cloth—and some new ones, all done with that instinctive and often unpredictable flair for color that had made the original silks such a sensation. The prints caught on immediately and were soon being seen in high-fashion houses throughout Europe and America, as well as in most of the other silk companies of Bangkok, who established a custom of snapping up a new Thompson design within a few days after it appeared on the shelves of his shop. The printing process was entirely new to him and proved an ideal therapeutic to take his mind off his recent difficulties. It was in many ways like the early days of the silk industry, when unexpected problems and gratifying successes were constantly coming up to keep things from settling into the routine production he found so exhausting.

He enlarged his already sizeable menagerie of pets—the inevitable dogs, a pair of Siamese cats, a flock of bantams, and a couple of ill-tempered geese who served as excellent watchdogs—with the addition of a docile, sulphur-crested cockatoo, which quickly assumed supremacy in the household. A gregarious bird, it regularly joined the dinner parties (it was partial to after-dinner liqueurs) and afterward entertained the guests by performing a curious little dance to symphonic music played at top volume. A later acquisition for the aviary, a dazzling red and blue loriket whose colors reminded Thompson of a costume in Petrouchka, was less successful at winning friends; indeed, it was extremely aggressive, and inflicted so many nasty bites on guests, as well as on its owner, that it was eventually banished to a cage in the garden.

Edwin Black, the army friend who had introduced Thompson to his wife as well as to the OSS during the war, came to Thailand in the mid-sixties as a brigadier general and as commander of U.S. Support Forces in the country, a group that was steadily increasing as the war in Vietnam widened. Black's headquarters were in the northeastern city of Khorat, where the majority of American troops were also stationed, and Thompson made a number of trips with him through the northeast to help the general get better acquainted with the area. Thompson found the experience exhilarating, for, as he told friends, it reminded him of his early days in Thailand, when he made so many trips through the same region with his Laotian friends, only this time he was the old hand rather than the newcomer.

Every year he went back to the States, going in the late summer and coming back, usually through Europe, in the early fall. These were supposedly family visits, though he invariably managed to get in a lot of business on the way, and he saw his three sisters and his brother, as well as a large collection of nieces and nephews. And twice he escaped Bangkok's sweltering hot season briefly by going to the Cameron Highlands in Malaysia with his old friend Mrs. Mangskau to spend the long Easter weekend with Helen and T.G. Ling at their restful bungalow in the cool mountains.

18

The first three months of 1967 were typically busy ones for Thompson. They were, in fact, even busier than usual, for after nearly fifteen years in the cramped little building on lower Suriwong Road he had finally bowed to the demands of progress and built new quarters, on the same road but farther up in a newly fashionable shopping area. For the design of the building he chose to copy a simple but elegant sixteenth-century structure in Ayutthaya and in doing so greatly enhanced an otherwise nondescript section of the city. It was not a simple matter to get municipal permission to put up such an unmodern construction. The building permit was finally granted on condition that the company also erect a tall office building in the rear of the property; but these and other difficulties were overcome and the grand opening of the shop was held on March 17.

It was an occasion of some consequence, for in a way it represented the final step in Thompson's remarkable business career in Thailand. The handsome white building with its graceful rising roof was a visible symbol of what he had accomplished since that day in 1945 when he had climbed off a military plane in a strange airport crowded with enemy soldiers. The bolts of brilliant silk stacked neatly on the shelves of the shop would have equaled almost the entire annual output of all the weavers in Thailand twenty-two years before; now they were only a fraction of the millions of yards produced, of which Thompson's own company exported a quarter of a million yards per year. The number of people who could claim to earn a living through the production of silk in 1945 had been tiny, if, indeed, there were any at all who could make such a claim in those days. In 1967, the total number of weavers alone exceeded 20,000 and thousands of other Thai people derived their income from the silk industry in less direct ways. From the part-time plumber who had obligingly woven a few lengths for Thompson to test in New York, the number of looms weaving for him had increased to 500, and each loom employed four people to keep it going. The silk was on sale in almost every capital of the world, and it had not only brought a new and large source of income to the country but also goodwill of the sort few public relations companies could have gotten at any price. More people in the West associated Thailand with silk than with any other single product.

Soon after the building opened, Thompson underwent another experience that would have seemed unlikely twenty-two years before but that had now become commonplace: he was interviewed by a camera crew for an American television company. It was the latest—and, as it turned out, the last—of hundreds of interviews he had given out to journalists from all over the world, and he answered the questions with a professional ease born of much practice. Like most celebrities, he knew what the questions were going to be, and his answers to them. He talked of how he had come to Thailand, of how the silk business had been started, of the changes he had seen over the years—in other words, the Thompson legend, which never seemed to lose its fascination.

He devoted a good deal of time during those months to one of his current projects, a revised and considerably expanded version of the book which was sold for the benefit of the Blind School on public days at his house. This was to be a fairly expensive affair—Thompson paid all the printing costs on the books—with handsome color photographs by Brian Brake, a gifted New Zealander who had been introduced to Thompson by the Japanese company that was printing the book. Brake had come to Bangkok on several visits and had taken an impressive collection of pictures of the house and its contents, the first prints of which he sent in early March. Thompson was enthusiastic about them and looked forward to seeing the completed book in the summer.

Toward the end of February he heard from Mrs. Mangskau that the Lings wanted them to come down to the Highlands again for Easter. This was welcome news for several reasons. He was exhausted from all the problems of moving into the new shop and felt in need of a rest. In addition, he had agreed to go to Singapore to meet a businessman named Edward Pollitz, who was looking into the possibilities of starting a textile industry there; the Cameron Highlands, he thought, would be a perfect place to stop for a few days on his way.

On March 21, he celebrated his sixty-first birthday with a small dinner for a few close friends. The one the year before had been, according to local tradition, a highly significant one, for lifetimes in Thailand are divided into cycles of twelve years and the completion of the fifth cycle is considered especially worth observing, no doubt because in the old days comparative few people ever reached sixty and those who did could usually not look forward to a sixth-cycle party. In recognition of this, Thompson had given a party for all the employees of his company, who had presented him with an enormous teak elephant with real ivory tusks as a symbol of longevity. The sixty-first affair, however, was of no special importance and he made no occasion of it.

Two days later, he and Mrs. Mangskau left for their holiday in Malaysia. No one later could recall anything unusual about his leave-taking. Thompson went to his company on the morning of his departure and worked for a few hours until it was time to go to the airport; when he left, he said goodbye only to those friends and employees he happened to pass on the way out. To most, he said he would see them the following week. Within a few days, though, they would be trying to recall that last morning, searching for possible clues in those innocent goodbyes.

Part Three: The Making of a Legend

1

For all her plans to have a good nap after their picnic lunch that Easter Sunday afternoon in the Cameron Highlands, Mrs. Mangskau slept only fitfully in her room at Moonlight Cottage. A little before four, she later remembered, she decided to do some of her packing since they were planning an early start the next morning for a leisurely drive to Singapore. The Lings could actually have made a longer holiday of it in the Highlands, but they were making the drive especially for Thompson, to show him the countryside and also to get him to Singapore in time for his dinner engagement with the American ambassador and the businessman Edward Pollitz.

While she packed, Mrs. Mangskau heard nothing unusual, nor did she expect to; she assumed the others were also in their rooms, resting. She came out around four-thirty and found Dr. Ling reading in the living room. They spoke briefly, and he remarked that he and Mrs. Ling had heard Thompson go out for a walk a little after three. Thompson's suit jacket was hung over the back of a chair on the veranda. He had also left his cigarettes and lighter and, in his room, the pills he took to quell the pains from the gallstone attacks he had been prone to in recent months. These suggested he could not have been planning a very long walk, as did the hour of his departure.

Darkness falls early in the Highlands—around six-thirty at that time of year—and they assumed Thompson would be back shortly to join them for tea, which was generally served about five. After talking with Dr. Ling, Mrs. Mangskau went back to her room and stayed there until teatime. Mrs. Ling was up by then and out in the garden cutting roses to take with them to Singapore. The three of them had a cup of tea and then resumed the flower cutting. There was still no sign of Thompson: the road leading down the hill, up which they expected to see him coming any moment, remained empty.

Around six, with the shadows lengthening and the air starting to turn chilly, the first doubts began to enter their minds. Not really serious doubts—they were all three familiar with Thompson's love of walking—but enough to make them look at their watches and wonder what could be keeping him so late. Dr. Ling was of the opinion that he had walked down the hill to the golf club and proposed driving down to bring him back. The ladies decided to stay at the house, in case he came from another direction, and Dr. Ling therefore went alone in the car. When he returned, a quarter of an hour or so later, he was troubled. Thompson had not been at the gold club, nor on the road, nor had anyone at the club seen him that afternoon. Mrs. Mangskau then telephoned the Smokehouse Inn, where some of their friends from Bangkok were staying, and talked with Dr. Einer Ammundsen, Thompson's doctor, who was up for a weekend of golfing and who said he hadn't seen him either.

It was dark now and nearly seven-thirty, four hours after Thompson had left the bungalow, and mild anxiety turned to active worry. Something clearly was wrong. Dr. Ling recalled the incident of the previous day, when he and Thompson had gotten lost on their way following a trail down the hill. By day the jungle was treacherous enough with its slippery rocks and unpredictable trails, but by night it was inky black and full of hidden dangers; more prosaically, it was also cold, the temperature dropping into the forties, and Thompson was wearing a short-sleeved shirt. In alarm he called, first the couple who served as rental agents for Moonlight Cottage and who knew the area well, and then the police in Tanah Rata, the main settlement in the Highlands. The police asked him to come down and make a report, which he did, and they said they would send word around to the villages in the vicinity to be on the lookout; if Thompson hadn't turned up by morning, a fullscale search party would be sent out.

Soon after Dr. Ling returned to the bungalow for the second time that evening, the Dutch rental agent arrived, accompanied by a British major, who happened to be visiting him when the message came and who brought along his dog, a cocker spaniel that had been vaguely trained in hunting. The two of them conferred briefly with the Lings and Mrs. Mangskau and then set off for the hill where Thompson had stumbled across the hornet's nest on his first visit to the resort, about three-quarters of an hour's walk by daylight but considerably longer in the dark. Thompson had revisited the site on his second trip and had mentioned going back again this time. It was the only definite direction anyone at the house could say he might have taken.

At this point, and for several days thereafter, the Lings and Mrs. Mangskau—and most of the other searchers as well—accepted the simple explanation as the most probable: that is, that Thompson was either lost on one of the myriad trails and could not get his bearings in the dark, or that he had had some sort of accident, a gallstone attack, perhaps, or a fall into one of the all but invisible ravines that are common in those jungled hills. No one mentioned, or really considered, the possibility of anything more sinister.

The agent and the major returned about midnight with disappointing news. They had covered the distance from Moonlight Cottage to the hornet hill, shining flashlights and calling Thompson's name, and had also alerted anyone they saw along the way. There had been no response; no one had seen anything. They rested for a while and then went out again in another direction for several hours, with the same results. Until professional reinforcements came from the police in the morning, there was nothing more to do. The dispirited people in the bungalow resigned themselves to wait the remaining hours until sunrise, each with his private vision of Thompson thrashing through the darkness, lying in pain in some gully, trapped by some nameless creature in the black underbrush.

2

The official search for Jim Thompson began early the next morning, some fifteen hours after he was last seen, with the arrival of four or five policemen from the Tanah Rata station. They studied the photograph of him in his passport, which Mrs. Mangskau had been keeping for him at his request after he had almost lost it in the taxi coming up from Penang. (He had been carrying it in the pocket of his jacket, and during one of their stops, Mrs. Mangskau had noticed it lying on the seat; she had cautioned him and he had suggested she put it with hers in her handbag.) Before that first day was done, nearly 100 people were involved, including local police, a group of British soldiers on convalescent leave in the Highlands, and a number of guests from the hotels like Dr. Ammundsen and some of the other friends from Bangkok.

It was an immensely difficult undertaking, partly because no one really had any idea what direction he might have set off in but mostly because of the wild terrain. The jungle at some points was so thick that visibility was limited to a few feet, and high grass obscured the wandering trails. Paths occasionally led straight up slippery slopes covered with moss, with sheer drops of twenty to fifty feet down to stream beds peppered with sharp stones. Cries of "Jim!" echoed through the forest and were answered by other cries of the same name; groups of searchers, hearing encouraging sounds, stumbled suddenly on other groups who were doing the same thing.

They looked for any signs that the missing man might have used the trails—trodden grass, broken branches, a bit of clothing, a handkerchief, anything—realizing that this first day was probably the crucial one, not only because of Thompson's personal safety alone in the jungle but also because within a day or two the searchers themselves would have left too many signs of their own along the paths. A few of the more pessimistic ones watched the sky, too, for the wheeling vultures that signaled a death in the jungle. Neither group saw anything.

At Moonlight Cottage, which was serving as a sort of command and relief post for the search, it was decided that the news now had to be broken to Bangkok. Dr. Ammundsen cabled his wife Rita, who relayed the message to Charles Sheffield, Thompson's assistant, in the late morning at the Thai Silk Company. He decided to wait until later in the day to tell the company's employees, but he did call General Edwin Black, both because Black was a good friend of Thompson's and because it was probable that if the first day's search proved fruitless some sort of official aid might be needed urgently. Through military channels Black and another friend, Colonel William Bond—whose wife had known Thompson back in the OSS days—arranged for helicopters to join the search the next day.

Just after closing time, the staff of the silk company heard the news in shocked silence; then, as other people all over Bangkok were to be doing the next morning when they read it in the newspapers, they tried to reassure one another with memories of Thompson's extensive jungle experience, his love of walking, the fact—or, at any rate, the hope—that people didn't really get lost at a celebrated resort like the Highlands where hiking was one of the principal forms of recreation.

The news had also gone out internationally through Jack Foise of the *Los Angeles Times*, who was on holiday at the Highlands and was, in fact, taking part in the search. By the next morning it was on the front pages of papers throughout the world.

In the Cameron Highlands itself, police and volunteers were going about asking if anyone had seen Thompson at any time after three-thirty the previous afternoon, when the Lings resting in their bedroom had heard the sound of footsteps going down the graveled path that led from Moonlight Cottage to the narrow road. They soon had several responses, but the information gathered was contradictory and of doubtful value. One person, for example, claimed to have seen a man answering Thompson's description at a place a good hour's walk from the house at around four, which conceivably could have been possible if he had gotten a ride at the foot of the hill. She described him, however, as wearing a sweater and carrying a camera, neither of which Thompson had with him. Another person said she thought she had seen him even farther away talking to two Malays.

The most likely sighting, in the eyes of the officials, was by a

Malay cook at a Lutheran mission cottage located on another hill but fairly near Moonlight Cottage. The cook said that at about four she was in the kitchen of the mission house when she saw a man who looked like Thompson come up the road, take a look at the garden, and then go back the same way he had come. Still another servant, at another mission house—this one of the Overseas Mission Fellowship—told a story that seemed contradictory but that was also judged worthy of consideration. At about four, she had seen a man who might have been Thompson standing on a small plateau opposite the house; he stood there for about half an hour, she said, and then he "just vanished." Beyond the plateau, the searchers found a track which after some distance forked, one segment forming a circle and coming back into the original trail and the other leading deeper into the jungle. They marked the latter for special attention.

Was the man any of these people saw really Thompson? The question has never been satisfactorily answered and later, when the accident theory began to lose favor, the sightings were more or less forgotten, or at least ignored. Yet it is not unimportant, for if either of the mission servants was correct then several of the most popular subsequent theories must be discounted. The cook from the Lutheran mission was quite definite in her identification of Thompson from a photograph, though she erred in her description of what he was wearing at the time; she said he had on gray slacks when in fact they were dark blue.

Monday's efforts were unavailing: other than the alleged sightings, not a single clue was uncovered. On Tuesday, the search expanded to proportions never seen before at the Highlands or, indeed, anywhere in Malaysia. Something like 325 policemen were now involved, including members of the Malaysian Field Force Police in their green jungle uniforms and in addition about thirty aborigines who lived in the jungle and knew its trails and hazards intimately were enlisted as guides. (Nearly all the reporters writing about the search, Malay as well as foreign, referred to these aborigines as Sakai, giving the erroneous impression that this was the name of a tribe. Actually, sakai is a Malay term of contempt, meaning "inferior person," and is used rather as "nigger" is used in the United States. It is not used by anthropologists, who correctly refer to the aborigines of Malaysia by one of several different tribal names.) There was also a sizeable group of amateur searchers composed of the convalescent soldiers and hotel guests who had helped on the first day, together with pupils from the Dalat American School, a school for children of American missionaries from all over Southeast Asia. Altogether, over 400 people took part in the search.

As a result of the efforts of General Black and others of Thompson's friends in Bangkok, several helicopters arrived to assist, though their limitations were soon apparent in the thick jungle, where it is impossible to see the ground from even a very low altitude. It was felt, though, that if Thompson were lost or injured he might be able to make some sort of signal, and the machines continued to hover over the area for most of the first week.

Thompson's eminence and the wide publicity his disappearance was stirring up in the world at large, together with the fact that his sister Elinor's husband, James H. Douglas, had been the secretary of the air force in the Eisenhower administration, assured his case of more than ordinary official attention. James Bell, the American ambassador in Kuala Lumpur, was reported to have conferred twice with Prime Minister Tunku Abdul Rahman and the permanent secretary of the Malaysian home office, who had directed the field force police to join the search. (The prime minister had met Thompson several times on visits to Bangkok and was very interested in the American's success with the silk industry.) Bell also sent his administrative officer, Robert Bliss, up to the Highlands during the search and was the recipient of a stream of queries from Washington about the progress of the investigation.

(Nearly twenty years later, after his retirement, General Black was quoted in a *Life* magazine article about the disappearance as saying that the American embassies in Bangkok and Kuala Lumpur "showed a singular lack of interest in doing anything remotely active...They were completely unhelpful. The State Department was afraid of making political waves. Their attitude was, the sooner the Thompson case was forgotten, the better." Like many of the latter-day comments, this is not supported by records or by the recollections of others on the scene. At the time, indeed, they were impressed by the degree of official interest, which was far greater than any ordinary case would have received.)

A number of people were convinced that if Thompson had had some sort of accident, the first twenty-four hours of searching would almost certainly yield a clue, however small. When nothing had been found by Tuesday, this group—largely composed of reporters and friends back in Bangkok—began to suggest other possibilities. Though there were stories about hikers having disappeared in the Highlands jungle in the past, they were hard to pin down with facts and dates. Somebody, for example, remembered something about a nun who had gone walking and never came back, but no one seemed to know exactly who she had been or when it happened. Even if such a tragic precedent existed, though, it had not been recent; local officials and business people were emphatic in their denials that walking in the jungle was unduly hazardous, and were sensitive to suggestions that the trails were not as clear as they ought to have been. Anyone who stuck to a main trail was quite safe, they said firmly, and the aborigines who lived in the area were friendly, more likely to help than ignore a lost stranger, particularly a European stranger.

Since no trace of Thompson had been found, wasn't it possible something else had happened, something less simple? The something else mentioned most frequently at this early stage was a kidnapping for ransom, though even then there were some who mentioned still darker things. Kidnapping had long been a fairly common crime in Malaysia, with the wealthy Chinese of Singapore and Penang as favored victims, and in the years just prior to Thompson's disappearance, it had reached such proportions that the authorities had made the payment of ransom itself a felony in an effort to diminish its appeal. The stratagem had not been altogether successful, however, and Chinese millionaires still occasionally vanished and reappeared after their families had turned over large sums, preferring to break the law rather than receive their loved ones back in sections. As far as anybody could remember, there had never been a case of a European falling victim to one of the extremely well-organized kidnap gangs, but, it was felt in some quarters, they might well have decided to branch out into the foreign market. There were stories, unconfirmed but persistent, of a gang that supposedly operated a short distance northwest of the Highlands, and Thompson's reputed wealth, of course, was widely known. On the other hand, there had been no sort of story in the Malaysian papers stating that he was coming to the resort nor, outside his circle of friends, was it widely known in Bangkok, though a passing mention had appeared in the social column of the *Bangkok World*.

Then, there were the haunting memories of the terrorists who had once been so common along these very trails and even at Moonlight Cottage, according to rumors. Could some of these still be up their old activities, or perhaps embarking on a new offensive to frighten the government? An employee of the Malaysian embassy in Bangkok thought it was at least a possibility and told a local reporter, "Nobody has ever turned up missing there before to my knowledge. If he were kidnapped by any terrorists who might have been left over from the Emergency, he would be the unluckiest man in the world." The man then went on to suggest another possibility which, it is safe to say, had occurred to no one at Moonlight Cottage. Thompson was "a very busy man," he said, and perhaps he had just taken a side trip for business purposes, inconveniently forgetting to mention it to the others.

The police officials on that second day, at least in their statements to newspapers, were inclined to dismiss these sinister possibilities. They still apparently favored the more ordinary explanations, that Thompson had either gotten lost or had had an accident in the jungle. The most bizarre possibility that they were willing to mention for publication was that he might have come across a leopard, a wild boar, or even a tiger, which, while not common, were also not unknown; tiger tracks had reportedly been seen in the vicinity of Moonlight Cottage several years before.

Very likely this is what the senior officials felt on this second day of the search, but more than a year later, certain persons who had been present suggested that among many of the ordinary soldiers who were hacking their way through the jungle in search of Thompson, a definite mood of pessimism had set in after nearly forty-eight fruitless hours. What these sources were saying, in effect, was that at least some of the searchers more or less gave up after the second day, having become convinced that the man they were looking for was simply not there. Such an allegation is unproveable, of course, but if true, it would be a natural enough reaction. Certainly after the third and fourth days, by which time rumors of conspiracies and stories of Thompson's wealth were flying through the area, the soldier-searchers must have developed serious doubts about the accident theory, as indeed many people outside the jungle were doing.

2

The second day also saw the introduction of another element which in the future was to assume quite as much importance as the idea of foul play and which was to make the Thompson case irresistible to newspaper editors. This was the supernatural. Late that afternoon, a man of about thirty came up to Moonlight Cottage and introduced himself as a well-known bomoh, a term which is usually translated as "witch doctor" though it has none of the connotations of the English expression. He asked permission to use his powers to discover Thompson's whereabouts. Given it, he proceeded to go into a trance and presently announced that Thompson was alive and in good health, but was being held prisoner by certain evil spirits in the jungle. The bomoh, who was exhausted by his efforts, then went back to his home in a neighboring village, where his regular employment was painting houses, but he returned to the bungalow the following day with news of a more encouraging vision: the American was being held under a tree, he said, and he readily located the site on a map being used by the searchers. A party went at once to the tree and were disappointed not to find Thompson there waiting for them, though unable to move, of course, because of the spiritual bonds. The failure did not shake the bomoh's composure; he said the spirits had clearly moved the missing man and, in another trance, informed his audience that Thompson would return "on his own" to the bungalow by nine o'clock the following morning. When that, too, resulted in disappointment, he decided that his powers, great as they had proved in the past, were inadequate to the demands of the present problem and said he was going down to Ipoh to get advice from a much-respected medium there.

This was the first of a long and extraordinary procession of bomohs, clairvoyants, soothsayers, astrologers, palmists, dowsers, and other practioners of occult arts who have been attracted to the Thompson case. They have come in such numbers, and in such variety, that a book devoted solely to their activities would provide a fairly complete picture of the state of these arts in the world today, not only in the simple society of a Malaysian village but also in the sophisticated West. Here we are concerned primarily with their effect on the search for Thompson, and for a reader to comprehend the importance of their role—in particular, the great influence they had over many of the people concerned—it is necessary to realize that in much of Asia the supernatural is taken for granted and forms an integral part of daily life.

Nearly every Malaysian village, for example, has its resident bomoh—often it has several—who earns a comfortable living by being available for consultation on all manner of problems, from locating missing wives to relieving impotency, and who is a perfectly respectable member of the community. In Thailand, animism and astrology are intricately intertwined with the philosophical tenets of Buddhism, so much so that it is difficult for an outsider to tell where one leaves off and the other begins; some of the most eminent clairvoyants in the country are also monks. The jungle of Southeast Asia are believed to be teeming with spirits of all sorts, good and malignant, and most of the country people—and not a few city dwellers as well—are convinced that everything from sickness to bankruptcy is somehow caused by them. There are amulets to ward off the worst spirits and to attract the more beneficial ones, and other amulets (along with a dazzling selection of tattoos) that are supposed to protect the wearer from bullets, knives, and other deadly weapons. About the time of Thompson's disappearance, one of Bangkok's English-language dailies ran an advertisement for a bulletproof amulet, calmly noting that "a practical test can be arranged at your convenience"; whether anyone applied is unknown, but the only really exceptional thing about the notice was that it appeared in a paper with a European readership. Bandits in Thailand are traditionally adorned with protective tattoos, and such is the widespread belief in the potency of these markings that the Thai government once felt compelled to publicly execute an especially vicious bandit leader to prove that he was as mortal as the next man. It is doubtful, though, that the demonstration had any serious effect on the tattoo industry. As the Thompson case was to show with numerous examples, one of the characteristics of such practices is that their occasional failure can be readily explained away, for the supernatural is not bound by anything as humdrum as scientific laws.

These beliefs are by no means confined to the more unsophisticated levels of society. In one form or another, they exist on almost every level, up to and including the governmental: in Malaysia, Thailand, Laos, Cambodia, and Burma there are official astrologers attached to the court or the government, and they are looked upon as vital in determining the most auspicious date and time for all important acts, such as the signing of a constitution or the opening of a parliament. When the late Sarit Thanarat, then the prime minister of Thailand, went to the U.S. for a serious operation, the exact moment for his plane to leave Bangkok was carefully charted, and the farewell ceremonies at the airport were not allowed to interfere with it.

Perhaps the one really significant difference between East and West in these matters is that in the latter most educated people tend to be nervous about the supernatural outside the safe confines of traditional religion. There have been cases where clairvoyants have been called in to assist a police investigation—most notably, perhaps, in the Boston Strangler case—and some celebrated people, like Sir Arthur Conan Doyle, have dabbled in mysticism; but by and large the occult is looked upon as vaguely disreputable and undeserving of serious attention. The average Westerner, outside his church, likes rational, scientifically provable explanations. Asian faith and skepticism, on the other hand, are not too neatly separated, and thus in the Thompson investigation it was quite natural that when ordinary methods were unsuccessful, others were employed. It was also quite natural that the results of these methods would be soberly considered and, if possible, acted upon.

The assorted mystics who have figured in the Thompson case have not been lunatics or even eccentrics. Nor, with a few notable exceptions, have they been simple charlatans, out for money and publicity while taking the gullible for a ride; it is perhaps instructive to note that of the few who probably fall into this category, at least one was European rather than Asian. For the most part, they have been respectable, sometimes famous members of their communities, following an ancient and honorable tradition.

Although the official search for Thompson lasted ten days, the third and fourth days, Wednesday and Thursday, might accurately be described as the most vital; for on Wednesday hope of finding him in the jungle began to wane perceptibly and by the end of Thursday, despite a large number of searchers still at work, it was as good as gone for many people, thus opening the door to a wide variety of other explanations. The greatest number of people were involved in the search in the first three days, and they had combed the jungle more exhaustively than it had ever been. The very magnitude of the search, together with the total absence of any clues whatsoever, led many to the conclusion that it was inconceivable for him to be in the Highlands area dead or alive, and nearly all the subsequent theories proceeded from this assumption. Yet was it all that impossible for him to be there? One member of the local police, in a statement that is sometimes forgotten, or ignored, by theorists discussing the case, said that it would take "a full regiment of men working for about a month" to truly cover the jungle around the resort, and even that would have been useless had he somehow wandered out of the immediate area. Considerably less than a regiment of trained men was involved even at the peak of the search, and their efforts were more sporadic than intensive after the first week. After five days, a police official told a reporter that he thought there was "little hope" that Thompson would be brought out alive.

By the third day, however, when nothing at all had been found to suggest that he had ever gone into the jungle—not a single bit of cloth snared on a twig, not a vulture circling in the sky—people began to wonder, and some of them began to ask questions that had been more or less ignored on the first day. If Thompson were a heavy smoker, as all his friends said, why did he leave his cigarettes behind at the bungalow? Why did he leave his "jungle box" of pills when, according to his doctor, he was prone to severely painful attacks that could render him quite helpless? And, if he had really gone for a walk in the jungle and had an accident as was at first supposed, how was it that he had managed to get so far away that the search had not discovered him?

Or did he not go for a walk at all? Had someone signaled to him when he was sunning himself on the lawn, or perhaps been waiting on the road just out of sight of the house? If so, who? And why?

Attention began to be paid to a story reportedly being told by a garage attendant in Tapah, the same garage where Thompson and Mrs. Mangskau had been forced to change taxis for the last leg of their journey from Penang. The attendant was said to have noticed a rather unusual thing on Sunday, the day of the disappearance. At about three-thirty that afternoon, he claimed, he saw five cars bearing Thai license plates going up the road to the Highlands. According to news reports, his memory of this incident was remarkably vivid: there were (he said) two Volkswagens, a Volkswagen bus, a black Chevrolet, and a Cortina with a white top and a maroon body. At five-thirty in the afternoon, the same cars had come back down the hill. To reporters, the next question was obvious: had Thompson been in one of them on the return trip?

(It may be just as well to dispose of this interesting story now, before it gains even more believers than it already has. It was repeated often in the first weeks of the case and included in the *New York Times* piece already mentioned, and it is still often offered in theories as an uncontested fact. It is nothing of the sort. It was investigated thoroughly by the Malaysian CID, who are convinced that it never happened. Apparently it was one of the several stories that were being woven out of the widespread gossip of those first few days and that, through repetition by progressively more reliable people, slowly attained the substance of fact. This is a phenomenon that occurs is almost every widely publicized mystery, but in the Thompson case, where real clues were simply nonexistent, the tendency was even more pronounced than usual. As a result, there are today (1998) at least a dozen "facts" that are solemnly brought up in most discussions of the case and that have contributed greatly to the general confusion.)

Attention, too, began to be paid to Mrs. Mangskau's story of the drive to the Highlands, in particular to the changing of cars at Tapah and the two unknown Chinese who wanted to ride with them. "Was it an abduction attempt that failed?" the *Times* reporter asked a week later, echoing a question that was commonly heard in Bangkok and Singapore. (Again, according to the Malaysian CID, the answer was definitely no; the drivers were carefully checked out and their explanations were apparently true. Changing taxis was certainly common enough not to be sinister to many who had made the drive to the Highlands before. But these explanations did not come until later and were never given very widespread publicity. The idea that there was something very peculiar about the whole business was firmly planted in many minds, and still remains there.)

In Bangkok, Monday and Tuesday had been dark days. The Thai Silk Company had remained open, as much to serve as a center of communications as because everybody agreed that Thompson would have wanted it that way. Personal calls by the staff were discouraged, and Sheffield and the others waited with a hopeless feeling, expecting every ring of the telephone to bring some real information. The ban on calls was ignored, however, by numerous friends, who called off and on all day long to see if any news had come in; others came to the shop and simply stood around, sharing the grim vigil with the employees. "Apart from feeling so useless," one member of the staff remembers, "the worst thing was the tourists who either didn't know Jim or hadn't heard the news. The first group would go on with their shopping while the sales people looked like members of the family at a funeral. The others heard the news and got the same look. It was like some dreadful wake at which half the guests had come by mistake, thinking it was a cocktail party."

On Tuesday, an old-time Thai employee of the company could bear the waiting no longer and said he wanted to go down to Malaysia and take part in the search. He did so, taking authorization from Sheffield to act on behalf of the company if any financial assurances were needed in connection with offering a reward. A couple of days later, two other old friends, General Black and Dean Frasche of Union Carbide, went to Malaysia, accompanied by Black's aide, Lieutenant Denis Horgan. By this time, hope of a quick solution was very dim indeed, and Black and Frasche had been empowered by Sheffield to make a reward offer of $10,000 for any information leading to Thompson's recovery. The amount was suggested by the Malaysian authorities and was, by local standards, large. In the weeks to come, it was raised several times and finally came to $25,000.

The two friends stayed four days at the Highlands, spending most of it in the jungle with aborigine guides while maintaining radio contact with Lieutenant Horgan back at Moonlight Cottage. Unlike anyone else who had taken part in the search until then, they had both been on walking trips with Thompson in Thailand, and they hoped they might be able to recognize trails and vistas that might have particularly appealed to him. They followed dozens of such trails looking for signs, and after several days their hopes were as low as those of the police. There was nothing, General Black told a reporter, to show that their friend had ever been in the jungle.

But if he was not there, still he must be somewhere. Black and Frasche were unable to offer any suggestions as to where, but others were already beginning to see tempting possibilities in the mystery.

5

One of them had been roused to action on Wednesday, when the first whispers of foul play were beginning to appear in news reports of the search. On that third day, Dr. Ling had to return to Singapore for an important business engagement; Mrs. Ling and Mrs. Mangskau stayed on for another week at Moonlight Cottage. The doctor drove down, and shortly after he arrived at his apartment he received a disquieting telephone call from a man who spoke good but not fluent English and who identified himself as one Michael Vermont. He had information about Jim Thompson's whereabouts, he told Dr. Ling, and would like to come by and discuss it.

When he came over, he proved to be a well-dressed young Eurasian; Dr. Ling was not sure of the mixture, but thought possibly the Asian part might be Indonesian. Vermont—which was almost certainly not his real name—told the doctor that Thompson was being held in a house not far from Tapah, at the base of the hill leading up to the Highlands, and that if Dr. Ling would go with him they could arrange for the American's ransom. The proposal sounded vaguely fishy to Dr. Ling, who had only just arrived and said he had to be present for his business meeting. However, he told Vermont that two close friends of Thompson's (Black and Frasche) were arriving in the Highlands the next day and that he would ask them to meet Vermont at Tapah. Vermont agreed but said he needed money to get to Tapah; Dr. Ling gave him fifty Malaysian dollars. After the Eurasian left, he called the Highlands and told Mrs. Ling about the incident. Two days later, Black and Frasche went to a meeting place in Tapah mentioned by Vermont. He failed to show up.

Vermont called Mrs. Ling at the cottage the next day and tried to arrange another meeting, but by this time strong suspicions had been aroused and Mrs. Ling asked for some guarantee that he was telling the truth, or at least of his identity; she suggested he give her his identification-card number. (All residents of Singapore and Malaysia are required to carry such cards, and the numbers are registered with the police.) Vermont readily gave her a number, which on investigation turned out to be nonexistent. Thereafter he passed out of the case, though not before again calling Dr. Ling at home and delivering an ugly warning to get out of Singapore if he valued his skin.

This unpleasant little hoax was the first of several inspired by the stories of Thompson's wealth and the willingness of his company to pay a large reward. Most of the others followed similar patterns: a vaguely plausible story (which grew increasingly easier to concoct as time went by), a modest first request for money, a sudden thickening of the plot, and the eventual disappearance of the contact, often with something to show for his efforts. During the first month, the Lings in Singapore were subjected to a number of calls and letters, some of them threatening. One caller asked Mrs. Ling to meet him at an isolated spot outside the city, an invitation she prudently declined.

As the first week of the search drew to a fruitless close, the absence of clues began to fan the fires of imaginations far more creative than Michael Vermont's. A Thai newspaper in Bangkok, seizing upon the widely reported story of Thompson's previous encounter with the hornets, came up with a front page exclusive stating that the missing American had once been abducted by the notorious "Wild Hornet Gang" and that it was very likely these evil bandits had been at work again.

Headline writers around the world paid a good deal of attention to phrases like "Thai Silk King" and "American Millionaire," the implication clearly being that silk kings and millionaires offered tempting targets to kidnappers. It was so freely assumed by most people that Thompson had made millions in the silk business that later Sheffield felt obliged to try to clarify the matter for a reporter, explaining that Thompson's financial holdings in Thailand were relatively modest outside of his famous art collection. One thing that he did not mention was the rather disillusioning truth that when the silk king went to Malaysia he had a bank balance in Bangkok of slightly more than fifty dollars. This was typical, for though he was paid a good salary by the silk company, he spent nearly all of what he earned on his collection.

The *New York Times* took stock of the mystery at the end of the first week and analyzed at some length the reasons by then being cited to support the contention that Thompson may not have gone off voluntarily and might not be in the area at all. They listed the following points, which were the subjects of much speculation at almost every gathering in Bangkok and Singapore: "(1) Mr. Thompson was a chain smoker. Yet he supposedly went for a walk leaving his cigarettes and lighter in the bungalow. (2) He suffered from a gall-bladder ailment that caused severe spasms, yet had left his pills behind at the house. (3) A dead body is not usually hard to find in the jungle: dogs and vultures could find it."

Dr. Ammundsen, who had stayed on at the Highlands to help in the search for his friend and patient, dismissed a speculation that Thompson may have committed suicide. "He was a man very interested in his work," the doctor was quoted as saying. "I don't think there was anything in his mental outlook to make him do a thing like that." Mrs. Mangskau and the Lings agreed; they had noticed that Thompson seemed tired, but not that he was suffering from any depression.

In Bangkok, people recalled Thompson's background with the OSS, the wartime organization which later became the CIA. The question of who is and who isn't a "quiet American" is an endlessly fascinating subject of debate in most Southeast Asian capitals, and Thompson's name had frequently been raised in such discussions—mainly, it seemed, on the rather questionable grounds of "once an agent, always an agent." As the mystery of his disappearance deepened, the topic inevitably acquired more interest, though at first such speculation was highly tentative. It was to be several weeks before really inventive minds got to work on it.

Hope was found by some reports, and by some innocent readers, in a story told by Mrs. Mangskau about an experience Thompson had had a number of years before while on a visit to Nepal in the Himalayas. According to the very distorted version that appeared in most reports, Thompson had gone off on a walking trip in the mountains and disappeared for two weeks, coming back in good health and high spirits. If that could happen in the rugged Himalayas, couldn't a similar happy ending be in store for the worried friends in Moonlight Cottage? The truth of the Himalaya episode, unfortunately, like the truth of so many of the stories being told, was considerably less exciting, as most of the reporters could have discovered had they bothered to check the incident. Thompson had gone off on a walking trip in Nepal, and his return had indeed been later than expected; but he had been with a sizeable party of natives and his niece from America and they had never been lost at all.

With the spectacular lack of success of the conventional search, the mystics of Malaysia and Thailand began to play a more active role. A bomoh in Tanah Rata (a village which apparently supported quite a few) went into a trance and came up with the information that Thompson was being held by the Great Spirit of the Forest, who was still upset over all the bloodshed during the Emergency and was now having his revenge. Numerous other bomohs from the surrounding area found their way to Moonlight Cottage to lend assistance, setting up altars in the rose garden and poring confidently over police maps to pinpoint the location of the missing man. There was much disagreement over just where he was and why, but they were unanimous on at least one point: he was alive and would sooner or later be found. All their visions received respectful attention from the searchers and all the locations were visited; all were empty.

The Saturday after the disappearance, the native voices were joined by the first, but not the last, foreign clairvoyant, an English mindreader named Al Koran, who was finishing a series of nightclub performances in Bangkok. Koran had a depressing vision to report: Thompson, he said, had gone into the jungle like an elephant to find a secret place to die. "I felt this as strongly as I have felt anything in my life," he told reporters, and then flew off to give more performances in England.

The Thai mystics, spurred by the widespread interest the case was naturally arousing in that country, were by no means idle all that time. One morning during the first week an apparently well-educated young Thai woman came to Sheffield's office at the silk company and said that she possessed unusual powers for seeing things hidden to most people. She asked permission to use a room at the company for a demonstration which would, she said, reveal the missing managing director's whereabouts at that very moment. Permission was granted, and a group of the firm's Thai employees assembled before a square of white cloth which the woman hung on the wall of a semidarkened room. She lit candles and joss sticks below the cloth and informed the gathering that if they concentrated properly they, like her, would be able to see Thompson quite clearly on the screen, "just like TV." There is no reason to believe that serious and devout concentration was lacking in that room of murmuring employees, but still none of them saw anything beyond a few flickering shadows made by the candles. The girl was disappointed in their failure; she herself, with her powers, had seen Thompson quite plainly being held at gunpoint by two young men.

The Thompson family at their Delaware home in 1927. Standing behind the group on the left is Elinor Thompson and beside her Jim, then a student at Princeton.

Jim Thompson at 37 in 1943, just before his transfer from the Coast Guard Artillery to the OSS.

"The Thai Silk King".

Thompson working with one of his weavers.

Inspecting newly dyed silk yarn on the
klong opposite his house.

Jim Thompson at his Bangkok home, Cocky, his pet cockatoo, on his shoulder.

Jim Thompson's house under construction in early 1959.
The house was built with elements of six different construction techniques
of different provincial origins.

Thompson's house was built next to the klong. Most of Thompson's weavers
worked in their homesteads on the other side of the canal.

The entrance to the Jim Thompson House is flanked by two stone lions.

(Top) A panoramic view of the Jim Thompson house.
(Above) The drawing room.

(Top) The dining room. The Thompson blue-and-white ceramic collection is found in this room. (Above) Thompson's bedroom.

Reading in the study of the Thai house on the klong.

Thompson and Mrs. Connie Mangskau just before his disappearance in 1967.

Jim Thompson at the picnic on Easter Sunday, March 26, 1967,
a few hours before he disappeared.

Moonlight Cottage, Cameron Highlands.

Malaysian field force police during the search for Jim Thompson at the Cameron Highlands; note the terrain in which they had to work.

Various individual employees of the company were consulting their own favorite mediums who, like their Malaysian counterparts, were optimistic about Thompson's present condition. Several were paying close attention to a rather unlikely source, an elderly Portuguese priest who for many years had taught at one of Bangkok's Catholic mission schools. In addition to his spiritual and pedagogic attainments, the priest had acquired an impressive local reputation as a dowser, a talent he explained at some length in a pamphlet which is a mine of curious and often surprising information. It opens with a brief historical sketch, in which the author—possibly to forstall any religious criticism of his hobby—notes that "between the two world wars, a French priest, L'abbe Mermet, brought the art of dowsing to a high degree of efficiency and accuracy"; and then goes on to explain how dowsing can be used in finding water, prospecting for oil, diagnosing diseases and prescribing medicines, finding children kidnapped by gangsters, and determining the sex of unhatched eggs. Among the numerous bits of unexpected information offered are the following:

"Working with the divining rod is very tiresome and even may prove injurious to health when too much dowsing is done.

Wishful thinking is the dowser's greatest enemy. If he is bent on finding water at a certain spot the pendulum will turn, the stick will pull down on that spot, and most probably he will be wrong in the prognostications.

Suppose a plane crashed between Rangoon and Bangkok, in the Tenasserim range—and that is a very bad place to crash—a good dowser will point out on a map the exact place where the plane is, and how many people still survive, and how many are wounded. It goes without saying that those indications may occasionally prove highly useful.

In 1943 the Vatical forbade Catholic priests to use dowsing for prying into other people's personal affairs."

Obviously such talents would, as the priest put it, "prove highly useful" in the present case, and he put in a good deal of work with his divining rob and pendulum over a map of the Highlands area. The results, unfortunately, were less than satisfactory. He did determine that Thompson was still alive, though in a "weakened condition," but a search of the probable location he indicated proved fruitless, the result, possibly, of the kind of wishful thinking he had warned against in his pamphlet.

6

After searching an area estimated at slightly less than seventy miles in the vicinity of Moonlight Cottage, the police officially ended the search on the tenth day after Thompson's disappearance. That does not mean that subsequently no one went into the jungle looking for clues. For nearly a month, small groups of police made occasional sorties when a likely suggestion came up, and nonofficial searchers, attracted by the increased reward offers, continued much longer, even into the second year.

The search for Thompson became, indeed, a sort of sport for some, combining recreation with the lure of bounty hunting. In mid-April, for example, a group who called themselves the Perak Adventurers Club, from Ipoh, announced that they were going to see what they could do to solve the mystery. The twelve members of the club split into two groups at Tanah Rata and each set off in a different direction. The president of the group informed the press that the reward was not the Adventurers' only motive; the expedition, he said, would also provide valuable training for the members. The training was all they got, as it turned out, during the course of three days and two nights in the jungle.

A month or so later, a considerably more amateur effort was mounted by a Mr. Hiong Chong Hock, a businessman from Singapore. Mr. Hiong felt he had one advantage over the Perak Adventurers, for all their jungle expertise. This was his niece, a lady named Madam Wong

Yoke Sean, sometimes known as Lucy Vee, who by happy chance was a medium. Madam Wong obligingly put herself into a trance at her uncle's bidding and came up with the information that Thompson was in a cave not far from Moonlight Cottage. Mr. Hiong immediately set off in the general direction and in short order managed to get himself lost for two days. Undaunted, he went back several more times before the harried police were able to persuade him to abandon the search.

Independent endeavors like these are hard to evaluate, but it is, perhaps, worth asking how thorough the official search was, since its assumed thoroughness has provided the springboard for most of the subsequent theories: the faultless logic being that if he could not be in the jungle, then he must be somewhere else. Though some of the testimony is conflicting, and though even at the time opinions on the matter varied, two things can be said with a fair degree of accuracy: (1) given the incredibly difficult geography of the Highlands and an inevitably limited number of trained searchers, it was probably as thorough as humanly possible and far more so than it would have been had the lost walker been an ordinary visitor; but (2) it was not as thorough as many people later seemed to believe.

Of all the aspects of the legend which has been constructed around the Thompson disappearance, few have been presented with more solemn assurance than this question of the near infallibility of the search effort—an assurance that is surprising only if one forgets how necessary it is to the legend as a whole. The tendency, especially in newspaper accounts, has been to emphasize the efficiency of the search; and this has sometimes been done with a notable disregard for the facts of the matter. Writing a year and a half after the disappearance, for example, Richard Hughes, a well-known Hong Kong correspondent for the London *Sunday Times*, stated that "experienced jungle trackers" were "on the spot inside five hours": a small enough error, of course, but certainly one that gives a misleading impression, since actually no experienced trackers at all were involved until the next day and they were not really organized for a good twenty-four hours. Another considerably more significant misunderstanding concerns the matter of trained search dogs. During the search, and regularly ever since, news stories have referred to these dogs, first stating that they were going to be employed and later, quite firmly, that they had been. In fact, only one dog (apart from the cocker the British major brought up to Moonlight Cottage with the rental agent the first night) was ever used, and it was an elderly, overweight bloodhound which was brought up on the second day and failed to scent anything. There are contrary explanations as to why the much-publicized dogs were never used. According to one source, the regular police pack, which was kept at Ipoh, had shortly before been decimated by a disease; according to another, they had been taken off to Singapore for some reason and were not available. In any case they were not used, and while this may or may not have been a serious omission (by the time the dogs could have been brought there even from Ipoh, the trail would probably have been lost because of all the searchers), it does weaken the assumption that the search left nothing at all to be desired.

The simple fact, of course, is that no search anywhere can ever be called entirely infallible. Anyone who doubts this should recall the Lindbergh kidnapping in 1932, when despite the efforts of hundreds of people and possibly the greatest publicity in history, the body of the dead baby lay undiscovered in a shallow grave only five miles from the Lindbergh house—and this in country far less wild than the Cameron Highlands. Another point about the Lindbergh case may also be analogous: at least one reason the baby was not found earlier was that it was widely believed he had been taken out of the area by his kidnapper, and when the body was discovered it was accidentally. In the Cameron Highlands itself, shortly before Thompson disappeared, the wreckage of a U.S. Air Force C-47 that had crashed in 1947 was discovered quite by chance. It was only a few miles from a well-traveled road.

None of this is intended as criticism of the search for Thompson as it was conducted, for it was, in the main, highly professional and went far beyond what might have been expected. And there is, indeed, something to be said for the contention that if he had had a simple accident and fallen near one of the main trails, he would probably have been found. It is still necessary, however, to insert the qualifying "probably," for there are at least a half-dozen possibilities that could account for his being there, more likely dead than not, and remaining undiscovered. Some that have been raised are that (1) he fell into one of the animal traps reputedly dug, illegally, by the aborigines and on being found dead was simply buried, either there or elsewhere, by the terrified hunters; (2) he crept injured into the one of the many caves in the area and met his fate there; or (3) he managed, as lost people often do, to wander many miles, perhaps over several days, and was injured outside the area most thoroughly searched, in which case his discovery would be pure chance. For the benefit of those to go to the Highlands today (1998), it may also be worthwhile to point out that the landscape has changed considerably; what now seems relatively tamed was much wilder and more sparsely populated thirty years ago.

These possibilities, at first widely discussed and supported by a number of people close to the case, steadily lost favor with the end of the official search. By mid-April, the mood was right for a more satisfactory explanation of what happened. The tantalizing reports of the mysterious cars, the supposed kidnap gangs, the changing of taxis, Thompson's colorful political past (both real and imagined), and the repeated rumors that it had never ended—all combined with a vague frustration at the continuing conundrum to produce a desire to hear a story that would somehow fit the pieces of the puzzle together.

A story that seemed to do exactly that, and more, was not long in coming. As a kind of curtain raiser, a Malaysian bomoh named Inche Awan bin Osman informed the press that he had made contact with the Raja Kramar (king of the spirits) who had told him Thompson never entered the jungle: in other words, just what so many people were already murmuring. This attracted relatively little notice, mainly because even the local reporters were getting a bit weary of the ubiquitous bomohs and their conversations with the spirit world which, thus far, had proved singularly unhelpful in its replies. They were to pay considerably more attention to a new entry in the psychic competition, a sort of Western bomoh who dealt in nothing so crude and old-fashioned as spirits.

7

Peter Hurkos was a Dutch-born mystic who claimed, according to a book once written about him, to have received extraordinary powers of extrasensory perception as the result of a fall from a ladder in Holland in 1943. Following his arrival in the United States after the war, he attracted a good deal of publicity because of his psychic powers and even some serious scientific respect, particularly in Southern California, where such phenomena are viewed less skeptically than in some other parts of the country. He acquired a number of admirers in Hollywood and a movie of his life was reportedly under consideration, with Glenn Ford in the leading role. His greatest public exposure was during the famous Boston Strangler case, when he was asked by the police to assist them in their search for the mysterious killer who strangled thirteen women in the Boston area in 1962 and 1963. Since there are several interesting parallels between his work on that case and on the Thompson disappearance, it is useful to briefly summarize what he did in Boston, as reported by Gerold Frank in his book on the subject.

Hurkos entered the Strangler case amid much skepticism on the part of the police officials, some of whom were understandably not overjoyed at the prospect of taking the "visions" of such a controversial figure seriously. Perhaps because of this, on his arrival in Boston he immediately set about impressing the various officials with whom he was to work by telling them things about themselves and their families they were convinced he could not have prepared beforehand; according to Mr. Frank, the strategy worked, and he gained quite a few converts to his unorthodox approach to detection. He then proceeded to the work for which he was being paid a fee of $3000, which was, of course, to identify the strangler. His method was to hold some object that had been connected with one of the murdered women—stockings, scarves, blouses, etc.—or to visit the scene of a crime and, thanks to his gift, "see" or "feel" what had taken place. He saw a lot, including, he claimed, the man who had committed the murders, and he gave a detailed description of his appearance as well as his background and mental state. He gave a harrowingly vivid account of how several of the murders were done, and, by way of factual evidence to support what he had "seen," even pointed to a doorway where he said the killer had waited and smoked; on investigating it, the police found a pile of cigarette butts. Soon afterward, the investigators handed him one of the numerous confession letters that had come into their hands in connection with the case and, without opening it, Hurkos identified the writer as the murderer. To the astonishment of the police, the writer of the letter did bear a certain resemblance to the man Hurkos had described earlier while holding the articles of clothing. All this was undeniably impressive; the only problem, from the police viewpoint at any rate, was that the letterwriter was not the man they ultimately decided was the strangler. Hurkos was later quoted as saying that he still thought he was right and that the wrong man was convicted of the crimes; but nonetheless his Boston adventure must in sum be counted a failure—officially, if not to his admirers.

Hurkos was recommended to Thompson's sister, Mrs. James H. Douglas, who decided that since the police search had ended in failure, unconventional methods might be worth a try. The contact was made through mutual friends, a substantial financial arrangement was agreed to, and on April 19, Hurkos left for the Far East, accompanied by an attractive young woman named Stephany Farb, who sometimes called herself Stephany Courtney and who acted as his secretary and general assistant. Although he was a large, heavyset, rather hulking man, Hurkos apparently needed some kind of assistant simply to cope with the minor necessities of life, of which he occasionally seemed not only unconcerned but unaware. In Bangkok, there were some who questioned the authenticity of this seeming vagueness, suggesting that he was taking in more than he seemed to be, but at least one person who was close to him for most of the trip was convinced that it was genuine and that Miss Farb, or someone like her, was truly necessary.

On the way to Thailand, the pair stopped briefly in Hong Kong, where, according to the report Miss Farb wrote of the trip, "Hurkos wished to avoid the press and also to check out the border between Red China and Hong Kong." Since at that time nobody knew he was coming other than the Douglases and one or two people in Bangkok (who had been asked to keep it quiet, and did), there can have been little danger from the press, so perhaps the main reason was to "check out" the border. If so, it did not meet with any success: Hurkos said he "felt" nothing there connected with the missing man.

They arrived in Bangkok early on the morning of the 21st and went straight to their hotel, where they later met with Thompson's friend Dean Frasche and General Black's aide Lieutenant Horgan. At the meeting, Frasche told Hurkos some of the theories being advanced to explain the disappearance, including one suggesting political motives that dated back to Thompson's early days in Thailand. He mentioned the name of Pridi Phanomyong, the former prime minister who was believed to be in exile in Communist China. Hurkos said at this time that he believed Thompson had been kidnapped by bandits and was being held just north of the Thai-Malaysian border, an "impression" he had received when studying a map of the region in Los Angeles, but that he would have to visit the Highlands to be certain his sensations had been correct. (Miss Farb, in her "complete report," as she described it, did not mention either the earlier impression or the fact that Hurkos had been told the political theories.)

In Bangkok, apart from meeting some of Thompson's associates, Hurkos' main objective was a visit to Thompson's house where, presumably, the vibrations would be strongest. He was taken there and, according to Miss Farb, did indeed receive a number of impressions. These were surprisingly vague compared with the detailed visions he was reported to have had about the murders in Boston. Miss Farb records him as saying, "I see that General Black slept here...(pointing to the bed in the far corner of the guest bedroom)...Sukarno was here...(still standing in the guest room)...there have been a great number of important people having meetings in here...(Hurkos now standing in the dining room) ... Thompson was playing with hot fire, associating with the wrong people...he just didn't realize...(Hurkos walked around the house, not saying anything more)."

Since General Black had often visited Thompson when he came to Bangkok from his upcountry headquarters, there was nothing very remarkable about the "impression" that he had slept in the guest bedroom. The only other point that could be checked was the visit of Sukarno, and this, Sheffield later confirmed, was correct. The Indonesian president had been to the house, though while Thompson was away on a trip; Sheffield had met him there at official request. Interestingly, however, Sukarno had not gone into the house at all—his real purpose in going to the compound, it proved, had been to take a boat across the klong to visit the Moslem silk weavers on the other side—and even if he had, he could not have gone into the guest room where Hurkos "felt" him because that room was only added several years later.

Plans were made for Hurkos to fly to Malaysia on April 23, and in the meantime he busied himself seeing various people in Thailand. He talked with Sheffield at the silk company; with Colonel Bond, chief of staff of the U.S. Military Assistance Command, who was a friend of Thompson's; with General Black at his headquarters in Khorat; and with Norman Hannah, deputy chief of mission at the American embassy and, at that time, the acting ambassador since the incumbent, Graham Martin, was in Washington on business. For the last three of these, Hurkos gave demonstrations of his ESP prowess, of which the one he staged for Colonel Bond's benefit was a typical example. In the colonel's office, he was given a photograph from Lieutenant Horgan's wallet and, without looking at it, gave a variety of details about the person in the picture; the young lieutenant affirmed that of the thirteen points mentioned, all were right as far as he knew. Similar readings were given for General Black and Mr. Hannah, and while the recipients did not say whether the impressions were correct in every case, they did admit that some were indeed accurate. As he had done in Boston, Hurkos was clearly eager to establish his bona fides before proceeding to more difficult problems, and he plainly impressed some members of his audience; again, though, as at the house, there was little of the startling insight that Mr. Frank says crushed the skepticism in Boston, where Hurkos told a young policeman, correctly, that he had been making love to his wife on the kitchen table a few hours before. Doubt remained in certain quarters in Bangkok when Hurkos went south, and as time went by it increased rather than diminished.

General Black gave permission for Lieutenant Horgan to accompany Hurkos and Miss Farb to the Cameron Highlands, though in a private rather than an official capacity, and Hurkos agreed to pay Horgan's fare out of his fee. On the 23rd, they flew to Kuala Lumpur and took a taxi to the resort—having, incidentally, to change cars at Tapah just as Thompson and Mrs. Mangskau had done five weeks before. They reached the Highlands after dark and put up at the Cameron Highlands Hotel.

In the fashioning of Jim Thompson's second legend, the following day proved to be perhaps the most significant since the afternoon he disappeared. Indeed, it would be possible to argue that the second legend did not really begin to flourish until that day; for while there had been rumbles before about a possible political explanation, prior to Hurkos' entry these speculations had been more or less informal, and barely an echo of them had reached the newspapers. The events of April 24 ended that, and afterwards the legend proliferated as luxuriantly as the Highlands jungle itself.

It may be recalled that Hurkos, or at any rate Miss Farb, had emphasized his desire to avoid newspaper publicity, or any public knowledge of his mission in Southeast Asia. If this desire was genuine, then their actions that first morning at the Cameron Highlands were somewhat peculiar, for instead of arranging with local authorities to give them privacy to conduct their investigations at Moonlight Cottage, they proceeded straight up the hill to the house and Hurkos performed before an audience consisting of their taxi driver, the servants, and three Malaysian soldiers who were using the place as a communications center for a search group still in the jungle. Thus his sensational revelations were hardly private and, considering their nature, it was not surprising that they very quickly traveled down to the world below.

The Dutchman began by walking restlessly about the house and garden, as if trying to catch a scent. Finally, with impressions apparently beginning to come in, he sat down on the veranda and laid out before him a photograph of Thompson he had been given in Bangkok and maps of the Highlands area and of Asia in general. He put his left hand on the maps and his right on the photograph. His face showed the strain of intense concentration. The others waited apprehensively. Then suddenly, as if unable to control himself, he began talking, and Miss Farb quickly switched on a portable tape recorder.

This is what he said, according to Miss Farb's report:

> "He was sitting in the chair...right there...he was not sitting
> in the house...the chair was on the veranda...ag, Prebi,
> oogh...Thompson ...Prebi, Pridi...fourteen people...fourteen
> people captured him... Prebe or Bebe...ora blunda Bebe...he is
> not in the jungle...I want to follow the route where they picked
> him up...he was sitting right there...his chair...there was nobody
> in, everybody was upstairs* ...there was nobody in the room
> (pointing to the living room)... they were upstairs... he was sitting
> outside in this chair... this chair... not in the jungle... car... fourteen
> people... one vehicle like a military vehicle... like a truck... I see
> truck... ah, truck, about from here on the road... he walks down
> the road... somebody woke him up... he was sitting outside and

* Presumably Hurkos (or Miss Farb) meant "inside," as they must have seen that all the bedrooms were on the ground floor.

somebody came in here... a friend of his... Bebe or Prebie... Pridi
has his own army... no bandits... nothing to do with bandits...
he walks about exactly half a mile, with Bebe or Prebie... truck
on the road... a truck on the road... fourteen people... one person
here, one person picked him up... he knows him... he was sitting
on the veranda and the men came in... asked for something, I
don't know... he went down the road... got morphine...
morphine... sleep in truck..."

He broke off, seemingly exhausted. At this point, it is worth noting
that Miss Farb's transcription of what Hurkos said on the veranda at
Moonlight Cottage differs in one significant aspect from the recollections
of Lieutenant Horgan, who also wrote a report of the Highlands trip.
Nowhere in his account does the lieutenant mention the name of Pridi,
which seems odd, to put it mildly, since of all the people there he would
have been the one most likely to recognize its importance; he did,
however, note that Hurkos mentioned someone named "Prebie."
Possibly Miss Farb inserted the name of the former prime minister
unconsciously when she was writing up the report from her tape, by
which time she was almost certainly aware of who he was.

After resting a bit from his psychic exertion, Hurkos clarified his
episodic impressions and a fairly coherent story emerged. Thompson,
he said, had been sitting on the veranda about three or shortly after and
was approached by a man named Bebe or something that sounded like
that. Bebe was dressed in civilian clothes, was about thirty-two or thirty-
five years old, had black hair and oriental features, and was known to
Thompson. The two men walked down the road together, and after
about half a mile the man suddenly knocked Thompson out with
morphine or, possibly, chloroform. A truck was waiting with thirteen
men in it, all dressed in green uniforms; the truck was disguised to look
like a military vehicle. The men were not in the Malaysian army, although
they were dressed in similar uniforms. They were Communists. The
driver of the truck was named Hassan. Hurkos was not sure who

"Prebie"—as distinct from Bebe—was, or what role he played in the abduction; the name had simply come into his mind. After putting Thompson into the truck, the men took him away somewhere and then moved him out of the country by plane.

It seemed that Hurkos had run out of impressions for the moment and the group ordered coffee from Mohammed, the Lings' cook and caretaker, who, along with the three Malay soldiers and the taxi driver, had presumably heard the strange recital. What they thought of it they kept to themselves—at least for the time being.

As they were drinking coffee, Hurkos suddenly jumped to his feet, went to the maps, and pointed at one of them. "There!" he cried. "That's where he is now! Cambodia! That's where he is. I'd give my neck on it."

If Miss Farb, the driver, Mohammed, and the three soldiers did not get the implications of this dramatic announcement, Lieutenant Horgan most certainly did, and he was properly alarmed by them; whether Hurkos was awared of them remains a matter of conjecture. Cambodia at the time was a neutral country, according to the frequent and impassioned statements of its premier, Prince Noradom Sihanouk. Nevertheless, it had no diplomatic relations with the United States (which it accused of interfering in its internal affairs) or with its neighbor Thailand (an old historical enemy). To publicly suggest that it was harboring a prominent American who had been kidnapped by Communists was an extremely grave charge, especially when the charge came accompanied by no stronger evidence than the impressions of a Dutch mystic sitting on a veranda in Malaysia. There was another point, too. Hurkos had been hired by Mrs. Douglas, whose husband had been a high official in Washington in the Eisenhower administration and who, while no longer connected with the government, still had friends there in prominent positions and was something of a public figure. It was at least questionable whether he and Mrs. Douglas would want such inflammatory statements aired so freely.

Lieutenant Horgan decided, therefore, that the semipublic

performance had gone on long enough, and he suggested to Hurkos that they walk down the road to see if he could get any sensations there. This they did, but the Malays—no doubt greatly intrigued by this novel European bomoh who hadn't mentioned spirits once—followed to see what further interesting things he might come up with. They and their companions had, after all, been working on the case for more than a month, and it was still the prime topic of conversation and surmise at the Highlands.

As they walked down the road, everyone expected Hurkos to stop at a rock where the cook from the Lutheran mission had said she saw Thompson sit briefly on the afternoon of his disappearance, but he ignored it. He stopped near the bottom of the hill, where the road to the golf course joined the one to Moonlight Cottage, and said that the truck with the thirteen soldiers had waited there.

Thompson had been watched for three days, he said, before the right opportunity came to get him, and the kidnappers had watched him the day before Easter, when he had been walking in the jungle with a woman. (As far as anybody knows, Thompson did not go walking with anybody, man or woman, that afternoon; he told the Lings and Mrs. Mangskau he had rested in his room, as they had done also.)

Then Hurkos made an announcement that must have impressed the Malay soldiers who had followed him down the hill. He said the truck had turned left and gone around the far side of the golf course to the main road that went through Tanah Rata and down from the Highlands plateau. The soldiers argued that there was no such road, and they were, supposedly, familiar with the area. Hurkos insisted there was. A quick survey revealed that there was indeed one, and it followed the route he had indicated.

8

Despite his full morning, Hurkos was eager to go on with his investigations. He wanted to go into the jungle and talk with Richard Noone, an Englishman who had been sent down several days before by the Thai Silk Company and whose findings—which, in many ways, were to prove even more influential than those of Hurkos—will be discussed presently. Noone was at that time at a camp a short distance away from Moonlight Cottage. The soldiers at the house were part of a team assisting him.

Before Hurkos could go there, however, a local correspondent for the Malaysian *Straits Times* greeted him in the lobby of the Cameron Highlands Hotel, where he and Miss Farb and Lieutenant Horgan had gone for lunch. Somebody, obviously, had been talking, and the reporter, whose name was Chou Chuan Sheng, was shrewd enough to see its news value. Hurkos, though, refused to make any statement for the press at that time. He really didn't have to; by the time he came out of the jungle later that afternoon, after a brief and uneventful meeting with Noone, the resourceful Mr. Chou had managed to collect nearly everything that had been said in the morning at Moonlight Cottage and announced that he was ready to send it to his paper for publication the next day.

Confronted by this highly unwelcome *fait accompli*, Lieutenant Horgan could do little but try to reason with the reporter, whom he had met on his previous trip to the Highlands with General Black and Dean Frasche. He could not talk him out of breaking the news of Hurkos' visit and giving the general outline of his "impressions," but Mr. Chou did agree to leave out the names the mystic had come up with and also, to Horgan's great relief, the supposed destination of the kidnappers. It is possible that the lieutenant's common-sense arguments were less effective in gaining the concessions than a dazzling performance which Hurkos gave to prove his powers to Mr. Chou; from a photograph given him by the reporter, he provided a wealth of information on past events, including details of an operation Mr. Chou's wife once had.

This demonstration not only removed any lingering doubts the journalist may have had but persuaded him to withhold publication of his edited story until after Hurkos had left the Highlands. Several weeks later, after his first story had run, he wrote a second piece informing his readers that he was absolutely certain the Dutchman had been correct in his impressions of what had happened to Thompson; anyone who could do what Hurkos had done with that photograph was clearly infallible in Mr. Chou's considered opinion.

Others were less certain. Lieutenant Horgan, for one, was not enthusiastic about Hurkos' expressed desire to go straight to Cambodia and locate Thompson at the place he had picked out on the map. He suggested a more practical course first: they would return to Bangkok and consult General Black and U.S. embassy officials before heading off to a country for which none of them had visas and in which the lieutenant, as a member of the American military, might possibly be unwelcome. Accordingly, the group went down the hill to Kuala Lumpur, spent one night there, and flew back to Thailand and what proved, by most standards, a fairly bizarre ten days.

These consisted principally of discussions, arguments, and confusion. With the aid of more maps, Hurkos amplified and refined his story, determining the means of transport used to get Thompson from Malaysia to Cambodia (a plane, definitely not a boat) and the precise town where the missing man was, he said, being presently held (a small place on the road between Pnom Penh and Angkor Wat). There were lengthy discussions with various officials over whom the mysterious Prebie might be, though why it should have posed such a problem is a minor mystery in itself. The name of Pridi was being freely mentioned in Bangkok as a possible clue in the case, and Hurkos himself, in expanding his Highlands impressions, identified "Prebie" as the mastermind of the kidnap plot and said that he lived in China. There could, it seemed, be little question of whom he was talking about, but still there was a strong official reluctance to come right out and name the former leader. Miss Farb, endeavoring no doubt to be helpful, thoughtfully pointed out that Hurkos worked partly in Dutch, interchanging b's and d's and that therefore Prebie just might be Pridi.

It was an extremely ticklish situation, for none of the odium surrounding Pridi's name had diminished in the years since the unsuccessful 1949 coup; if anything, it had increased, since among the Thai military in Bangkok it was widely believed that he was directing the Communist insurgency movement in the northeast. Perhaps wisely, the Americans dealing with Hurkos in Bangkok decided to ignore that difficulty for the time being and concentrate instead on another equally thorny one, which was whether Hurkos should be permitted to go to Cambodia as he wished. The answer, of course, rested basically on whether or not one believed what he was saying—whether or not, that is, one believed in his powers—and here is where the confusion deepened and where tempers, especially at the embassy, became considerably frayed. There is no real point in going into all the details of this odd dispute, which was probably without precedent at the embassy and which revealed that the Asian investigators were by no means alone in placing faith in mystic visions; it is enough to say that a good many cables flew back and forth between Bangkok and points in America, tentative overtures were made to a friendly country with representation in Pnom Penh to act as liaison should the decision be affirmative, and various people took firm positions for and against the enterprise.

During all this, the source of the controversy diverted himself by talking with various people about his theory (which, of course, he did not look upon as a theory at all but as simple fact) and enjoying the hospitality of an American woman, a long-time resident of Thailand, who shared his enthusiasm for psychic matters and who had gotten in touch with him as soon as she heard he was in Thailand. Hurkos managed to paint three pictures at her pleasant house, and she, naturally, supported the validity of his visions; quite possibly the two discussed some of her own experiences, which included regular communications with the spirit of her late husband. On May 4, word came that the

Douglases, after consultation with Washington, had decided against sending Hurkos to Cambodia. In other words, his mission was over.

Hurkos professed great disappointment with the decision and announced that he would leave Bangkok the next day. Back in America, he said, he hoped he would be able to persuade people to accept his views—if not Thompson's family then perhaps even President Johnson. On both scores he was unsuccessful.

Before he left, however, he had a fruitful meeting with one of the Thai mystics who had been working on the case, a Buddhist monk named Keo, who reputation as a clairvoyant was extensive.

He was held in particular esteem by certain Thai businessmen in the mining industry, some of whom refused to take any significant step without first consulting the monk and getting his opinion on its wisdom. Keo had already been consulted on Thompson's disappearance and had produced a number of impressions, including one that Thompson had been kidnapped for political motives. It was felt that Hurkos and the monk ought to get together and compare notes and, accordingly, they had a forty-five minute session at Keo's headquarters south of Bangkok.

One might expect a certain tension at such a meeting between rival mystics, but, in fact, the two men got along well and exchanged remarkably similar ideas through an interpreter. Their views on the matter differed in detail rather than substance, and the monk had gone one step further and provided a reason for the abduction, which Hurkos, at that point, had not done. (He was to make up for this oversight later.) Keo said that according to his impressions Thompson had been taken by four, not thirteen men, and transported by boat not plane, but that the destination was indeed Cambodia, just as Hurkos had said. He further believed that the disappearance was probably connected with the Vietnam war and that while he had not gone voluntarily, Thompson had changed his mind and was now cooperating enthusiastically in his captors' scheme. Some word about him would definitely reach his friends in Bangkok by June 15, and there would very likely be a temporary cease-fire in Vietnam by late October or early November of that year, due to whatever Thompson was doing.

Hurkos did not comment on these theories, though, as we shall see later, he may not have forgotten them when he came up with his own suggestions as to the why of the case; but he and Keo went over some maps and discovered that the monk's boat trip and Hurkos' plane route were very nearly the same and that both located Thompson in the same part of Cambodia. All things considered, it was an exceptionally successful meeting between East and West.

Hurkos and Miss Farb left Bangkok and direct participation in the Thompson case on May 5. It was not, however, the last time he was heard on the subject.

9

What can be made of this curious interlude? Was Hurkos a fake, out for publicity and a generous fee? Or did he have the remarkable powers of perception and clairvoyancy he and his supporters claimed, and, if so, was what he had to say about Thompson's disappearance the simple, literal truth? Or, as a third alternative held by at least one person who observed him closely, did the true answer lie somewhere in between the two extremes?

These questions are worth asking, and the possible answers are worth examining in some detail, because of the great influence the Hurkos findings had on the Thompson legend. It is necessary, though, to preface such remarks with the admission that none of the answers can be regarded as conclusive.

Opinions in Bangkok during Hurkos' stay varied widely, though it would probably be correct to say that with the passage of time his detractors came to outnumber the faithful—largely, perhaps, because nothing at all turned up to prove that a single one of his impressions was correct. At the time his "visions" became generally known, a surprising number of people were ready to accept them wholeheartedly. This was not so unusual in the case of some of the Thais and Malaysians involved, since their skepticism in such matters is naturally a good deal less than that of the average Westerner, but the roster of Hurkos believers was by no means exclusively Asian. Several quite worldly farangs were willing to believe him completely, and more were willing, though perhaps a little reluctantly, to concede that he "might have something"—a vague phrase that covered a number of things, from the possession of supernatural powers to the simple fact that what Hurkos said he had "seen" happened to coincide with what they had been inclined to suspect for reasons of their own. Some of the latter group recalled that there were, as a matter of scientific record, cases of people who could literally "see" through their fingertips—a schoolgirl in Russia was credited by scientists as being able to perceive the contents of a locked safe by merely resting her hands on it—and others who had remarkable degrees of what is usually called extrasensory perception. This sort of ability could explain some, if not all, of Hurkos' demonstrations. But they remained skeptical about his ability to sit on the veranda of Moonlight Cottage and "see" what had taken place there five weeks before.

Then there was a group willing to grant him nothing beyond a healthy ego and a sharper eye for public relations than his rather vague manner indicated. This group remained unimpressed by the "parlor tricks" he performed for influential skeptics in the course of his stay; a dozen other nightclub magicians can do the same things, they said, and the fact that they cannot be readily explained by the layman does not mean that they were inexplicable. Few people know just how Houdini got out of all those locked boxes, but that doesn't make the act miraculous. As for his impression of what happened to Thompson that afternoon in the Cameron Highlands, his detractors did not even consider that a very clever trick. They said he simply picked up a few names he had heard in preliminary conversations—the Prebie-Pridi business being the example most cited—and then wove them into a tale based on nothing more than a vivid imagination and perhaps too many cold-war spy movies, picking Cambodia as the kidnappers' destination because he knew he probably wouldn't be allowed to go there. If he had been allowed to go, without success, he would have had the same ready answer that had been heard so often in the Highlands when caves and hollow tree trunks had failed to yield the missing man: Thompson had been moved, by Communists in Hurkos' story, by spirits in the bomohs'.

As suggested before, it is impossible to say which view is correct, partly because nobody ever went to Cambodia and called Hurkos' bluff, if in fact it was a bluff. It is rather easier to come to a decision on Hurkos in his later appearance in the case four months later.

Two things can be said with some certainty, however, concerning Hurkos' visit. One, already mentioned, is that his performance in Bangkok and Malaysia was not up to the reported pyrotechnics with which he dazzled the police force of Boston. There he not only identified the killer (to his own satisfaction, anyway) but also went deep into his psychology, his motivations, and his personal habits; he also furnished intimate (and supposedly unpublished) details about several of the murders. In Thompson's case, he remained remarkably vague about the kidnappers and their motives and even about Thompson himself, except for a number of details that were already common knowledge in Bangkok. The blame for this incomplete vision could not, apparently, be laid to any language difficulties. In his brief second appearance in the case, Hurkos claimed that he spoke fluent Malay and Chinese, though he gave no indication of such fluency during his Asian stay.

The other thing to be said about his visit is that, intentionally or not, it opened the floodgates on the theories of political conspiracy, which would later come to occupy center stage in the case, officially as well as privately. By dropping Pridi's name into the controversy and by making the kidnappers Communists, Hurkos put all sorts of ideas into all sorts of heads. Nearly every political theory that has followed his— including, paradoxically, some advanced by people who had no faith in the Hurkos "impressions"—has freely borrowed details from it, and most of them have observed his useful precedent of drawing conclusions that are almost impossible to prove, or, worse, disprove. One man close to the case (and not, needless to say, an admirer of the Dutchman) is convinced that had Hurkos not come forth with his story, most of the subsequent theories would never have been heard, much less taken seriously. "He muddied the waters," this man says, "and as a result we may never see bottom now."

Not surprisingly, the Hurkos version of Thompson's fate did not sit well with most official minds, especially at the American embassy in Bangkok, who generally accepted neither his methods nor his conclusions. Like their predecessors in Boston, they were faintly embarrassed at having to seriously consider the words of a mystic, however celebrated he might be, and there was a collective sign of relief when he finally left. An expert of a very different sort, and a man much more to their taste, was Richard Noone, the Englishman with whom Hurkos had spoken briefly in the jungle at the Cameron Highlands.

Noone was working in 1967 as a planning officer at the Southeast Asia Treaty Organization (SEATO) headquarters in Bangkok, and though he had never met Thompson, his credentials for giving an opinion in the case were highly impressive. A graduate of Cambridge, where he studied anthropology, he had been with an Australian division in Johore when the Japanese invaded Malaya and had just managed to escape in time. He returned to Malaya in 1952 to join General Gerald Templer, who was leading the fight against the Communist insurgents, and worked as an adviser to the aborigines department for the next nine years, during which he organized a regiment to help eliminate the terrorists. Much of his time had been spent in or near the same jungle where Thompson had disappeared, and he had become particularly close to the native tribes who knew it best.

In his own personal history, Noone also had a story that was almost as strange and remarkable as Thompson's and that had itself been the subject of widespread speculation. It concerned his older brother, Pat, who before the outbreak of the Pacific war was the curator of the local museum at Taiping, Perak, a state that borders on the Highlands area. By the beginning of the war in 1941, Pat Noone was already a somewhat legendary character in Malaya: a high-spirited Irishman who knew the jungle like his backyard and was fond of vanishing into it occasionally, emerging just when everyone was getting worried. According to his contemporaries, he was an anthropologist of great talent, his chief interest being an aborigine tribe known as the Temer, who came in time to regard him as a sort of father figure and, possibly, even as a god. He married a Temer girl, which no doubt drew him even closer to the shy, primitive people who so fascinated him and among whom he was to meet his mysterious fate.

When the Japanese began their thrust down the Malayan peninsula in December 1941, Pat Noone, quite characteristically, stayed behind and disappeared into the Perak jungle to organize a resistance force, presumably with the assistance of the Temer and other aborigine tribes with whom he had worked. He was never seen again by anyone outside the jungle. In 1942, another Englishman, F. Spencer Chapman, who had also escaped capture by the enemy and decided to do behind-lines resistance work, made a long and harrowing journey through the wild country in an effort to find Noone and join forces with him. He succeeded in finding the Temer, but they refused to tell him anything about the anthropologist—not, apparently, because they knew nothing but because they did not choose to talk. In 1943, Noone was officially declared dead.

After the war, in the late forties and early fifties, strange rumors about him began to circulate through Malaya. It was said that he had not died during the war after all, and seemingly reliable reports had him alive as late as 1949; in 1948 and 1949 a white man was reported to be a member of one of the terrorist bands then operating in the jungle, and some people thought he might be Pat Noone. Others believed that he had died, or been killed, sometime after the end of the war—by a Chinese Communist who was afraid of Noone's knowledge of the insurgency plans, according to some; by one of the Temer, according to others. In 1951, a young English soldier named Tom Stacy made a journey through the jungle and later wrote a book about it (*The*

Hostile Sun); in it he described a Temer ceremony he attended where he suddenly became aware that the name Noone was being chanted, like a religious incantation. Stacy became fascinated by the legend of Noone and tried to get the aborigines to say what had happened to him. He went so far as to allow the Temer to believe that he was Noone's son by an English marriage, but they still remained evasive on the subject. The nearest he got to a solution was when he was told by an English officer serving with the Malayan police that in 1948 the officer had been taken by an aborigine guide to a grave which was pointed out as being Noone's.

In 1952, when Richard Noone became an adviser to the Malayan Aborigine Department as part of an effort to get the aborigines to help in the Emergency, he, too, decided to see if he could discover what had happened to his brother. His attempt was described in a book by another Englishman, Dennis Holman, entitled *Noone of the Ulu*; the Noone of the title was Pat, and ulu is a Malay word generally used to mean the interior jungle. After a good many months of wandering through the territory and gaining the confidence of its inhabitants, Richard Noone finally learned his brother's fate—at first through veiled hints, at last from reliable informants whose testimony he found convincing. It was not a pretty story. Pat Noone, the aborigines said, had been murdered during the war by one of his closest and most trusted friends in the tribe. His killer had felled him with three poisoned darts, two of which had struck him in the thigh and the third in his eye, and had finished him off with a parang, the large, razor-sharp knife carried by most natives. The motive was probably Noone's aborigine wife, who later disappeared. Noone's Temer friends had buried his body with suitable ceremonies and then, according to the one who told the story many years later, "We agreed that a taboo should be made of the matter."

Noone was recommended to Sheffield by a man at the American embassy who felt that the Englishman's expert opinion on the situation would be a valuable addition to the search efforts. His main object would not be so much to search for Thompson, for that had already been done with far greater resources than he could command, but to talk to the aborigines of the area. If, as some people were suggesting, they knew something they were afraid to divulge to the police, Noone could possibly get it out of them, just as he had gotten an admission of his brother's death when numerous others had failed. Sheffield agreed, and the silk company paid for Noone to go to the Highlands shortly before Hurkos arrived on the scene.

In Malaysia—where he emphasized to reporters that his trip "had nothing to do with SEATO"—Noone stayed at Moonlight Cottage, where he was joined by two of his old assistants from his service days. One was a former border scout from Sabah, in North Borneo, and the other was an aborigine bomoh with the resounding name of the Toh Pawang Angah Sidak. The bomoh, Noone said, had been successful in locating a missing man in the jungle once before, in 1960 after a plane crash, and he had also helped discover a secret route by which a group of Communist terrorists had escaped the police in Pahang. Noone was quoted as saying, "Because of these two incidents so accurately pointed out to me by the Toh Pawang, I am taking him with me again."

Noone and his two companions did not remain in the Highlands jungle long; they came out, in fact, after only a little more than thirty-six hours. During this time, they went deeper into the forest than the field force searchers had gone and talked with a number of aborigines. The proven powers of the Toh Pawang were not, as it turned out, of much use, but even so, Noone's conversations and observations were apparently persuasive enough to make him willing to commit himself to a fairly sweeping statement. "I am fully convinced," he said, "that Mr. Thompson is not lost in the jungle."

Though a skeptic might question how he could come to such a firm conclusion after so short a stay, no one could really question his integrity. The objections that could be raised to Hurkos did not apply to Noone. He received no money other than his expenses, he was certainly not interested in publicity, and he was an acknowledged expert on the jungles of Malaysia. His conclusions, therefore, were not to be dismissed lightly, nor were they. If Hurkos provided the fantasists with a wealth of material to aid them in their imaginative speculations, Noone's conviction that Thompson was not in the jungle was profoundly influential in persuading many more soberminded observers to abandon their accident theory. With his return to Thailand, the general acceptance of a conspiracy advanced another step, and a major one.

11

During the summer months of 1967, the Thompson case was punctuated by false alarms, mystical visions, further theorizing, and events that must be classified as simply inexplicable, or at any rate more than passing strange.

In the latter category, perhaps, should be placed the very curious experience of Edward Pollitz in Tahiti on May 27, two months after the disappearance. Pollitz was the businessman Thompson was scheduled to dine with on the evening he was to come down to Singapore from the Highlands. The two men were not close friends or, indeed, friends at all except in a business sense, but they had met several times and Thompson had entertained Pollitz in Bangkok; Pollitz certainly had no doubt that he would know Thompson if he saw him, and that, so he thought, was exactly what happened in Tahiti.

On the 27th, he said, he was sitting in the manager's office of the Tahiti Hotel in Papeete. He happened to glance out the window during the conversation and there, to his great surprise, he saw Jim Thompson, going out the door of the hotel. Pollitz called out to him and ran out of the office, just in time to see the man get into an automobile with a gray-haired woman and drive off. He was sufficiently sure he had not made a mistake to contact the local Pan American manager and make inquiries around the island. There was no trace of Thompson, but neither could Pollitz find the man who had driven away from the hotel with the gray-haired woman.

He reported the strange incident later to Thompson's family, who were inclined to consider it a perfectly natural case of mistaken identity;

after all, Pollitz certainly had Thompson on his mind at that time, and the missing man was not all that distinctive in appearance. Pollitz admitted the possibility, but six months later, on a trip through Bangkok, he was still almost sure he had been right. Neither he nor anyone else could suggest a good reason why Thompson should have been in Tahiti or, if there and presumably in hiding, why he should have gone to the island's leading hotel.

In mid-May, Noone again lent a helping hand, but this time he went to Singapore, Kuala Lumpur, and Ipoh instead of to the jungle. Actually, he was doing a follow-up job on an aspect of the case he had gotten involved in on his previous visit to Malaysia, which concerned negotiations with a somewhat mysterious woman from Singapore, who shall here be called Mrs. Florence Wong. Mrs. Wong was a Eurasian who had reportedly once stood, unsuccessfully, for municipal office in Singapore, and she had been interested in the Thompson case since early April. At that time she had sent several cables to Sheffield in Bangkok offering her assistance in locating the missing man. Her motive, she declared, was "based on love for God and justice" rather than any desire for the reward money, which she discreetly said would be "merely appreciated." The exact form her assistance might take was unclear, which was what prompted Sheffield to ask Noone to make contact with her on his earlier trip. In this first meeting, at the end of April, she suggested that she had certain friends who might know something, and she was particularly eager to talk with General Black, having read about him in the newspapers when he had gone to the Highlands to assist in the search. Black was unavailable at the time, and it was arranged for her to meet Noone again, with the understanding that he had authorization to take any action he considered desirable.

Mrs. Wong was a lady of generous proportions (in one of her several requests for plane passage to Bangkok, she had specified first-class accommodations since, she said, she could not fit comfortably into a tourist seat), who lived in cramped quarters with a large number of cats and dogs and who had a wide and clearly colorful circle of acquaintances. Among them, she told Noone, were several procurers who, for some unexplained reason, made a specialty of supplying girls to the crews of Norwegian ships calling at Singapore. From these sources, she had learned that Thompson had been taken aboard a Norwegian cargo ship and carried to Hong Kong, though for what reason she did not yet know. She was eager to discuss all these interesting matters with the people in Bangkok, who she hoped would be kind enough to give her something to defray her expenses.

Noone listened to this bizarre story and said he would pass it on for possible action. In the end, no action was taken, mainly on the advice of the Malaysian authorities, who already knew about Mrs. Wong and were inclined to view her and her information with a good deal of skepticism. One of her varied circle of friends, it seemed, was a certain Singapore medium who did her business with a crystal ball and who was known to be at work on the Thompson affair. They tactfully suggested that if Mrs. Wong came up with any really hard information she should turn it over to the police officials who were handling the case. With that Mrs. Wong reluctantly faded out of the picture, but only for the time being; like so many other characters in the mystery, she did not accept defeat calmly but only bided her time until a new opportunity presented itself.

While he was in Malaysia, Noone also met Santokh Singh, the police officer who had been placed in charge of the Thompson investigation from his headquarters in Ipoh. Santokh, a Sikh, was the first Malaysian to graduate from an American police school conducted by the FBI and had taken a considerable interest in the case, which was certainly the most widely publicized thus far in his career. Since assuming direction, he had followed down a number of seemingly promising leads, but all of them, he told Noone, had proved negative. The report of the five mysterious cars with Thai license plates seen going up to the Highlands on the day of the disappearance had been thoroughly investigated and dismissed: no such cars had come into Malaysia at all, according to the border authorities. The Malay caretaker of Moonlight

Cottage had also been investigated, and the police were convinced he knew nothing about Thompson's fate. The body of a man found in a park near Kuala Lumpur on May 15 was definitely not that of Thompson. In brief, the case was still wide open, the mystery as total as it had been on the first day.

In May, too, Mrs. Douglas and Thompson's older brother, Henry, came and spent several weeks in Bangkok and Malaysia, talking with various people who had worked on the case. Shortly before they left to return home, they gave a dinner in the celebrated Thai house for some of their brother's close friends. It was the first time most of the friends had been in the house since the dreadful news had come, and some of them anticipated a trying emotional experience; indeed, one very old friend decided she was simply not up to it and regretfully declined the invitation. Yet as it happened, one guest remembered, it did not prove a sad occasion after all: the beautiful drawing room, ablaze with lights and rich colors, looked so much as it always had that the tragedy seemed unreal. It was as though Thompson was merely away on one of his trips and would return soon to the objects he had assembled so lovingly, to the assorted animals that roamed freely about, and to the servants, who thus far had refused even to entertain the possibility of his not coming back.

In fact, the idea that he was still alive gained rather than declined in strength as the months passed, encouraged by a variety of seemingly hopeful rumors and reports. On July 3, the Malaysian and Bangkok newspapers proclaimed in large headlines that the search for Thompson was concentrating on Hong Kong, and while the story that followed was extremely vague many people felt there must be something behind it. The telephones at the Thai Silk Company rang all day with anxious friends wanting to know how true it was. They had to be told there was only a grain, and a very small grain at that. The Malaysian police had sent a routine request out through Interpol, the international police organization, to be on the lookout in various cities, and the security officer at the Hong Kong Hilton had mentioned the fact to a newspaper reporter. Yet even this fairly unexciting development stirred up speculation: if the Malaysians were notifying Interpol, didn't it suggest that they believed Thompson was no longer in their country?

A Kuala Lumpur correspondent for the London Observer sent in a report containing the following information, which was based almost entirely on gossip being aired at every Bangkok social gathering: "Many people say that Thompson was involved politically in Thailand, and that he was a U.S. agent using silk as a screen for his intelligence work. But others maintain that Thompson is more Thai than American, and that his presence in Bangkok was causing Washington some embarrassment. It is well known that Thompson got to know many Communist agents during the Japanese occupation of Thailand."

People were indeed saying some of these things, but what the correspondent, like most of the other reporters writing about the case, conveniently neglected to point out was that there was not the least evidence for any of these opinions. If Thompson were a CIA agent— and, as we have seen, this is denied by the organization's own files— then it was one of the better-kept secrets in an organization that, contrary to popular opinion, is surprisingly well known in the areas where it operates. The wife of the CIA station chief in Bangkok was a friend of his, and served as one of the guides in his house; but to claim this as a significant clue, as several were to do in coming years, would be to implicate all her many friends in Bangkok. Also, it was quite a trick for him to "know many Communist agents during the Japanese occupation of Thailand" since he had not arrived there until after the war ended. And, for that matter, what did the writer mean by "Communist agents"?

An article that caused a much wider stir was one which appeared in the Asian (but not the American) edition of *Life* magazine. After a discussion of the mysterious nature of the whole affair, the writer then went on to quote a fairly startling theory from a source identified only as "a man in a highly responsible U.S. government position." The theory ran as follows:

"The number one Communist propaganda effort today is directed at bringing the bombing of North Vietnam to an end. Obviously this is not a goal accomplished overnight. It will take a well-planned, extended effort. Now, consider the role of Thailand in the war. Many fighter bombers striking North Vietnam come from here. The presence of B-52s now enables the U.S. to double or triple their raids with much greater ease. These forces pose a great threat to the Communist side. An obvious effort would be to immobilize the bases in Thailand.

"Now here's Jim Thompson, well known, close to the Thai people, admired because he put silk weavers in the business. If Thompson could be captured, brainwashed, perhaps cast in the role of a defector, the Communists could surface him. He might say something like he couldn't stand what's happening to Thailand and he wants to help the Thai people. Well, that would be quite a Communist propaganda coup."

Hurkos had helpfully explained the how of Thompson's disappearance; here was a suggestion as to the why, one that dovetailed in many interesting respects with the monk Keo's feeling that the disappearance was somehow connected with the war in Vietnam and that, moreover, apparently came from an eminently respectable, if unidentified, source. Given the world of conspiratorial adventure we live in—few novelists would have dared invent the character and career of Kim Philby—it seemed to many people quite logical. The case was not progressing at a very encouraging rate in terms of hard, provable facts, but as far as speculation was concerned it was entering its baroque period, with the foundations for the second Thompson legend already firmly in place.

12

One night about three months after Thompson disappeared, an old friend named Elizabeth Lyons, who was staying temporarily in his house while on an assignment in Bangkok, decided to have a small dinner party. There had been few entertainments in the house since the one given by his sister and brother on their trip, and Miss Lyons felt it might be good for the servants, who appeared to be getting depressed by the unnatural stillness of the place; after all, when Thompson was there, scarcely a night passed without people coming for drinks or dinner.

Accordingly, she sent out invitations to a few other old friends, and, as Thompson usually did if the weather was good, set the candlelit table outside on the stone terrace that overlooked the klong. As the guests gathered, giving the open stagelike living room some of its old glamour, they suddenly became aware of something happening on the other side of the water. They saw, to their astonishment, that the rickety boardwalks running along the canal were thronged with people, whispering together excitedly, and others were pressing for a view through the windows of the waterfront houses. In a short time, there was a large crowd, all chattering and looking across at the Thompson living room.

Miss Lyons asked Yee, Thompson's long-time houseboy, to see what was wrong; only some disaster, she thought, could assemble so many people so quickly. When he came back, he had a sad but not really surprising story to report: a rumor had swept through Bangkrua that evening that Thompson had returned, and, seeing the people gathered at his house, the villagers had decided it must be true.

Informed of their mistake, they disappeared as quickly as they had gathered, moving away from the windows and slipping down the dark alleyways through the houses. In a few minutes, everything was quiet across the black, oily waters. The dinner party on the terrace that evening was a subdued one.

13

While the imaginative theorists were busily concocting elaborate political schemes to explain the disappearance—one that made the rounds had Thompson in Canton as a houseguest of Pridi—another, less vocal group still clung stubbornly to the hope that if he had been kidnapped from the Highlands it could still turn out to be an old-fashioned, non-Communist ransom affair, with the kidnappers waiting until some of the police activities died away before making their demand. This hope was sustained, though not very strongly, by a number of leads throughout that summer.

Most of these began with a letter, sometimes in Thai but generally in rather uncertain English, and all that looked in the least promising were followed up by the Bangkok law offices of a young American named Charles Kirkwood, whom the Thai Silk Company had retained to handle the reward offer and various other aspects of the case. (In the early summer, a group of Thompson's friends had gotten together and added substantial contributions of their own to the company offer, thus more than doubling the original $10,000 reward.)

A typical one, in early May, started with a communication from a Thai man named Narong, who advised the silk company to get in touch with a woman in Bangkok named Chuchit if they were interested in information about Thompson. Chuchit said that she had been told by Narong, whom she considered reliable, that Thompson had been kidnapped by Communists but later released by them. He was at present suffering from an unknown ailment that affected both his legs and was being treated by a doctor in the southern part of Thailand, near the Malaysian border. The doctor wanted 3,000 baht (about $150 at the time) and for this surprisingly modest sum he would turn the American over to Narong for delivery to his friends. Investigation showed that the woman had a good reputation and property of her own, and it was decided to risk giving her the money. It was a mistake. Further requests for money followed, the mysterious Narong remained elusive, and the affair was finally written off as a hoax.

This was the general pattern: an apparently respectable initial contact, a tale that was sometimes odd but that was usually not outside the bounds of possibility, a gradual increasing of the demands for "expense" money, an ultimate dead end. The only subject most of the informants seemed really knowledgeable about was the reward offer, and about that they were often very well informed indeed: one had worked out a complex scheme for depositing it in various accounts in both Thailand and Malaysia, and spent so much of his communications in explaining this system that he more or less overlooked the question of finding Thompson.

One would-be contact at least could be dismissed with little investigation. This was a man from Songkhla, in the far south of Thailand, who wrote that he had seen Thompson on the Malaysian side of the border and recognized him easily since he was "of medium built, oval-shaped face, thin hair (light brown), tends to limp when walking, and speaks Thai fluently." In more than twenty years in his adopted homeland, Thompson had never managed to progress beyond a few simple phrases of Thai.

Of all the supposed leads that came up in the first year of the case, the one that seemed most promising originated with a letter received in September by the Kirkwood office. It was from Haadyai, near the border, and was written by a man named Khed, who wanted to know if the reward offer was still effective. On being assured that it was, he wrote back to say that he could lead them to Thompson in the Ipoh area of Malaysia. Unlike nearly all the other informants, he frankly admitted that his motive was the collection of the reward. He set down terms of how and when it was to be paid should he deliver Thompson as promised but said he would accept nothing unless Thompson's associates in Bangkok were satisfied. These indications of good faith were further strengthened by the results of a discreet investigation by the Thai police, in which it was found that Khed owned a private school with about 300 students and was considered locally to be an honest, reliable citizen.

Early in October Khed came up to Bangkok for further talks on his proposal. The story he had to tell was a curious one, and, on the surface, not very credible. He said that Thompson had dyed his hair red and was living in a market area near Ipoh, posing as a fortuneteller. No one in Bangkok really believed this tale—after all, a red-haired farang fortuneteller would certainly have attracted notice before then— but they decided to go along with it on the theory that the kidnappers, afraid to come forward themselves, had delegated Khed to act as their emissary and might indeed bring Thompson to the marketplace to release him. Khed said that on three days' notice, he could take anyone designated to the market and point Thompson out; if the identification were satisfactory he would then be eligible to collect the reward.

Both the Thai and Malaysian authorities felt the lead was worth following up, and it was agreed that Sheffield, Kirkwood, and another American, Harvey Price, from Kirkwood's office would meet Khed in Ipoh on October 15. It was also agreed (though needless to say not with Khed, who was already suspicious at dealing with so many farangs) that Santokh Singh and his men in Ipoh would be alerted in case the kidnappers might be planning to abduct Sheffield or one of the others.

The first part of the trip was straight out of a melodrama. Through indirect, official channels, Santokh advised Sheffield and his party to arrive dressed in casual clothes and, if questioned by anyone, to say they were on a holiday. They flew to Penang first, then drove to Ipoh for a secret meeting with Santokh at the Station Hotel. From there they proceeded to a rather dingy Chinese hotel, where they registered with their first and middle names only and used their American addresses. On an earlier trip, soon after the disappearance, Sheffield had registered under his full name and had quickly been discovered by newspaper reporters; Santokh wanted to avoid a repetition at all costs.

That evening, Friday, the three Americans dined with Santokh at a private club and discussed the plan for the meeting with Khed, which had been scheduled for Sunday morning. Khed would meet Sheffield and the others, he had said, at a Buddhist temple not far from the market at ten on Sunday, and would lead them from there to Thompson. No one knew how many men he would have with him, but it was hoped he would have at least one. This was a young Thai named Surachai, Kirkwood's office boy, who had gone back to Haadyai with Khed after his visit to Bangkok as a sort of hostage to insure that his employer and Sheffield would show up in Malaysia. Before he had left, Surachai had been instructed in a signal to give the border guards when he and Khed crossed into Malaysia so that they could be trailed to Ipoh.

Santokh Singh had worked out elaborate plans for keeping the foreigners under surveillance at their temple meeting. They would be accompanied by a police officer, a Eurasian named Stuart Moreira who had only recently joined Santokh's staff and whose face was unfamiliar in Ipoh. He was to pose as "Mr. Stuart", Sheffield's silk representative in Kuala Lumpur, and had supposedly been asked to join the rescue party in case a Malay-speaking translator was needed in the negotiations. All roads leading out of the temple area would be watched by covered trucks, each containing a dozen armed police, and one of the trucks would follow the party when it left the temple to go to the market. A number of plainclothesmen would be in the vicinity of the temple itself: one posing as a tourist taking pictures, one painting an ice plant across the street, another repairing an automobile in front of the temple gate. Hidden spotters would be in constant communication with Santokh by radio.

The following day, Kirkwood and Price drove up to the Cameron Highlands to look at Moonlight Cottage, which they had not seen before, and Sheffield remained in Ipoh, going over the plans with Santokh and Moreira. They looked perfect—assuming, that is, that Khed showed up at the temple and that he was as truthful as he seemed. If he were, then perhaps by the next afternoon the mystery of what had happened on Easter Sunday at the Highlands would be solved, and all the theorists could take a well-deserved rest.

On Sunday morning the three Americans and Moreira proceeded

to the temple, driven in a borrowed car by an armed policeman in civilian clothes whom they had supposedly "hired" in Ipoh. They arrived a little before the appointed time. Khed was not there. Nor did he come at ten, and as the minutes slowly passed it began to look as if this lead like all the others had led to nowhere. At ten-thirty he arrived: he had forgotten to change his watch to Malaysian time, which was then half an hour ahead of Thailand. He was accompanied by a driver, three friends, and, Kirkwood was relieved to see, the office boy Surachai.

Khed announced that they would go to the market at eleven o'clock, and to pass the time until then he and his friends went to have a bath in the monks' quarters of the temple. When he came out, he had changed his mind: only he and one of his friends would go to the market with their driver to meet their contact, and the others would wait for word at the temple. After an hour the driver returned with bad news. Khed had gone into the market area and disappeared; he had no idea what had happened to him. The discouraged foreigners remained at the temple for some time, watched by their numerous hidden guards, and finally went back to their hotel in the hope that Khed might communicate with them there.

The car and driver were trailed all that afternoon and Sheffield, at the hotel, received several telephone calls from Santokh's headquarters; the driver had driven all over Ipoh and at one point had circled the hotel. About six o'clock a messenger brought a letter, saying that a stranger on the street had paid him to deliver it. It was from Khed, and he was apologizing for his failure to make contact with his friends in the market. Sheffield sent an answer to the hotel where Khed had said he had stayed the night before, saying they understood and asking him to call them.

Early the next morning, Kirkwood and his associate left for Bangkok. Sheffield decided to stay as long as Khed was in the vicinity, which could not be very long since his Malaysian visa expired the following day. Around nine o'clock that morning, there was a knock on the door of his room and, opening it, he found Khed and his entire party. Problems had arisen, Khed said; the group that was supposed to deliver Thompson had been frightened two days before by a foreigner who had allegedly driven "to every corner of Ipoh" inquiring about Jim Thompson, and, as if this weren't enough, three other foreigners had been asking questions in the town. As a consequence, the group had decided to lay low.

There, for all intents and purposes, the promising lead came to a stop. Sheffield suggested that Khed contact the police if he had any further information from his mysterious friends and told him that the police were willing to guarantee that no one who found Thompson, under any circumstances, would be prosecuted. He then returned to Bangkok. During the following several months there were two or three letters from Khed about the matter; in the final one he said he believed his friends had taken Thompson out of Malaysia, to where he did not know.

Was Khed telling the truth? On reflection, Sheffield and the Kirkwood office were inclined to think he probably was—as far as he knew. He gave every appearance of being genuinely surprised when his friends failed to produce Thompson at the market. They felt that he was very likely the victim of a confidence game in which the Malaysian group extracted advance payments from him through the promise of turning the missing man over and sharing the reward with him. When called upon to deliver, they simply faded away.

14

Al Koran, the British mind reader with the nightclub act, had been the first professional entertainer to discover the publicity value of the Thompson case, but he was by no means the last. Of the several who have enjoyed brief headlines with their sensational "discoveries," none was more persistent than an Australian, a former major in the British army, named Robert McGowan.

If McGowan were telling the truth about the extraordinary things he said happened to him in his pursuit of the truth about Thompson—quite apart from what he said had happened to Thompson—he will undoubtedly someday rate a biography of his own; if he invented them, he may well have an unexplored career ahead of him as a film scriptwriter. His periodic involvement with the case stretched out over a year, and his pronouncements, made more often than not within hearing distance of a newspaper reporter, not only earned him a number of performing engagements in various Southeast Asian capitals but also a rather surprising amount of serious regard from several people closely concerned with the mystery. It is only fair to note that most of them later tempered their enthusiasm considerably, but that he managed to get their ear at all with what he had to say is testimony to his powers of persuasion.

In 1967, McGowan had a nightclub act consisting of himself, his son Peter, and a girl with short, straight hair called Curley. McGowan did various mind-reading tricks with his son and, perhaps to enliven the act a bit, threw knives at Curley—"from not very far away," according to an unimpressed member of one of his audiences. He played mostly engagements around Southeast Asia and in June of that year was doing jobs in Kuala Lumpur and Singapore. It was in the latter that certain of his "impressions" concerning the Thompson disappearance found their way into the local papers, though in small, not very prominently displayed stories. His coverage improved considerably in July, when he was able to inform a reporter that he had been "threatened" to keep away from the case by a couple of Asians and an American who claimed to be a CIA agent; worse, someone had tried to stab him as he was walking innocently along Singapore's Bugis Street, a popular late-night meeting place for sailors, prostitutes, and assorted toughs, but with quick thinking he had fortunately been able to deflect the knife. McGowan announced that he was undaunted by these sinister incidents. Indeed, he was stimulated by them to go on with his "investigation" and was, in fact, going to Bangkok to see what he could find out there.

Soon after his arrival in the Thai capital, McGowan made the acquaintance of another receptive reporter, on the *Bangkok Post*, and he had a good story for him, too. He said that he and his son—who, he claimed, had much stronger powers of ESP—had a strong impression that a certain Mr. Seng knew something about the disappearance. After a diligent search of the city, they had managed to locate a man named Mr. Peng Seng, who, by a truly remarkable coincidence, had an antique shop right next door to Thompson's silk company on Suriwong Road. Furthermore, this Mr. Seng (as McGowan insisted on calling him, though no one else ever had) proved to be an old friend of Thompson's and had told a story that McGowan and Peter found extremely significant. It was this: on the morning he went to Malaysia Thompson had come into Peng Seng's shop to pay a bill, and he had said goodbye not only to the owner but also to the rest of the staff. McGowan quoted the shopkeeper as saying that this multiplicity of farewells was unusual. "We feel this is a very important clue," the mind reader told the reporter, and then added, "Our impressions are coming in very strongly, and we believe we're getting closer to the answer in this case every day."

If so, it was by a very roundabout route. McGowan spent a good deal of time talking to people interested in the case, including the American woman who had entertained Hurkos during his stay, all the time maintaining close contact with his reporter friend, who was clearly enthralled by all the mysterious goings-on. Then, if McGowan is to be believed, the plot got much darker. He said he received a telephone call from a South African who had once before contacted him in Singapore. The caller advised him to go to Laos and said that there he would be given proof that Thompson was still alive. McGowan, of course, passed on this newsworthy information to his reporter friend, with the encouraging comment, "Our investigation is going perfectly, slowly, step by step. We receive an impression, follow it through, and confirm it by fact. And so far, every one of our impressions have been proved correct." He did not explain what impressions he was referring to.

The two McGowans and Curley set off for Vientiane, the capital of Laos—where, conveniently, they had a nightclub engagement— and there, according to a report he later wrote in the hopes of getting financial support for his "investigations," the plot became even knottier. The task of untangling it is perhaps best left to his future biographer, but some suggestion of its dramatic flavor may be seen in the fact that several key scenes were played in the Third Eye, a psychedelic nightspot populated mostly by the European hippie community who were attracted by its ready supply of drugs and run by a young American nonconformist who talked about forming a rebel U.S. government in Laos. For added color, if any were needed, there was the strange South African (McGowan described him, with an uncharacteristic lack of originality, as "reckless, devil-may-care") and a curious-looking Chinese who was "completely bald on the front half of the head, with a line of hair from ear to ear in the rear." As a result of numerous shadowy meetings and whispered conversations, McGowan claimed to have discovered that Thompson was in, of all places, Cambodia, where he had been brought to meet, of all people, former Prime Minister Pridi. Pridi, it seemed, hankered to return to his native land (a piece of news McGowan hardly had to journey to Laos to uncover, since almost anyone in Bangkok could have told him) and he had wanted Thompson's assistance. Thompson had told him he would not be welcome in Thailand (a fact Pridi could have learned from reading the newspapers) and therefore Thompson was being held to keep him from talking too much before a projected coup was staged.

This information was given sober consideration in Bangkok, mainly by the group that had been inclined to accept the Hurkos impressions. It was some time before active disenchantment with McGowan's sources of information began to set in—not, in fact, until he claimed he had gone through various other hair-raising experiences (attempted murder in a Bangkok slum, for one) and announced that Thompson had been moved from Cambodia to Switzerland. In due course, interest began to wane, or perhaps the plot became too complex even for a theory, and McGowan like his predecessors faded out of the picture, either a highly imaginative man or a grossly misunderstood one, with an ample sheaf of newspaper clippings.

In 1984, a journalist named Robert Sam Anson wrote an article about the case for the American edition of *Life* magazine, apparently based on interviews with Thompson's nephew Henry, the American woman who admired Hurkos in Bangkok, and the by then retired General Black. In it, he brought forth one bit of information that had not been known by Sheffield and others at the time. McGowan, he claimed, had been quite specific about the place where Thompson was being held in Cambodia: a two-story house in Stung Treng, clearly identifiable because it had a wagon wheel leaning against it. The American lady and "a pilot for the CIA's Air America," according to Anson, were so impressed that they hatched a bold plan for the pilot to fly over Stung Treng, feign engine trouble, land, and rescue Thompson with the help of a Gurkha lieutenant who had been drawn into the scheme. The plan was stopped at the last minute by the CIA, but "undaunted, the Gurkha lieutenant made his way to Stung Treng and spent two weeks there in a vain search for a two-story house with a wagon wheel leaning against it."

15

Political skullduggery has been by far the most popular element in the explanation of what happened to Thompson, with ransom kidnappings coming in second place, but imaginations were also at work along other trails. As one clueless month succeeded another, the case stubbornly refused to die away as a popular topic for debate in most of the capitals of Asia and, because of Thompson's extensive circle of friends, outside Asia as well. Experts appeared unexpectedly on the inner workings of the CIA, on Thompson's love life, on the jungles of Malaysia, on aborigine customs, on the Communist mentality, and on the habits of tigers and assorted other wild beasts with regard to human beings. The beauty of the case was that it was so marvelously flexible; it could be adjusted to meet almost any theoretical need, and it is clear that some of the needs were considerable.

There was, for example, the solution offered, quite seriously, by a Malaysian businessman to a reporter in Singapore. He said that it was possible Thompson had been kidnapped by a love-sick aborigine woman from one of the tribes who lived in the Highlands area. "It's not as crazy as it sounds," he said. "Shortly before World War Two a wealthy man from Johore fell into the hands of such a woman and never returned. Once you fall into their hands and once they fall in love with you, they never let you go. Besides, some of the Sakai women are quite beautiful, and I think a man might be tempted to stay with them rather than strike out into the dangerous jungle to escape." If this dire fate had befallen the American, he said, the only real chance of release would be if the aborigine woman tired of him.

A Singapore-based reporter for the *San Francisco Chronicle* came up with another theory. "When the rewards for finding Thompson climbed to more than $10,000," he wrote, "I decided to vacation in the Highlands. Driving up the 35 miles of hairpin turns, I craned my neck looking for a 63-year-old (sic) hitch-hiker. All I saw was a woolly headed, wild-eyed, betel-nut-chewing Sakai hunting with a long blowgun. At once it hit me. Thompson was felled by a silent dart of death, blown by an aborigine hunter."

The aborigines figured in several of the theories being aired in Bangkok. In addition to their odd romantic tendencies and their blowguns, their alleged habit of digging and concealing pits for trapping animals was thought by some to offer a possible explanation. Suppose, it was suggested, Thompson had stumbled into one of these traps, the bottoms of which were sometimes studded with lethal spikes. On discovering that they had killed or seriously injured a white man, would it not be the most natural thing for the hunters to bury him quickly, eliminate all traces, and pretend total ignorance to the searchers, even to Richard Noone?

Nature itself was popular in other theories, as well as the nonhuman inhabitants of the jungle. Past visitors to the resort recalled the precipitous ravines of the area and the large number of caves in the mountainsides; could not an injured man fall into a ravine or creep into a cave and, for all intents and purposes, simply vanish? Was it really possible to search every ravine and cave in that wild territory? And what about the wildlife? Tales of tigers abounded, and while it was difficult to get precise information on the subject, nobody doubted that there could be tigers, and leopards, too, for that matter. There were also wild boars, which could be just as unpleasant to encounter along a narrow trail at sundown. If the attack had taken place some distance away from the bungalow, the animal could have dragged the body to a convenient lair—one of those caves, perhaps—that might not have been visible to the searchers.

The principal difficulty with the wild-animal explanation was the total absence of clues—bloodstains, bits of clothing, etc.—which such an attack might have been expected to leave behind, wherever the animal took its victim. One armchair detective in Bangkok came up with a theory that neatly solved that, however: Thompson, he said, had been swallowed by a python. It was a bit farfetched, since pythons do not ordinarily swallow grown men, but it was just as plausible as some of the others.

16

By the end of the summer, though the discussions went on over dinner tables in Bangkok and Singapore, the case had mostly died out of the newspapers, except an occasional rumor or prediction by a nightclub performer. Few of Thompson's friends and associates were ready to give up—the Thai Silk Company, while deciding to name Sheffield managing director, nonetheless voted to continue paying Thompson's salary into his bank account—and both the Malaysian and the Thai authorities were still actively pursuing every lead. But there was, all the same, a perceptible sense of hopelessness along with the frustration. The monk Keo's June date had come and gone (as his date for the Vietnam settlement would also come and go), with nothing heard. The kidnap leads had all ended negatively; if the Communists were really holding Thompson for some political purpose, they were taking their time about revealing what it was. The bomohs continued to make pronouncements and to haunt Moonlight Cottage (the Lings finally had to ask for police assistance to keep them from ruining the garden) but their visions were attracting less enthusiasm than in the early stages. Nothing had been discovered to prove a single aspect of the celebrated Hurkos impressions, nor had the McGowan investigations produced anything that could be described as evidence. At this point, the unhappy Thompson family received a second blow that returned them, and the case of their missing brother, to the front pages.

On the morning of August 30, a cleaning woman reported for duty at the isolated Pennsylvania home, about halfway between Philadelphia and Wilmington, of Mrs. Katherine Thompson Wood, Thompson's eldest sister. She let herself into the silent house, went to Mrs. Wood's bedroom on the ground floor, and came upon a horrifying sight. The seventy-four-year-old woman was dead; she had been savagely beaten to death with what the police later conventionally described as "a blunt instrument," while her two trained watchdogs, a German shepherd and a golden Labrador retriever, had apparently stood by without attacking the killer.

Mrs. Wood was a retiring, somewhat eccentric woman whose past life had not been altogether happy. In 1922, she had married Osborn Cutler Wood, the son of the well-known General Leonard Wood, who had been governor-general of the Philippines and, in 1920, an unsuccessful aspirant to the Republican presidential nomination won by Warren Harding. Osborn Wood made a large sum of money on the stock market in the early twenties, but the marriage was not a success; after three years and two sons, the couple were divorced. Since then Mrs. Wood had lived quietly but in some style. She was prominent in Philadelphia and Wilmington society, and her large and comfortable house was set in a fourteen-acre estate, a quarter of a mile from the nearest neighbor. She kept the two dogs and a gun in her bedroom at night, but she did not seem overly concerned about her safety since, according to friends, she often left the house doors unlocked at night.

Although Thompson had not been as close to Mrs. Wood as he was to Mrs. Douglas, the sister nearest to him in age, there was no sort of estrangement, and he nearly always came to see her when he made his annual late-summer visit to the States. It had, in fact, become something of a tradition for him to come to her house for Labor Day. Mrs. Wood had talked with her sister, Mrs. Douglas, only a few days before and had remarked how wonderful it would be if their brother turned up after all, though neither believed it would happen. Mrs. Wood had repeated part of the conversation to her maid, which may have been unfortunate, for after her murder the maid mentioned it to the police and the news stories, twisting the anecdote slightly, said that the dead woman had been expecting Thompson to appear—a misstatement that, like numerous others, quickly established itself as a fact.

The murder was front-page news, partly because Mrs. Wood was a socially prominent figure in her own right but mostly because of the still-fresh memories of Thompson's disappearance. Suggestions of a sinister connection were not long in coming, and the police, prodded by reporters, announced that they were considering the possibility of "an international plot." One of Mrs. Wood's sons (who would later commit suicide in the same house) was quoted as saying he thought the two mysteries might be related. And Peter Hurkos, who had remained quiet in California throughout the summer, saw the murder as tragic proof of his Highlands impressions and also as an opportunity to give them another public airing.

He did this through the medium of another *Life* article, which again ran exclusively in its Asian edition. The piece labored mightily to suggest a relationship between the murder and the disappearance— even going to far as to run side-by-side pictures of Mrs. Wood's house and Moonlight Cottage—and closed with a long interview with Hurkos, who clearly favored the international-plot angle. He also added a few details to his previous revelations about Thompson's disappearance and about his own activities in the Far East.

"I know for sure that Thompson was alive when I was there and is still alive," he was quoted as saying. "He is still where I marked the spot on the map. When I found out what country and town he was in, I wanted to take him out by force. I know the town, I know what it is like, I can speak Chinese and Malaysian perfectly. I wanted to do it with five Thai—not American—soldiers. I can get him out. But I was not allowed to go in after him. When I got back here I got a note from Bill Bundy, the Assistant Secretary of State. He said that he didn't want us to go into that other country, that we cannot use force against a country we are not at war with—it would be an act of aggression."

Hurkos did not explain, and the reporter did not question, how his fluent Malay would be useful in Cambodia, which of course was the country he was talking about. Nor did he elaborate on his generous offer to use Thai rather than American soldiers to free Thompson—an offer which, if made, must have seemed odd in view of the fact that Thailand had not then had diplomatic relations with Cambodia for more than eight years.

Hurkos' only other public mention of the case came in an interview he gave in February of 1968, in which he announced his intention to stop giving himself to scientific study ("I should spend all my life in a laboratory testing for this and that? It's loco.") and to form a nightclub act which would bring him $5000 a week in places like Miami Beach and Las Vegas. "Thompson," he told his interviewer, "is still alive. I would stake my neck on this."

17

The murder of Mrs. Wood caused a flurry of renewed speculation in Bangkok as well as in America, for followers of the case in the Thai capital found it just as difficult to believe that two such total mysteries in a single family could be simply a coincidence. And, as the months passed, it became clear that Mrs. Wood's death was going to be almost as clueless as Thompson's disappearance. The police in charge of the case interviewed a number of former employees of the dead woman and strangers who had been reported in the neighborhood on the fatal night, but their investigations, like those in the Highlands, seemed to lead nowhere. An inventory of the house confirmed the first report that nothing at all was stolen, which appeared to rule out robbery as a motive. Some of the newspaper accounts mentioned "a litter of papers" in her bedroom, implying that her killer might have been looking for a document, but this notion was scotched by family members; Mrs. Wood's desk, they said, always looked like that, and nothing on it had been disturbed.

Why had the dogs not attacked the intruder, as they were supposedly trained to do in such emergencies? Was it another example of the famous Sherlock Holmes story of the dog that didn't bark, and, if so, what familiar person didn't they bark at? Pointless (and unsolved) murders of prominent people are not exactly unknown in American life, but human nature resents coincidence in a mystery and many people were reluctant to put Mrs. Wood in that category; Hurkos was not the only bystander to insist there must be a connection. But if there were one, it has not yet been found.

Among the more fanciful suggestions of a relationship between the two cases at the time was that the murderer was searching for some documents concerning Thompson, which Mrs. Wood was supposedly safeguarding. This, of course, raised the question of what the document could have been, and the theorist had a ready answer: it was the second will Thompson had drawn concerning his Thai property, which was, unaccountably, missing.

The idea that anyone would murder Mrs. Wood to obtain this will—or even that Thompson would have given it to her—is patently absurd for a long list of reasons, but the question of the will's whereabouts remained one of the minor mysteries of the case for nearly two years and figured in a number of the theories. It had been written as a consequence of the unpleasant experience with the Fine Arts Department concerning the five limestone heads. At the time, it will be recalled, Thompson had revoked his original 1961 will in which he left his Thai property to the Siam Society; he wrote a letter to the Society informing them of his action and, at the same time, resigning from the Society's council. (This resignation was neither accepted nor rejected; it was simply ignored, and, in time, after the initial bitterness had passed, Thompson's interest in the Society's affairs returned to some extent, though he never again attended the meetings of the council.) Wills in Thailand are supposed to be deposited at the offices of one's amphur, the rough equivalent of a police district office in the U.S., and after revoking the first will, Thompson went to his amphur and retrieved the original signed and witnessed copy. He did not, however—perhaps because he had forgotten about it—retrieve a second copy which he had sent to the Siam Society at the time the will was drawn. He remained without a will for several years until, shortly before going on one of his regular trips to Europe and America, he decided to make one. He did not call a lawyer in but simply copied the wording of the first one, replacing the Siam Society with his nephew, Henry Thompson III, as sole beneficiary of his possessions in Thailand except for several small bequests to his servants; the property covered included his house and the land on which it stood, his collection of art, and his shares in the Thai Silk Company. The will was witnessed by Sheffield and two Thai employees of the silk company, and Thompson said he would drop it off at the amphur's office himself.

There the matter rested until after his disappearance. Sheffield assumed the second will was duly deposited, but did not discuss its contents with anyone since Thompson had expressed a desire to keep it confidential. (Thompson himself, however, did discuss it with several people, among them the English writer Ludovic Kennedy, who interviewed him in a connection with a book he was doing about people who lived in faraway places.) When it became apparent that Thompson was not going to be found quickly in Malaysia, the company's lawyer was sent to the amphur to get the will so that a temporary administrator could be named for the estate. It was not there, nor could it be found among any of Thompson's personal papers at his office or in his house. In the amphur's registration book where documents are recorded as they come in and go out, there was no record of its ever having been received, though there was a record that the first will had been taken out at the time it was revoked.

There was, at the time, much speculation about the whereabouts of the second will. Did Thompson simply forget to take it over to the amphur, as he had a habit of doing with such administrative matters? Or did he, as some people thought, have a change of mind and destroy it, intending at some future date to write a third will?

There seemed to be no answers to any of these questions, and the absence of the will raised a delicate legal question which, during the second year, was to arouse a certain amount of controversy. The immediate question was not so much who was going to get the property eventually as who was going to administer it for the seven-year period that both Thai and American law required before Thompson could be legally declared dead. Certain persons at the Siam Society felt that their copy of the first will entitled them to the administratorship and, in time, the property, since the second will could not be found. (The Society, incidentally, was the only group who could conceivably benefit from the continued absence of the second will, and while some found their actions unseemly, it would require a considerable effort of the imagination to accuse the highly respectable members of that august organization of beating an old lady to death to get a document that she almost certainly neither had nor knew about.) Thompson's lawyer was of the view that since the second will had been duly witnessed and since the witnesses were willing to testify to its contents, it was in fact a valid document. A legal dispute between the family and the Society thus loomed as a distinct possibility.

For the first year after the disappearance, Thompson's older brother, the father of the nephew named in the second will, was named temporary administrator. A more permanent administrator would be appointed when the year was up, and that was when the legal questions of the matter would be considered.

As far as Thompson's family was concerned, the prospects of a court fight over the estate were anything but attractive. There were Thompson's wishes to be considered, of course, and he had made it decidedly plain, in conversation and in writing, that he did not want the Society to have the property. Certainly this was the way he had felt during and immediately after the affair of the limestone heads, and if he had had a change of heart later, he had kept it secret and never, apparently, made it legal. There was, however, another side to the issue. No one ever really tried to evaluate Thompson's art collection in terms of the prices it would bring in such centers as New York and London, for the simple reason that any figure arrived at would be wholly unrealistic: the pieces that would bring the highest prices—and some would bring very high prices indeed on today's inflated market for Asian antiquities—would not be allowed out of Thailand, and hence could never be put up for sale unless they were smuggled out. Even then, they would be quickly recognized since they had been widely photographed, and their appearance outside the country would cause a scandal. Thompson's family never had any idea of selling the collection, though; both Mrs. Douglas and Henry Thompson made it clear, when they came to Bangkok in May after the disappearance, that they firmly intended to keep the property intact and in Thailand, as they believed their brother wanted done. Yet if they—Americans and non-residents of Thailand—found themselves embroiled in a dispute with a non-profit Thai organization, it could possibly generate some ugly misunderstandings and misrepresentations in the Thai press. Thompson had countless Thai friends, both high and low; he had also, like most men, made some enemies, both socially and in business, some of whom were not above using such an issue as a means of damaging his reputation. It was not an appealing thought, yet as 1967 drew to a close, it was one that had to be faced.

There was one other noteworthy development in the case before the end of that year. A niece of Thompson's by marriage, Mrs. Earl Galleher, who lived in Baltimore, had become intrigued at the frequent mention of Cambodia in the various political theories—Hurkos, the monk Keo, and McGowan had all named it as the place where the missing man was being held—and, on an impulse, she decided to write to the Cambodian premier, Prince Noradom Sihanouk, and ask for his assistance in the matter. She did so, and after some time received an answer, in French, from Sihanouk himself, which he also had published in a French-language newspaper in Pnom Penh. He said he could not imagine why anyone thought that Thompson would be in Cambodia but that he would investigate and see what he could find out. Later he wrote a second letter in which he said that his inquiries had uncovered nothing and that he was convinced the missing man was not in Cambodia.

No one was happier to see 1967 end than the various boosters and officials of the Cameron Highlands, upon whose heads the Thompson case had dropped an avalanche of decidedly unattractive publicity. They had remained loud in their assurances that hiking in the resort presented no unusual perils and had, quite naturally, eagerly espoused the suggestion that the American had been the victim of a foreign plot. They were just beginning to breathe easily again when, in the first month of the new year, they found themselves with yet another disappearance on their hands.

A pretty young American schoolteacher named Jean Laing, who taught at the Dalat missionary school that had been moved from Vietnam to the Highlands, vanished along with three of her students while on a hike in the jungle. After three days and four nights of frantic searching—and, inevitably, public musings as to a possible connection between the two disappearances—a group of aborigines came upon the terrified group only three and a half miles from the main house of a large tea plantation. Miss Laing and her three charges were understandably shaken after their nightmare experience but were otherwise in surprisingly good condition. Questioned by a reporter, she did not really think Thompson's disappearance could be compared to her own. "If he'd been an ordinary person like us," she said, "I'd say he was lost. But a millionaire..."

To Miss Laing, as to so many others, millionaires were a very special class. They did not get lost in the jungle.

18

At one point during the hectic months just after the disappearance, a friend and associate of Thompson's in Bangkok wondered, rather wistfully, whether the extraordinary interest in the case would still be keen if Thompson remained unfound for an entire year. Would the newspapers still be looking for fresh angles? Would the soothsayers still be consulting the occult and coming up with startling discoveries? Would the theorists still be taxing their imaginations about what took place that afternoon twelve months past? The first anniversary arrived, and with it his answer.

The *Bangkok Post* dispatched an enterprising reporter named Amy Stone to the Cameron Highlands to do an anniversary roundup. Miss Stone interviewed a number of people at the resort, went down and talked with the police at Ipoh, and found that "the myth of Jim Thompson is still as vigorous as ever." She saw Mohammed, the Lings' servant at Moonlight Cottage, who told her he did not think Thompson had simply gotten lost; of what did happen, though, he could offer no suggestion. She also saw a European friend of the Lings who had lived at the Highlands for many years and who firmly scotched the notion that Thompson had disappeared voluntarily. "Jimmy Thompson wouldn't do such a thing," she said. "I saw him at church the morning he disappeared and he can't be such a cad as to disappear and cause the Lings all that worry. Of course, all that anyone knows is pure, pure hearsay."

In Ipoh, Miss Stone called on Santokh Singh but found him less willing to venture opinions. "I'm a professional policeman," he told her, "not a telepathist." He added that he felt everything possible had been done and that the case was still considered very much open.

The indefatigable McGowan turned up again, this time in Hong Kong, with an anniversary message on the subject; it was imparted, as usual, to a reporter. Thompson, he said, was being held by a left- wing group on the Thai-Cambodian border; the group was trying to arrange a meeting between the American and "a former Thai Prime Minister" in Europe, probably in Switzerland.

McGowan did not have the Hong Kong scene entirely to himself. A local English language paper, the *China Mail*, with a greater fondness for sensation than for hard news, displayed a doublepage spread under the headline WHAT'S HAPPENED TO THOMPSON? According to the anonymous author, "the man they called Lord Jim" was in fact "a leading operative with the CIA" and may well have been the chief of "the CIA's network of agents in Southeast Asia." Other than this rather startling disclosure, the piece consisted largely of a rehash of previous articles in other publications and never made any effort to answer its headlined question. It concluded on an ominous note: "But observers say that they have been told—off the record—that the file is not closed, that the man they call Lord Jim, the man with a nation's secrets in his head, will be hunted, if necessary, to the ends of the earth."

In America, reporters interviewed Mrs. Douglas, who told them that the family had no desire to remove Thompson's art collection from Thailand but would like to see it established and administered as a foundation. She also said that her hopes of seeing her brother again had suffered a decline. "I have felt until very recently that he is still alive. But after a year now I have begun to doubt that. He was either kidnapped or met with foul play."

Nor had the Asian mystics given up on the case despite the passage of time. In June of 1968, the Bangkok newspapers reported the arrival of an Indian expert in astrology, palmistry, and yoga, who said he was working on the case and who, before he finally left Thailand, managed to generate a good deal of excitement if not much enlightenment.

His name was Dadi Balsara, and he was an intense, rapid-speaking man with a neatly-clipped beard and a beguilingly direct manner, which was somewhat misleading since he had a habit of telling different stories to different people and of casually dropping possibly slanderous remarks about certain people who had figured in the case. He claimed to work for the ministry of finance in India and to be president of an organization called the Institute for the Advancement of Indian Sciences, which, he said, specialized in astrology, palmistry, numerology, and mysticism, and sought to give these arts a proper scientific standing. According to Balsara, the members of the institute were wary of such designations as "palmist" and "astrologer," with their connotations of tearoom gypsies and nightclub performers, and preferred the term "destiny scientist," which he defined for a reporter as "a man who deals in the science of human destiny."

Balsara's particular interest among the institute's sciences was what he called "medical palmistry," by means of which, he said, a number of diseases like cancer, kidney trouble, heart ailments, and high blood pressure could be diagnosed in advance of conventional symptoms by a proper reading of the lifeline on a man's palm. He felt strongly that doctors should be trained to use palm impressions as part of their routine diagnostic techniques. It was astrology, however, rather than palmistry that led him into the Thompson case. He said he had first become interested in the mystery when news of it appeared in the Indian papers, several days after the disappearance, and he decided to draw an astrological "birth chart" on Thompson, based on various bits of personal information about the missing man he had read in the press. Such a chart, which with some variations is more or less standard among astrologers all over the world, tearoom and otherwise, is divided into twelve sections or "halls," each containing different kinds of data, sometimes in surprising combinations. Section five, for example, not only provides information about wisdom (as distinct from intellect, which is in another "hall") but also about children and sexual problems.

The nature of the information concerning these qualities is determined, of course, by the various groupings of the stars, which astrologers, or "destiny scientists," are supposedly trained to decipher.

It was the eighth section that attracted most of Balsara's interest on the chart he prepared for Thompson, for here lay what the stars had to say about death and disappearance, among other things. First of all, he found that Thompson could not die before he was eighty, which was obviously newsworthy since it meant he was still alive wherever he was. Balsara also found that Thompson had not disappeared voluntarily but had been abducted and that, further, the abduction had been prompted by personal rather than political reasons.

Other things he saw in the chart were puzzling, he said, and one of these was Thompson's reported age, which according to the newspapers (and his birth certificate) was sixty-one. Thompson simply could not have been sixty-one, Balsara insisted, and have arrived at the position he had in life: the stars proclaimed that he could not have risen above a fairly low position. His true age, according to the chart, was in the seventies, though there was an unlikely possibility he could be in his forties. When asked about birth records and the like, Balsara easily shrugged off the question. "Such things," he remarked to an interviewer, "can be forged."

The Indian said he had brooded over his astrological revelations for more than a year, building up a collection of newspaper clippings about the case and reading the disappointing pronouncements of the other experts who had been called in. (Hurkos, he said, was "a fraud"; the institute did not think much of ESP and other fancy Western innovations.) Then he was invited to come to Singapore to give some lectures on yoga to several groups like the Rotarians and the Lions. He liked to speak on his subjects to such people, he said, because in that way he could reach the "intellectuals" of the community and thus raise the general level of understanding. In the course of one of his speeches he happened to mention some of his findings about Thompson, and these were duly reported in the local papers, which continued to print just about everything anybody had to say about the case.

Now from this point on, Balsara's story tended to be occasionally vague and not always consistent, but apparently one of the readers of the stories about him was Mrs. Wong, the lady in Singapore with the wide circle of unusual friends who had tried to interest the Thai Silk Company and Richard Noone in her findings—or, at any rate, her beliefs—a year before. She had not abandoned her efforts, despite the lack of enthusiasm they had inspired, and she still kept a bulky file on the case. (She had marked one folder "Bastard Sheffield," Balsara later cheerfully told Sheffield, to indicate her displeasure with the new managing director for failing to be as cooperative as she had wished.) Naturally enough, she was interested in what Balsara had to say on the subject so close to her heart and she invited him to call on her. He did, and as a result had what must have been a remarkable experience.

In Bangkok a week or so later, Balsara was to tell several versions of this visit to at least five different people, including a journalist who had no real connection with the case at all, cautioning each of them to keep it confidential. Needless to say, they did not and the inconsistencies were very soon revealed. The general outline was pretty much the same in all the tellings, however, and even with certain features censored in deference to the libel laws—of which Balsara seemed blissfully unaware—it was a tale that deserves an honored place in the Thompson folklore, certainly as much so as the more publicized Hurkos story.

According to Balsara, Mrs. Wong—whom he also referred to at various times as "Madame X" and as "a certain millionairess"—took him to see a prostitute who had information about Thompson. This lady was described sometimes as being Chinese and sometimes as Norwegian (a nationality for which Mrs. Wong seems to have had a weakness), but in either case she produced some photographs purportedly showing her and Thompson together; in one, Balsara said, they were with a European who looked Scandinavian. Mrs. Wong had said the woman would not show the pictures for nothing, and after some haggling fifty Malaysian dollars was agreed on as a fair viewing price. The woman said the pictures had been taken in 1959 or 1960 and that she and Thompson had been lovers. Balsara said he asked her if he could have the pictures but she refused "with tears in her eyes," saying that though she loved Thompson and wanted to help him, she also valued her life. She then told a strange story.

On March 27 of the previous year, she said (or at least Balsara said she said), which of course was the day after Thompson disappeared, four men appeared at her place. They were known to her as customers, and, to her great surprise and horror, who should they have with them but her old lover, in a drugged and almost unconscious state. They did not know of her acquaintance and naturally she was careful to avoid any sign of recognition since she had read about the disappearance only that morning and, being a perceptive woman, knew something odd was going on. The men wanted her to keep Thompson for a few hours while they made some arrangements; they would return later to get him. She could do nothing but agree, and did her best to make him comfortable while she waited. It was a scene right out of an early Hitchcock movie, without, however, the last-minute happy ending, for no friends or police came to the rescue, nor did the prostitute figure out a way to outwit the kidnappers. Instead, the men came back and took Thompson away. The woman had, however, been doing some fast thinking while they were away on their sinister business, and as soon as they left the second time she called a taxi-driver friend, who sometimes assisted her in her work, and asked him to trail them and report where they went. The friend did so, and said they had gone to the Changi area of Singapore (the site of the notorious World War II prison camp and now of the international airport), where they had put the drugged man in a boat bound for an offshore island. He had been taken away from there, the woman said she later learned, to one of the several hundred Indonesian islands.

To some, but not all, of the people he told this story to in Bangkok, Balsara said the woman had kept Thompson's clothes and showed them to him; from the newspaper accounts, he said, he recognized them as the ones the missing man had been wearing that afternoon in the Highlands. To at least one listener, he added another detail: he claimed he had gone to the Changi area where the men supposedly put Thompson in the boat and had actually succeeded in finding a coolie who had assisted in loading the drugged man. The coolie had not known what he was doing, or who Thompson was, but Balsara said he readily picked the American out in a group photograph; apparently, putting drugged foreigners in boats was a common occurrence in Changi.

After exposing Balsara to these interesting experiences, Mrs. Wong, who had clearly revised her thinking on the matter of compensation, suggested that he go to Bangkok and see what interest he could arouse. If he were successful they would split the reward fifty-fifty. But before he left Singapore, though, Balsara said he got a telephone call at the Raffles Hotel from a Eurasian who asked if he were interested in the Thompson case. When he replied in the affirmative, the voice said, "Don't be interested, if you want to leave here in one piece." The supply of threatening Eurasian voices in Singapore seems to have been inexhaustible, and their message was always the same.

In Bangkok, Balsara's knowledge of yoga got him several speaking engagements, his publicity got him several lucrative "readings" of the palms of local believers, and his provocative tale of Thompson's abduction got him an introduction to most of the people close to the case, such as Sheffield, Frasche, General Black, and Mrs. Mangskau. With Sheffield he paid a visit to Thompson's house, where he meditated on the problem by lying for a long time on the missing man's bed; whatever he discovered there, he kept to himself. In the end, however, his visit was unproductive. Partly this was because of his admitted association with Mrs. Wong, whose admirers in Thailand were few; partly it was because of certain highly questionable accusations he made without the slightest evidence to support them; and finally, there were the numerous inconsistencies in his stories, which also lacked evidence. When, after several days of protesting purely altruistic motive, he finally got around to asking for some expense money, it was refused, and he flew off to India and silence.

About the time that Balsara was spinning his tale in Thailand, a member of the Malaysian parliament raised the question of Thompson's disappearance in Kuala Lumpur. Mr. Hadj Mokhtar bin Haji Ismail asked to be enlightened on the results of the government's investigations and, in particular, whether the home affairs minister could tell him whether the American had been kidnapped either by an international syndicate or aborigines, killed by wild animals, or lost in the ravines. Predictably enough, the home affairs secretary replied that he could tell him nothing; despite extensive and continuing investigation by the police, no evidence had been discovered to confirm any of the rumors mentioned, or an additional one suggested by another parliamentarian that Thompson might have been working for the Communists.

19

In the late summer of 1968, the legal future of Thompson's house and collection was finally settled, though not before some of the unpleasantness that the family had feared when the problem of the missing will was first raised. This came from two sources. One, apparently was the Fine Arts Department, and may or may not actually have had anything to do with the art collection. It came during the summer and took the form of several articles in some of the Thai newspapers and magazines, in which the director general of the department was quoted as saying that Thompson had been one of the leaders of a group that was systematically looting ancient Thai temples upcountry. Other Thai papers did not report the alleged accusations, nor did Bangkok's English-language press, but a number of reporters from European and American newspapers got wind of them and wrote stories suggesting that perhaps the government was contemplating an effort to claim the whole collection. There is no evidence that this was true; if it were, the effort was apparently abandoned, for nothing further was ever done.

The other source of difficulty was the Siam Society. Several members of the council decided to contest the application for the administratorship which had been filed by Thompson's nephew, using as a justification the fact that the second will had not been found and that the Society was in possession of a copy of the first one. Other members strongly opposed the filing of a counterclaim, but they were overruled and the claim was duly filed. The Thai court, confronted with two conflicting claims on the property, instructed the two sides to try to reach an agreement, and to the considerable relief of nearly everyone this was done on a visit Henry Thompson III made to Bangkok in early September. According to the agreement, the property would be jointly administered by the Society and representatives of the Thompson family, through a committee, for the period until Thompson could be declared legally dead, after which a foundation would be formed to maintain the house and collection as a permanent memorial.

After the agreement had been reached, the president of the Society called a meeting of members to explain it to them. The president, a high-ranking Thai prince, had been a friend of Thompson's, and he was clearly upset by the rather formal wording of the agreement, which gave it a tone of funereal formality. In an effort to lighten the atmosphere of the gathering, he said that he was sure the members joined him in hoping that the whole thing would turn out to be entirely unnecessary. Thompson, he reminded them, was by no means officially dead yet, and there was still ample reason to hope that he would "come walking in again through that door." Almost to a man, the membership turned to look at the door he had indicated, and they seemed disappointed at finding it empty.

20

In 1970, three years had passed since that Easter afternoon. Thirty-six months of professional and amateur investigation, of extrasensory perception and spiritual consultations, of highly imaginative theories and common-sense logic, of large reward offers and extraordinary publicity, had yielded, in sum, not a fragment more of positive knowledge about what happened in the Cameron Highlands than what was known the evening of the first day. All the things known were entirely negative, things that did not happen, and there were precious few even of those.

The investigating authorities in Malaysia never came out publicly on the side of any of the theories, but according to reliable sources they did have one, and perhaps still do, which they arrived at by a process of elimination. The theory went something like this: (1) If Thompson had been killed or injured or had gotten lost in the area where he was supposedly walking, he would have been found during the search or subsequently by the aborigines; he was not found, nor was any trace of him, hence he was not killed, injured, or lost in the area. (2) If he had been kidnapped by an ordinary gang for ransom purposes, some attempt at collection would have been made; no such attempt had been made, hence his kidnappers were not of the ordinary variety. (3) To have pulled off such an abduction would have required perfect timing and superb organization, and therefore the group behind it must have been extraordinarily well-trained and disciplined. (4) The only group that met these requirements of discipline, organization, and obvious lack of interest in money was the Communists.

Many Thais also thought that the Communists were responsible for Thompson's disappearance, and a number of them said—off the record, of course—that there must have been some cooperation on his part. The most common rumor in Bangkok was that he was in Canton, the supposed residence of former Prime Minister Pridi Phanomyong, and the obvious implication was that Thompson's business in that city had something to do with the aging political figure. What it had to do with Pridi was unmentioned.

It took close to twenty years for Thompson's first legend, as the king of Thai silk and the prototype of the Good American Businessman in Asia, to become firmly established. It required less than three for his second, as a mysterious figure who may have been a spy and may not, who may have been kidnapped and may not, who may still be alive somewhere and then again may not. Legends are notorious for obscuring the truth, as Thompson's second legend, now past its thirtieth anniversary, has provided ample evidence.

Since so many of the theories concerning Thompson's disappearance seemed to have been prompted by popular fiction, it was only fitting that in mid-1968 there appeared a French thriller which had been inspired by the case. It was called *S.A.S. Gold of the River Kwai*, a title that might, to the uninitiated, suggest a guidebook published by the Scandinavian Airlines System. In fact, it was one of a James Bond-type series by a writer named Gerard de Villers dealing with the improbable adventures of one S.A.S. Malko, a golden-eyed prince (he wears dark glasses to avoid recognition) who works occasionally for the CIA to get money for repairs on his castle in Austria. Whoever de Villers was, he had plainly been to Thailand or had friends who knew about the place, and he also knew a good deal about the Thompson affair. In the book, Thompson becomes a silk merchant named Jim Stanford, who has disappeared on a trip to the River Kwai (thus hooking up with another popular legend). There are other familiar figures, too, such as a sister of Stanford's who has been mysteriously murdered and a certain Colonel White, who is the head of the CIA in Thailand. Stanford lives in a Thai-style house, and the telephone number of his silk company is the same as that of the Thai Silk Company in Bangkok. The plot is splendidly preposterous in the true Fleming style, with beautiful girls who turn out to be double agents, Chinese mistresses, and chases through Buddhist temples. At the climax, Stanford, who has been hiding out, is killed in the war cemetery at the River Kwai, and as he expires asks to be buried in one of the numerous graves there so that no one will ever find his body. So far, the book has not been translated into either English or Thai. If it ever is, it will have a guaranteed audience in Bangkok, and possibly the war cemetery may have to hire extra guards should local readers take it too literally.

One mystery that was finally solved, quite by chance, was that of the missing will. A sizeable number of people had applied their talents to trying to find it in the months just after the disappearance and, as in the search for Thompson himself, the search for the will progressed from the logical to the fanciful, from the probable to the remotely possible.

His personal papers at the silk company and at the house had, of course, been carefully gone through, and when these yielded nothing, more imaginative efforts were mounted. One friend leafed through every book in the library, on the chance he might have stuffed the missing document inside one of them; another looked inside all the covered bowls in the extensive Bencharong collection. Why Thompson should have put the will in either of these places, or, indeed, why he should have hidden it at all, remained unanswered questions. It was suggested, by more than one person, that he had quietly destroyed the will, intending to make another when he could find a suitable heir to oversee the property in Thailand and keep it intact as he obviously wished. The most imaginative suggestion of all was that the murder of Mrs. Wood was somehow connected with the missing will, though just how apparently strained even the inventive powers of the theorist.

Then in March, 1969, just two weeks short of the second anniversary of the disappearance, Charles Sheffield had occasion to take out the plans of Thompson's Thai house because of a minor repair job being considered. As he opened the folded blueprints, which had been in the company safe all along, a single sheet of paper fell out. It was the will, duly signed by Thompson, witnessed by Sheffield and two other employees, leaving the Thai estate to his brother's eldest son. The plans had been shuffled through during the search, but no one, apparently, had thought to look inside them. It was, however, as one associate remarked, a logical enough place for Thompson to put the will for temporary safekeeping and then, characteristically, to forget about it. The finding of the will did not change the family's plans for the future of the house and collection, but it did give them the legal security that had been lacking before.

Three years later, his house was much as it was the day he had left it except for one change that Thompson would have immediately noticed and regretted had he come back. One night toward the end of 1968, his favorite of his dogs, an elderly bitch of mixed ancestry, disappeared. Everyone who lived along the narrow street leading to the compound knew her since she had been there as long as the house, but none had seen her on the fatal night. She simply vanished.

Part Four: Postscript on the Evidence

"O ne thing this town doesn't need," a Bangkok resident said several years after the disappearance, "is another theory on the Thompson case." Though the implied hope is probably futile, given the irresistible temptations of an almost total mystery, there can certainly be little argument that the theorists have already worked overtime on the case, often with only scant regard for common sense, and they have doubtless come up with the right solution somewhere along the line. Unless one has the visionary self-assurance of a Malaysian bomoh or a Peter Hurkos, however, there can be nothing approaching a firm decision on which it might be.

Discounting angry spirits and celestial destiny as being outside the realm of objective inquiry, the four explanations that have been offered most frequently are these: (1) that Thompson was kidnapped for ransom by one of the gangs known to operate in Malaysia, (2) that he committed suicide for one of a variety of alleged personal reasons and did so in such a way that his body could not be found, (3) that he was kidnapped, or went off voluntarily for some political purpose, and (4) that he had some sort of accident in the jungle—several kinds have been suggested—and that his remains are still there. These four general theories, which are, of course, subject to numerous variations, have the advantage of taking in almost every remotely plausible possibility. They all share the considerable disadvantage of being unsupported by the smallest shred of evidence, even circumstantial, which might make one substantially more attractive than others. They also share another disadvantage: even viewed hypothetically, each has a number of weaknesses which can be exploited to effect by its nonadherents. Some of these weaknesses are so obvious that they have been widely perceived; several, rather surprisingly, seem to have been overlooked, despite all the time spent on them; and a few, possibly, are not as great as they have been made to appear. It may be instructive to examine the four theories more closely, in the light of over thirty years' experience and, as far as possible, through known facts.

The Malaysian authorities in charge of investigating the case, as already noted, more or less discarded the kidnap-for-ransom theory, mostly for the simple, and logical, reason that no one with any kind of valid evidence ever came forward to try to collect the reward despite an offer of immunity from prosecution. For all their occasional successes, kidnap gangs are generally not made up of the criminally elite, and if one took Thompson at the Highlands it must have been a fairly large one—probably with connections in Thailand—composed of a variety of types. Given the exceptionally large reward offer (which remained in effect for ten years), it is almost inconceivable that at least one member of the gang would not have found the lure too tempting to resist. Somebody, somewhere, the police felt, would have said something over the years, and one small crack is all it would take to break the wall of silence. Just possibly, the leads that took Sheffield to Malaysia and others on similar missions to southern Thailand may have been the result of such talking, but this is considered extremely doubtful for the ends they came to were too absolutely dead; if one of them had been a lead, it would have been followed by another.

This same argument would apply to two variations of the ransom-kidnap theory that have been suggested: one, that the gang decided to eliminate Thompson when they saw the racket they had stirred up, and another, rather more ingenious one that the intended victim was not, in fact, Thompson at all but his host, Dr. Ling. This mistaken-identity variation is interesting because there was a certain resemblance between the two men, especially from behind and at some distance, and it is at least conceivable that a hired gang might make the error. It would also answer the nagging question of how a Malaysian kidnap gang would pick Thompson up when his presence at the Highlands that weekend was not exactly a matter of public knowledge. Dr. Ling could have been a target for one of the Singapore gangs that specialized in wealthy Chinese, and it would have been a simple matter for them to find out that he was going to the Highlands for Easter. Yet again, even if they had disposed of Thompson once the mistake was discovered, it is improbable that everyone involved would have kept quiet. Inevitably, there would be degrees of guilt in such a crime, and one of those with less to lose would find it hard not to make a try for the reward money.

Silence, then, is the outstanding weakness of the kidnap-for-ransom theory, plus the known characteristics of local kidnap gangs, and with the passage of time the weakness has increased: people who are willing to abduct a man for money do not suddenly lose their greed because they happen to have killed him.

Al Koran, the English mind reader who made a brief appearance in the case during the first week, was the first theorist who brought up the question of suicide. Dr. Ammundsen had quickly and firmly scotched the notion and so had the Lings and Mrs. Mangskau. After that, the possibility was not aired very widely, yet there still persists a small group, some of them knowledgeable, that maintains that the theory is not as farfetched as it may first appear. One of this group, who did not present it necessarily as his theory but as worthy of serious consideration, was a man who knew Thompson well and who was a frequent guest in his house in the year or so before the disappearance. In summary, the argument this man presented to support the theory was as follows:

Thompson's life had become too much of a routine for him, and he was a man who detested routine. The development of the silk industry was an accomplished fact; even the printed silks, which he had welcomed as a diversion and a new challenge, were becoming less a creative than a production job, capable of being continued without his presence. The business side of the company had always bored him and now, with success, it was mostly business, and highly complex business at that. His "mission" in Thailand was thus complete; at sixty-one, he was unlikely to live to see the completion of another one. Nor, since the episode of the five heads, were his house and collection quite the source of joy they had once been. A similar disaster might befall him at any time, the property was no longer going to remain intact as a legacy to the country, there was no assurance now as to what would happen to it. Added to these unpleasant realities was the recurrent evidence of his diminishing vitality. He had had numerous bouts with pneumonia and other pulmonary disorders in recent years, and his bathroom shelf was laden with an assortment of pills for such ailments as amoebic dysentery and gallstones; even when he traveled he was forced to take along his "jungle box" to save him from the crippling pain of a gallstone attack. For a man who was uncommonly proud of his stamina and hated being ill, these signs, however common in men of his age, must have been depressing in the extreme, and to several people in Bangkok he had remarked that he would prefer a quick and painless death to a long old age of ill health. All these factors, according to the theory, had combined and perhaps been sharpened by physical exhaustion to create an acute depression that led him, perhaps on a sudden impulse that Sunday afternoon, to go into the jungle and destroy himself.

Against such an hypothesis must be placed the Lings' and Mrs. Mangskau's impressions of the last three days before the disappearance, when, as far as they could tell—and they were old and perceptive friends—he seemed normal and in good spirits. His letters to his family in recent months had indicated no great, or even slight, depression, nor did his friends and associates notice any very alarming signs in the weeks before he left. Thompson was never particularly noted for concealing his feelings—indeed, he had a reputation for expressing them rather freely and openly, even when they concerned quite personal matters—and his closest friends felt almost certain that they would have observed something out of the ordinary. According to Dr. Ammundsen, Thompson's health, while not perfect, was not unusually bad; he was still extraordinarily active, and the gallstone attacks could be stopped by a relatively simple operation which he had agreed to have soon after his return. The doctor knew Thompson well as a friend and as a patient, and he gave no credence to the idea of suicide, impulsive or otherwise; after thirty years, he still feels the same way. Finally, there is the quiet, but compelling statement of a member of his family: "If he were going to commit suicide, he would never have done it in a way that would cause so much inconvenience to others. He wasn't that kind of man."

If silence is the weakness of the ransom-kidnap theory, it is, in the opinion of many, the strongest point in favor of the idea that Thompson was abducted for political reasons. Among ordinary criminals the financial motive is paramount; among revolutionaries, as everyone knows—or at least believes—it is secondary, if it exists at all. The Malaysians, as we have seen, reportedly believed that Communist agents were behind the disappearance and so, probably, do most Thai today. So do a sizeable number of Thompson's farang friends, including some of the most knowledgeable; not long before his own death, in the mid-eighties, General Black told the journalist Robert Sam Anson of his feelings that the CIA was holding something back. So widespread is this belief that it is very seldom questioned any longer and almost never examined for the sort of weaknesses that are discovered in all the other suggested possibilities.

The general theory—of which there are enough variations to keep a writer of thrillers supplied with plot material for years—maintains that it was a very carefully planned operation, perhaps with Thompson's connivance, perhaps not, but in any case an extremely well-organized undertaking that very likely required days, probably weeks, of preparation. On exactly why Thompson should be kidnapped or choose to disappear for political reasons, the theories for the most part tend to be somewhat vague but there is fairly common agreement that it was in some way connected with his activities in Thailand: his work as an OSS agent or as a possible CIA operative, his alleged friendship with and admiration for former Prime Minister Pridi, his association with dissident nationalists from Vietnam and Laos who gathered in Bangkok in the late forties. The disappearance was arranged either because Thompson was still an agent, or because some of his old friends felt he could be of use to them in their present work, or because he had become politically dangerous in some way and had to be eliminated, or because he thought, for reasons of his own, that he could help in some project of personal significance.

Despite the tenacity, not to say passion, with which the political theory is held by numerous intelligent, well-meaning people, including some members of Thompson's own family and many of his close friends, a close inspection of it reveals a surprising variety of serious shortcomings. The most glaring one, which, oddly, is rarely questioned, is why either he or his abductors should have chosen the Cameron Highlands vacation for his disappearance.

Moonlight Cottage is at the top of a hill, at the end of a dead-end road. The Lings' bedroom window overlooked the road and, had they been about that Sunday afternoon, the servants, too, could have seen it. It was simple luck, or bad luck, that no other servants, from Starlight Cottage say, or random walkers happened to be on the road below the house or down where it came to the golf links. Peter Hurkos suggested that one of the Lings' servants may have been an accomplice, yet exhaustive investigations by the police convinced them that this was not true, nor has any such link been discovered since. Yet one is asked by the political theorists to believe that a well-organized group chose this particular site, with all its hazards, for an abduction that could have been made with almost no risk at all in Bangkok or even, the following day, in Singapore with its crowds of people and its plentiful opportunities for escape by sea. Thompson's routine in Bangkok was well-known and a would-be abductor could easily have picked a time when interference would be a minimal danger. In the Highlands, he was alone exactly twice during his stay except when he was sleeping and, assuming he did not go with his kidnappers voluntarily, both times were the result of more or less impulsive decisions and the possibilities of failure were practically endless. Suppose he had decided not to take a walk? Suppose the Lings and Mrs. Mangskau had decided not to take a nap? Suppose the Lings had looked out their window? Suppose someone had been walking up the hill? It is asking a lot to imagine that the skilled and dedicated gang envisioned by the authorities would deliberately invite so many risks if their motive was simply to kidnap

Thompson or even to eliminate him; there are too many relatively safe ways to dispose of a person in Asia.

The only thing that makes the choice even remotely plausible is the wildness of the Highlands jungle at that time and its obvious dangers: if he could be made to disappear there, people would think he simply had an accident of some sort and would not suspect that political motives lay behind it. If this were the case then his abductors were not only daring but sadly mistaken, for some of the searchers seized on politics within a couple of days.

It has been suggested, especially in Bangkok, that Thompson cooperated in his disappearance, that, in fact, it had all been planned with his assistance and possibly at his instigation, and that he went to the Highlands expressly for that purpose. But the same risks as above would still apply, for how could he be sure he would be left absolutely alone, that the road would be clear, and so on?

Would it not have been infinitely simpler just to vanish from his hotel room in Singapore the following day, or from Penang two days earlier?

Some people have found what they took to be evidence of his complicity in his apparent desire to wind up the Easter picnic and get back to the cottage, and in his failure to take a nap like the others although he had indicated he was going to. Did not this suggest he was trying to make some appointment? Not really, according to friends who were familiar with Thompson's personal habits and tastes in walking. He preferred walking alone, or at least with a companion who could keep up with his rapid pace and was willing to undergo a little hardship in the interests of exploration. Despite his affection for the Lings and Mrs. Mangskau, none of them was really his kind of walker; the ladies, indeed, were not walkers at all, and Dr. Ling, apart from the fact that he was in his seventies, had injured his leg the day before and would not be game for the sort of rough terrain Thompson especially enjoyed. His eagerness to get back to the bungalow that afternoon could, therefore, be ascribed to nothing more than a simple, but quite characteristic, desire to take advantage of his last opportunity go off by himself for a solitary ramble, something he had done on both his previous visits to the Highlands.

Nor did his friends see anything very significant in the fact that he had left both cigarettes and pillbox behind, though this is still regularly cited as suspicious. He was trying to cut back on his smoking and the pills he regarded as a sign of weakness that he preferred to ignore.

Another, far more persuasive argument against Thompson's planning his own disappearance is the haphazard manner in which he approached the Malaysian trip. Would a man involved in such a complex scheme, which would have to be plotted weeks ahead, neglect such elementary travel requirements of the time as a cholera shot and his Thai tax clearance and thereby endanger the whole enterprise? As a matter of fact, of course, he had not even planned the trip himself; it had been suggested by Mrs. Mangskau after she heard from the Lings and he had agreed because he had to go to Singapore anyway to meet Edward Pollitz.

The weakest point in all the theories of abduction for political reasons comes with the inevitable question of why. This is where nearly all of them become markedly vague and farfetched, and even Peter Hurkos, the man who might be said to have given the political theory its greatest boost, did not attempt to say why in his first appearance in the case; it was not until the murder of Mrs. Wood that he began to see a design but even then it was a rather sketchy one. He suggested that the Communists were trying to make Thompson "talk"; but talk about what? This vagueness is not surprising when one looks closely at some of the attempts that have been made.

For example, there is the regularly heard allegation that Thompson was a CIA agent who was off on an all-important mission or who was wanted for secrets he supposedly possessed. Now, Thompson could have been an agent (anybody could, as our current literature makes clear), one of the few whose identity was not fairly common knowledge in Bangkok, though this was denied by official sources at the time and has never been revealed through any files obtained by researchers since; as noted before, a former CIA agent who says he saw the files claims that all involvement ceased toward the end of the forties, when Thompson's anti-colonial sentiments were deemed contrary to the agency's views at the time. In any event, even if he were an agent, he cannot have been a very active one, considering the amount of time he was known to spend on his silk business and on entertaining visitors— approximately 90 percent of his waking hours, according to one source— and it is highly improbable that he was privy to more secrets than many other people in Bangkok, whose abduction, or elimination, would have been more profitable.

Thompson did enjoy talking in general terms about his OSS past, and he did maintain contact with several people who had been associated with him in that adventurous period; to one, who was down on his luck, he frequently lent small sums of money. But this is surely not necessarily so significant as some people have made it out to be: former intelligence agents are notoriously sentimental about their wartime past, and there is almost as much pleasure in seeming to be behind the scenes of big events as in being behind them. In his early days in Thailand, Thompson had not only gotten a fairly comprehensive education in the politics of Southeast Asia from his Laotian and Vietnamese friends but had also served for a time as a political adviser to the American ambassador. He had clearly felt personally involved in the struggles then taking place, particularly those against the French colonialists. But that was more than twenty years ago, and both he and Asia had changed enormously in those years. He had become more and more immersed in his business activities; he lost, it would probably be accurate to say, a good deal of his earlier romanticism with regard to the political complexities of the region. In more recent years, especially with such friends as General Black, he often reminisced about his activities in the forties, but he did not seem very interested in the contemporary situation. One friend, for example, remembered that he had little or nothing to say about the Vietnam war, except that he had a generally hawkish attitude toward it, which was hardly surprising since General Black introduced him to most of that war's leading military figures. At one of his dinner parties, he strongly rebuked Marietta Tree, who was visiting from New York, when she condemned the American role in Vietnam as immoral.

In those days, and perhaps now, the better-known—or better-suspected—spies in Bangkok nearly always had extremely ill-defined jobs which allowed them an unusual amount of time for "holidays" in the provinces. There was once, in fact, a certain American organization which was well-known as a front for agents, who seemed to be free practically all the time. If the Thai Silk Company was Thompson's front, then it must certainly have been the most exhausting one ever devised in the history of espionage.

Then there is Pridi, the former prime minister, whose name flickers so enigmatically through so many of the political theories. Pridi was living in China at the time, reportedly in Canton, and was in his seventies; he subsequently went to France and remained there until he died. To many Thais in the 1960s, however, he still represented a distinct threat, and he was said to be behind various Communist activities in the border areas of the country, particularly in the northeast and in the far south near the Malaysian border. It should be emphasized, however, that there was no evidence to support this then, nor has any been produced since.

Both Hurkos and the ubiquitous McGowan, to mention only two of many, brought up Pridi in connection with the disappearance, and even today in casual conversations with nonofficial Thai it is not uncommon to hear such remarks as "Thompson? He went off with Pridi, didn't he?" accompanied by a knowing smile. Even more people have placed him in China without directly connecting him with Pridi. These rumors found their way as far afield as *Women's Wear Daily*, which, in a gossip column note in February, 1969, observed, "Jim Thompson, head of Thai Silk, who reportedly took a walk in the jungle a couple of years ago and disappeared, is rumored to be in Peking. Making China Silk?"

Given all these easily made references—none of them, of course, based on anything more than hearsay—it is only reasonable to ask: Why? The most obvious place to begin in searching for a possible answer is in Thompson's past association with Pridi. They are generally described as being friends, and no doubt they were, though the term may be misleading to an outsider. In the period Thompson knew him, Pridi was, briefly, prime minister, then a high official enmeshed in one of the greatest scandals in his country's history, and within two years (a substantial part of which Thompson was away) he was ousted in a coup. One is forced to the conclusion that there cannot have been much time for friendship as it is usually understood. Thompson certainly admired Pridi when he first came to Thailand. So did nearly all the American OSS people, as well as the British, to whom Pridi under his wartime code name of "Ruth" had become almost a symbol of the country and for whom they were willing to make all kinds of allowances they would not make for his predecessor (and successor) Pibul. Pridi, of course, returned this affection, and during his brief period of power just after the war, the ex-OSS agents in Bangkok enjoyed unusual access to various official ears; they were invited to all the social fuctions, they were asked for their advice in certain diplomatic matters, they felt that "their side" had won. Pibul was "the other side"; according to wartime propaganda, he was the collaborator. It is hardly surprising that Thompson and many of his friends felt a sense of personal defeat when he regained his position, and this sense was not diminished by the excesses committed after the 1949 coup.

Though a remnant, even a sizeable one, of Thompson's old admiration of Pridi may have lingered through the years, this is surely not the same as saying that he had any strong desire to see the former leader return; his closest friends in Bangkok had no recollection of his ever having expressed such a wish, or, in fact, of his talking much about Pridi at all except in conversations about his past.

Even assuming, for hypothetical purposes, that Thompson did

wish to have Pridi back in power, what could he have conceivably done to aid the restoration by disappearing or being abducted? He had little, if any, political influence in the Thailand of 1967, nor was he so misguided as to think he had any. However impressive his success with Thai silk, the mere fact that he was a foreigner would have weighed heavily, and probably decisively, against him in any sort of propaganda undertaking, including any directed at the Vietnam war operations. He was definitely not a Communist; even the most imaginative theorists have not alleged that seriously. What use, then, could he have been to either Pridi or the Chinese?

(Toward the end of Pridi's life in Paris, he received a number of visiting journalists, both Thai and foreign; asked about Thompson, he professed amazement that anyone could suggest a link between them. His reputation has since undergone considerable revision in Thailand, where a foundation in his memory has been established by his widow, his children, and former students.)

Quite obviously, the political explanation is not as solid as many people seem to believe. It does not provide convincing answers as to why the Cameron Highlands was chosen for the disappearance or, more crucially, why Thompson should have been considered either useful or dangerous to anyone of any political persuasion. It is remotely possible, of course, that there are answers to both questions which, if known, would be convincing. But the same thing can be said of all the theories, not excepting the one about the lovesick aborigine maiden—which was strongly challenged, incidentally, by a Malaysian newspaper reader, who wrote to the Thai Silk Company wanting to know why on earth such a girl would choose an aging farang over one of the strong young farmers that were in more easily available supply. As a hypothesis, the political theory is actually no stronger than the generally discredited kidnap-for-ransom theory, and possibly even less so.

The last of the explanations was, of course, the first chronologically—that Thompson had some sort of accident, or got lost. The list of possible accidents is endless, ranging from a slip on a moss-covered rock overhanging a deep ravine to an aborigine trap deep in the jungle, and getting lost in the tangled winderness was, of course, a simple matter, as the short walk taken by Thompson and Dr. Ling the previous day showed.

Both these possibilities have been quite firmly rejected by so many people, experts as well as mystics like Hurkos, that it is widely assumed that Thompson could not be in the jungle. Relative strangers to the case, not surprisingly—and these include nearly everyone who has written about it in the last twenty-odd years—are inclined to start their speculations with this assumption, as though it were an established fact, with the result that they almost always end up exploring one of the popular political explanations. Even in the early seventies, one reporter who came to Bangkok with the idea of doing an updated piece on the mystery had the impression that the Highlands jungle was a comparatively sparse one, in which the sort of search made for the missing man could accurately be described as exhaustive; more recent visitors, viewing a much-changed Highlands, sometimes come to the same conclusion. For a more accurate picture of what the terrain in question was like in 1967, the following description may be instructive. It is taken from a book called *The Jungle is Neutral*, by F. Spencer Chapman, the Englishman who tried to find Pat Noone during the war, and concerns a walk made by Chapman and several other "stay-behinds" quite near the Highlands area:

"I was now to learn that navigation in thick mountainous jungle is the most difficult in the world—and I had always rather fancied myself at map reading and at finding my way in all types of country, from Greenland to Australia. In the first place, it is quite impossible to find out where you are on the map; the limit of your visibility is fifty to a hundred yards, and even if you are on a steep hill-side, you are none the wiser, as one hill is exactly like another. There are no landmarks, and if there were, you could not see them. Another difficulty is that there is no way of judging distance: it took us more than a week to realize that we were taking eight hours to travel one mile instead of the three or four miles we imagined, judging by the amount of energy we were expending. Perhaps the greatest impediment to navigation is that, having decided to move in a certain direction, you are quite unable to do so owing to the difficulties of the terrain; we were continually forced off our course by swamps, thickets, precipices, outcrops of rock, and rivers. It was impossible even to follow a ridge unless it was very steep and clearly marked.

"The going grew worse and worse; sometimes we clambered up hills so steep that we had to hold on to the vegetation with both hands to pull ourselves up, and on the descents we had to lower ourselves from branch to branch. We seemed to meet every kind of thicket—bamboo, rattan, atap, scrub, and thorn. The worst going of all consisted of whole valleys full of huge granite boulders half covered with a treacherous layer of moss and roots, so that a false step was liable to land us in the stream below. Our packs seemed to get heavier and heavier, and the Tommy-guns nearly drove us demented. Though it was usually dry in the mornings, it rained steadily almost every afternoon and most of the night, so that we were never dry and the wet clothes rubbed away the skin in the most tender parts of our bodies, so that it was agony to start again in the morning. Though my boots were as good at the end of the crossing as at the beginning and I did not get a single blister on my feet, the others' footwear rotted away and by the end of the journey had almost completely disintegrated."

Chapman and his party of three had food supplies, weapons, matches, maps, and a compass, as well as supposedly suitable jungle clothing. Thompson was alone, was wearing a short-sleeved shirt, light silk trousers, and loafers, and, of course, he had no food, matches, or other kinds of survival equipment.

The whole assumption that Thompson could not possibly be in the jungle was based on the conviction that, if so, he would have been found, either by the searchers or by the aborigines who, reputedly, know everything that goes on in the jungle. This conviction derived from two sources. The first was the search itself, which was undoubtedly as thorough as was humanly possible under the conditions prevailing but which nevertheless may not have been quite as infallible as it later seemed to many people. The insistence on the absoluteness of the search is rather surprising in view of the obvious difficulties, and one can only guess at the motives behind it. There may, for example, have been a natural reluctance on the part of the search officials to admit that they could have failed to find someone who was there, perhaps even in the area that was searched, and of the Highlands authorities to be saddled with such a black mark in the record of "the Holiday Playground of Malaysia." There have, after all, been no other cases of permanently lost walkers in the Highlands' recent history (the Emergency, with its unnatural hazards, doesn't count), and it cannot have been difficult for these two groups to join the ranks of the political or kidnap theorists and thus diminish their sense of responsibility.

Some of Thompson's friends may have been motivated by an equally natural unwillingness to accept an accident explanation for an event that struck them as a major tragedy. Apart from being a remarkable person whose friendship was highly regarded by the many who enjoyed it, Thompson was also a legend, and legends, as an American official observed not long after the disappearance, tend to breed further legends when they are involved in any sort of mystery. He attracted such a large assortment of stories about himself during the twenty-odd years he spent in Thailand that it was probably inevitable that the process should not only go on after he vanished but even be accelerated, unhindered by troublesome facts. In the weeks immediately following the disappearance, Thompson's old friends searched their memories for anything that might point to a hopeful outcome, and what they discovered soon found its way into the second legend, usually in a distorted form. Mrs. Mangakau, as we have seen, recalled the walking episode in the Himalayas and this, in the hands of reporters and others, quickly assumed the highly inaccurate and misleading form previously mentioned. It became, in short, another piece of evidence that Thompson was not the kind of man who got lost or had an accident. Others remembered the OSS survival training program, and despite the fact that it had been twenty-two years in the past (and, according to Alexander MacDonald, not all that rigorous to begin with), this, too, received prominent play, giving rise to the erroneous impression that Thompson was a man in prime physical condition who was as unlikely to meet disaster in 1967 as he had been in 1945. Vague and not always accurate recollections of his political past, coupled with rumor and gossip, also provided useful alternative theories for those who disliked the idea of an accident. As time went by, those things which had pointed most tellingly in the direction of an accident—the absence of any suspicious-looking people about the resort, for example, and the sighting of the servant from the mission bungalow—were either forgotten or explained away, and the conviction that he had never gone into the jungle at all grew stronger.

The other source of this conviction was Richard Noone's firm, unequivocal statement that he was convinced the missing man was not in the Highlands, either dead or alive. This could not be laid at the door of wishful thinking, for Noone had never even met Thompson and could therefore approach the problem far more objectively than either the search officials or Thompson's friends. Furthermore, he was an expert on the region with an intimate knowledge of both the terrain and the aborigines who inhabited it. He stayed, as noted, only a brief time in the jungle, but when he emerged he was quite sure Thompson was not there, and he never changed his opinion.

His certainty was based on two facts, which he (and others) felt were conclusive evidence against the acceptance of the accident or lost theory: first, that there was simply no precedent, and second, that the aborigines said they had seen no sign of Thompson. Probably the second weighed most heavily in his conclusion, for the aborigines inhabit the jungle almost like its wildlife and their eyes have been trained over generations to observe things an ordinary searcher would miss; in his years of working with them, Noone had seen this skill in operation too many times to doubt it. The nightmare experience of Miss Laing and her students in early 1968 only provided further evidence, for when she was found, it was not by the official searchers but by a group of aborigines.

It has been suggested that if the aborigines were in some way responsible for Thompson's death, either accidentally or on purpose, they might be disinclined to reveal what they knew, even to a trusted outsider like Noone; they had, after all, kept silent for many years on the subject of his brother's fate. Noone, however, did not accept this possibility, perhaps could not in view of his long association with them and his strong belief not only in their jungle expertise but also in the powers of their bomohs; he thought the aborigines had told him all they knew even in such a short time, that they knew nothing, and that they would have known something if Thompson had been there. Nor, apparently, did he think that Thompson, lost, might have wandered out of the search area without leaving signs of his progress in the jungle, which would have been noticed by the keen-eyed natives.

In summary, the weaknesses of the accident theory are that no clue of any kind was found during the search, that no walker has ever disappeared so completely, and that the aborigines claimed to know nothing about the missing man. If they do not, on close examination, seem quite so serious as the weaknesses of the other leading theories, they are still serious enough to cast doubt. And this doubt has been, perhaps, the leading factor in the creation of the second Jim Thompson legend, for without it there would be no legend.

At this stage, after more than thirty years, there are unlikely to be further revelations. Beyond much doubt, Jim Thompson was either kidnapped, for ransom or political purposes, or he did away with himself, or he was the victim of some possibly simple accident that will probably never be explained. Not one of these theories is without flaws, not one is supported by anything a court of law would recognize as valid evidence. The best that can be said of any of them is that they might have happened.

It is some measure of the first Jim Thompson legend that it could leave behind such a rich variety of possibilities.

Afterword (1970)

While I have tried to make the foregoing account of Jim Thompson's career and disappearance as accurate as possible, some readers will have by now perceived that it is not entirely objective. There are reasons for this, or at least a reason, the usual one: the subject was a friend. Not a friend of many years, nor was our friendship a particularly close one; certainly not close enough to warrant the intrusion of the personal pronoun into the narrative, since if I was involved in any of the events described it was as nothing more than a bystander. Still, here at the conclusion, where a reader can conveniently pass over it without detracting from, or really adding to, his knowledge of the story, I should like to set down briefly my own personal recollection of the man.

I first came to Bangkok in the spring of 1959. I was employed at the time as a scriptwriter for a documentary film company, a job for which I had no qualifications at all other than a strong desire to visit the various Asian countries mentioned by the owner of the company when he rather rashly hired me in New York seven months before. This owner is now dead, but even if he were alive it would be no libel to say that his ignorance of documentary film-making was only slightly less than mine. Why he ever went into it in the first place, I was never entirely sure; perhaps it was only an interesting way to dispose of a considerable inheritance he had come into, or perhaps he enjoyed the role of producer, which he played with great relish. At any rate he clearly enjoyed it, and it gave him (and me) an eventful year or so.

Besides being an alleged scriptwriter, I had a number of other chores to perform for the company. One of them was to act as what my employer called an "advance man," and I suppose that is what it really was, though not in the usual theatrical sense of the term. It entailed my going ahead, alone, to various places where we had hopes of doing a film and establishing certain local contacts with people who were supposedly friends of the owner. This had definite advantages—for one thing, it didn't involve writing scripts, and, for another, it got me away from my employer, of whom I was terrified—but it had one serious drawback: the people I was told to look up, and on whom I was supposed to depend for many favors, almost invariably turned out to detest my employer. If he realized this, it bothered him not at all, for in the letters he gave me to present to them, he made all sorts of peremptory demands, from finding me a cheap place to stay to lending me money in case of emergencies. By the time I was sent to Bangkok, I had learned to be wary of these introductions, having been thrown out of an office in Hong Kong and subjected elsewhere to numerous unflattering evaluations of my employer's character.

There were places, though, where social, linguistic, and financial desperation made the risk of humiliation seem worth taking, and Bangkok proved one of them. This time, I was fortunate; of the several letters I had been given, the two I chose to present both led to lasting friendships. One was to Darrell Berrigan, then the editor of the *Bangkok World*, the other was to Jim Thompson.

Jim shared the general dislike for my employer, but I did not learn this until much later. The day I presented my introduction to him at his shop on Suriwong Road, he asked me for dinner at the little house he then lived in across from Lumpini House—a house I was to know well, incidentally, since I lived in it myself after I came to stay in Thailand later. The house was incredibly crowded with his collection, but somehow the effect was not one of clutter but of richness and an overwhelming sense of the Orient. I had come from a stay of about six months in Manila, which was a very nice but also a very American city, and I had not really felt far from home; I did in Jim's house, with its marvelous furnishings and a pungent klong just beyond the open living room and the distant jingle of pedicab bells from the park across the way.

Two very attractive young women from New York were also at dinner, and Jim entertained us with tales of his silk business and his life in Thailand. In the years to come I found that these were more or less his stock anecdotes, with which he entertained most of the constant stream of visitors he asked to his house, but there was nothing mechanical about the way he told them; his enthusiasm seemed genuine, and he obviously wanted us to share it. And we did: I left that first evening convinced I must find some way to come live in this wonderful place, and at least one of the ladies must have been similarly infected, for several years later, when she married a wealthy man, one of the conditions she placed on her acceptance was that he bring her to Bangkok for a stay of two years—which he did; he was a friend of Jim's, too.

I saw Jim regularly during the rest of my assignment in Bangkok. He found me my cheap hotel (which turned out to be an active and intriguing brothel), cashed my checks, and otherwise followed the demands in my employer's letter. He also did more: he took me on a tour of the silk-weaving village, got me a temporary membership in the Royal Bangkok Sports Club so I could swim at lunchtime, introduced me to many amusing and helpful people, and had me to the fabulous housewarming party in his new Thai house, which he moved into the week before I left. When I consider the sour reception that I am now inclined to give casual visitors in Bangkok—especially people with letters from people I dislike—I am amazed at the recollection of all this hospitality, which he dispensed as if it were quite ordinary and no trouble at all. (And it is trouble, as I can testify; simply getting across Bangkok in the hot season is an arduous undertaking, and to do so on behalf of a near stranger is indication of a truly generous spirit.) Nor was I by any means the only recipient: in the month or so I was in Thailand, perhaps half a dozen other friends of friends wandered through and were given the same welcome. The simple fact was that Jim liked people, and if you were not downright unpleasant or, worse, boring, he made you feel as if you were the most important and welcome visitor to hit town in years. Much later, when tourists to Thailand were numbered in the thousands rather than in hundreds and when he was not in the best physical health, there was a perceptible decline in the warmth of his hospitality; he even began to sound as if he meant it when he occasionally complained of having to entertain, night after night, people who would be gone the next day and the majority of whom would not even bother to write a thank-you note (though they were quick to let it be known back home that they had been entertained by Jim Thompson); yet even then, he had few rivals as a host in Bangkok.

Three months after his housewarming party I was back in New York, the bottom having fallen out of the documentary film venture. I had always thought, like the character in Dos Passos' *Manhattan Transfer*, that New York was the top of the world, that once it soured on you there was nowhere else to go. Now it had soured on me, and I knew exactly where else I wanted to go. In my office at the company where I had gone to work I found myself doodling little sketches that turned out, to my eye at least, to resemble Thai-style houses; I took to going to Chinatown for Sunday brunch.

I got one or two letters from Jim, and he did me a typically generous favor from long distance. The magazine *House Beautiful* had sent a photographer to take pictures of his new house, but as Jim had been out of Bangkok at the time, they had not been able to get a story to go with them. The editor wrote Jim to get the information and he, in turn, suggested that they get me to do the article, which became the first of many picture stories done on the house. Shortly before the piece appeared, I made a decision I have never regretted since: I went to the offices of a Dutch shipping company and bought a one-way ticket to Bangkok.

From 1960, when I moved permanently to Thailand, until his disappearance, seven years later, I saw Jim several times a week, sometimes at lunch at the Sports Club, sometimes at the silk shop (where I got my mail), sometimes at dinner at his house. I lived, as I have said, in his old house for a spell, sharing it with Charles Sheffield, his assistant, and this naturally brought us together fairly often. I was never one of that quite small— smaller than many people thought— circle to whom he really confided, but I was close enough to get a clear view of his more public side and to add to the rather sketchy impressions I had gotten on my original visit.

I saw a good many more examples of that kindness and generosity which had been my first experience of him, and I also saw what some of his friends referred to as his "difficult" side. Mostly this took the form of stubbornness, which would come out at unexpected times and in unexpected ways. While he could be marvelously flexible in certain areas—he rarely, for example, got as exasperated at the inscrutable ways of Asian bureaucracy as most other Western businessmen did— he could, and did, take positions on seemingly petty matters and hold them when they were clearly untenable. He once, for instance, brought a young American out to work for his company at a salary which proved inadequate to the rising cost of Bangkok living. A couple who were among Jim's oldest friends in Thailand sided with the young man in his insistence on the need for a raise, and, as a result of the dispute, were banished from his circle for nearly fifteen years. This particular break was healed to the extent where social relations were resumed, but the couple never really regained their former affection for Jim, who they felt had behaved foolishly.

I got a personal glimpse of his temper one day when I casually remarked that Germaine Krull, the former partner with whom he had quarreled on the Oriental Hotel venture nearly twenty years before, had approached me about working on a book she planned to write. His blue eyes immediately became cold; if I did such a thing, he said, he would never speak to me again. Only when I assured him I had no idea of working with Miss Krull, which was true, did he once more become the friendly Jim I thought I knew.

He could also be outspoken to the point of tactlessness on occasion. He earned himself several lasting enemies by this trait, which usually consisted of giving honest answers to questions asked in expectation of flattery. Even in the West this is not the best way to win friends; in Asia, where one never criticizes anyone to his face, it is a serious social sin and not easily forgiven. It is at least possible that Jim was unaware of the effects of some of his tactless answers, but

I am inclined to doubt it; he was too sensitive to criticism himself to be so obtuse and, in addition, the recipients of such remarks were nearly always in need of a comeuppance. He was never rude to anyone who might conceivably be truly hurt by it, or who had not earned it by excessive pride.

When I was talking to people in Bangkok in connection with this book, the most frequent fault I heard cited about Jim was snobbery. He was, a number of people told me, a great snob; anybody who was rich enough or socially prominent enough could get invited to his house for dinner, however dreary they might be in other respects. In view of my own experience, this surprised me, but thinking about it I realized that there might be a grain of truth in the accusation, though only a grain. Certainly Jim was attracted to the rich and the titled, and certainly he did have some friends whose bank accounts seemed (to me, at any rate) their only asset. Yet what many people in Bangkok forgot, if indeed they ever knew it, was that Jim had grown up in close proximity with the very rich, and if he had never been one of them financially in his early life, neither had he been a poor little boy with his nose pressed against the window. He understood these people, he spoke their social language, and he was inclined to be more tolerant of their intellectual failings than outsiders might be. There is another, more basic reason why the charge of snobbery seems unfair. A true snob not only seeks the company of the wealthy and the influential, he also avoids the company of the less fortunate on the grounds that they are not worth his time. On this count, no objective observer could judge Jim guilty. If he was fascinated by the very rich, he was equally hospitable to the very poor if he found them interesting, which he often did. It is significant, I think, that of his closest friends in Bangkok, few, if any, would have found the favor of a real snob.

A stubborn streak, a tendency to be too blunt at times, a tinge of what seemed to some snobbishness: these are really all the faults I can now recall about the man, and they do not seem so serious when set against such virtues as generosity, thoughtfulness, courtesy, and a vital presence that was not truly apparent until one realized it was gone. With Jim here, Bangkok was a more exciting place to be; without him, there is a curious vacancy that even after three years no one has come close to filling.

On the day we got the news of Jim's disappearance, I went down to the silk company and, like many others, derived a sort of comfort from talking about him with the friends who had gathered there to wait hopefully for news from the Cameron Highlands. As people do in such moments, everyone seemed to be remembering the last time he or she had seen Jim, as if by recalling the past the present could somehow be rendered more comprehensible. The last time I saw Jim was about a week before he left for Malaysia. I was doing the text and captions for the new picture book he was having done on his house and collection. The superb photographs had been taken by Brian Brake, and the first batch of color prints had arrived for his approval several days before. Jim was delighted with them, for they were the first pictures ever taken in which the rich colors of his house had fully come through. He was eager to get everything off to the printers in Tokyo as soon as possible so the books would be ready before the end of the year. Since I am no authority on Asian art, I was having difficulty with some of the captions and wanted him to check them before he went off on his trip, which was supposed to last about a week.

It was the kind of necessary but niggling detail that Jim hated, and he had made, and canceled, several previous dates to go over the captions. Once, about a week before, I had arrived by invitation ready to go to work only to find him entertaining about twenty visitors, a gathering I think he got up just to avoid the chore. On this last evening, though, he was as good as his word, and besides me only Charles Sheffield was present. We spent several hours measuring and identifying objects and finished up early, about ten, since Jim was obviously very tired. Although later, of course, I tried to recall the evening as clearly as possible, I found that I could remember little of what was said, largely, no doubt, because nothing of any significance was said. It was simply another evening with Jim, a quiet one for a welcome change but otherwise not unusual; we agreed to go over what I had written about the objects when he returned and then send everything off.

As he always did with guests, Jim came downstairs with us and said goodbye at the front door. He stood there, flanked by a pair of stone Chinese lions and surrounded by the usual confusion of dogs, in the warm, still, hot-season night, and when I thanked him for dinner he replied, as he usually did, "Thank you for coming." And we drove off, and that was the last I saw of him.

Postscript (1998)

This book was first published in 1970. For this revision, I have added a number of details, some that I have learned in the meantime and that clarified or corrected information in the original, others that I deliberately omitted out of what may have been a misguided effort to avoid intruding on the privacy of various people—misguided since it seems to have led to a certain amount of confusion. Otherwise, I have left the text substantially as it was and summarize here what has happened since the second Thompson legend.

About four days after the disappearance, Charles Sheffield came home to the house we shared for a change of clothes and a brief respite; we had no telephone, and he was both working and sleeping at the silk company to be on hand for calls from Malaysia and elsewhere. As we were having a drink in the garden, he suddenly said, "What if there's no news? Not only now, but never?" The very idea seemed absurd to me. There would certainly be some news, even if it was bad; it might take some time, I was willing to admit by then—the four days had seemed like an eternity—but one day we would know beyond a reasonable doubt what had happened on that Sunday afternoon in the Highlands.

I was wrong. Over the past thirty years, new theories have been proposed, old ones revised, but not a single piece of evidence has turned up to support any of them. No careless tongue or newly released secret file has broken the silence of any conspiracy, no aborigine has revealed any secret he or his tribe might have been concealing, no hiker or hunter has come across any bones in a jungle cave.

Most of the people mentioned in my account are gone. Charles Sheffield, who succeeded Thompson as managing director of the Thai Silk Company, died of cancer in 1973, personally convinced that his former employer was the victim of an accident in the Highlands. Richard Noone died of the same disease, in the same hospital, a few months later, equally convinced that he was right in his assertion that Thompson was not in the jungle, dead or alive. In their last months the two often met and discussed the case, neither persuading the other to abandon his position. Dr. and Mrs. Ling, the owners of Moonlight Cottage; Mrs. Mangskau, who was also a guest that weekend; Elinor Douglas, Thompson's sister; and General Edwin Black, his good friend—all have died, too. So has Cocky, Thompson's beloved white cockatoo, of old age according to some, of a broken heart according to others.

The Thai Silk Company, on the other hand, is very much alive and flourishing under the directorship of William Booth, an American who first came to Thailand with the military. On getting out of the service in the early 60s, Booth decided to go into the silk business in northeastern Thailand, which is where Thompson met him. The company now does vastly more business than it did in Thompson's day and is still regarded as the pace setter in the Thai silk industry.

Jim Thompson was declared legally dead in 1974 after the seven year period required by Thai and American law had elapsed. The heir to his Thai estate, his nephew Henry Thompson, established a foundation to maintain the house and art collection and keep it open to the public, with the proceeds going to various research projects related to Thai arts. Today around four or five hundred people visit it daily, and it is listed in every guidebook as one of the essential places to see in Bangkok.

Interest in the case also continues to flourish. On every anniversary—ten years, twenty years, etc.— there is a flurry of articles, a rehashing of theories. In 1996, a Singapore resident named Edward Roy De Souza published a book entitled ...*Solved! The Mysterious Disappearance of Jim Thompson, the Legendary Silk King*. Readers who bought the book on the basis of its title, however, might be forgiven for feeling a bit short-changed. De Souza's "solution" emerged in the words of a conveniently dead "ex-reporter" and an unidentified Chinese "ex-triad leader" who both claimed that Thompson was involved in drug smuggling, using his silk business as a front; in support of his charge, the "ex-reporter" asserted that Thompson was a regular visitor to the Highlands, easily identifiable since he wore "a white suit complete with gold buttons and a white topi."

On the thirtieth anniversary, I received telephone calls from half a dozen reporters all over the world, from Sydney to London, asking for update information to include in stories being prepared for newspapers and radio and television programs. Absolute mysteries, it seems, only improve with age, and there can have been few as absolute as Thompson's disappearance has proved to be.

Many inquirers, of course, still insist on an explanation, and the question most often asked me is: What do you really think happened to him? Since this is usually asked by someone who has supposedly read this book, it always surprises me. I thought I had made my choice of theories—and it can never be more than a theory—quite clear.

I would like to think it remains clear, though experience tells me I am probably as wrong about that as I was in my conviction that the mystery would be quickly explained. Beliefs are hard to shake once they become established, logic has little appeal. Memory is apt to play tricks even on those who mean well, as I have discovered again and again over the years that I have lived with the Thompson case. An example may be pertinent here.

Among the *farang* ladies who regarded it as both interesting and rather chic to work in Jim Thompson's shop was an American who for a time was my neighbor and is still a good friend. Not long ago we were at a party together and I overheard her telling of the last time she saw Jim. "I remember it very clearly," she said. "I was sitting in the window seat at that little crowded shop down on Suriwong Road. Jim came downstairs, walked through the shop, and went out waving. He was on his way to the airport and then to the Cameron Highlands."

Later I told her she was wrong. In 1967, she had already left Thailand, and the company had moved up Suriwong to its new offices; she was remembering quite a different departure.

She was startled, then aghast. "My God, you're right," she said. "I've been telling that story for years and I really believed it. It just seemed so right."